Digital Culture & Society

Vol. 6, Issue 2/2020

Anna Dahlgren, Karin Hansson, Ramón Reichert,
Amanda Wasielewski (eds.)
The Politics of Metadata

The journal is edited by
Anna Dahlgren, Karin Hansson, Ramón Reichert,
Amanda Wasielewski (eds.)

Editorial Board
Maria Bakardjieva, Brian Beaton, David Berry, Jean Burgess,
Mark Coté, Colin Cremin, Sean Cubitt, Mark Deuze, José van
Dijck, Delia Dumitrica, Astrid Ensslin, Sonia Fizek, Federica
Frabetti, Richard A. Grusin, Orit Halpern, Irina Kaldrack,
Wendy Hui Kyong Chun, Denisa Kera, Lev Manovich, Janet H.
Murray, Jussi Parikka, Lisa Parks, Christiane Paul, Dominic
Pettman, Rita Raley, Richard Rogers, Julian Rohrhuber,
Marie-Laure Ryan, Mirko Tobias Schäfer, Jens Schröter, Trebor
Scholz, Tamar Sharon, Roberto Simanowski, Nathaniel Tkacz,
Nanna Verhoeff, Geoffrey Winthrop-Young, Sally Wyatt

[transcript]

This special issue was made within the project *The Politics of Metadata* funded by the Swedish Research Council (Grant no 2018-01068).

Bibliographic information published by the Deutsche Nationalbibliothek
The Deutsche Nationalbibliothek lists this publication in the Deutsche Nationalbibliografie; detailed bibliographic data are available on the Internet at http://dnb.d-nb.de

© 2021 transcript Verlag, Bielefeld

All rights reserved. No part of this book may be reprinted or reproduced or utilized in any form or by any electronic, mechanical, or other means, now known or hereafter invented, including photocopying and recording, or in any information storage or retrieval system, without permission in writing from the publisher.

Cover layout: Kordula Röckenhaus, Bielefeld
Typeset: Mark-Sebastian Schneider, Bielefeld

ISSN: 2364-2114
eISSN: 2364-2122
Print-ISBN 978-3-8376-4956-7
PDF-ISBN 978-3-8394-4956-1
https://doi.org/10.14361/9783839449561

Content

Introduction
The Politics of Metadata
Anna Dahlgren, Karin Hansson, Ramón Reichert and Amanda Wasielewski   5

Institutional Metadata and the Problem of Context
Jane Birkin   17

One-Eyed Archive
Metadata Reflections on the USVI Photographic Collections at The Royal Danish Library
Mette Kia Krabbe Meyer, Temi Odumosu   35

Man, Woman, Child
Ethical Aspects of Metadata at the Pitt Rivers Museum
Rebecca Kahn   63

Pioneers and Feminisms
The Swedish Suffrage Movement as Archival Boundary Object
Rachel Pierce   87

Designing Digital Diagnostics
(Meta)data in Clinical Radiology
Kathrin Friedrich   115

Archiving the Leftovers of Science
Metadata and Histories of Scientific Institutions
Alina Volynskaya   133

Europeana, EDM, and the Europeanisation of Cultural Heritage Institutions
Carlotta Capurro, Gertjan Plets   163

Paradata in Documentation Standards and Recommendations for Digital Archaeological Visualisations
Lisa Börjesson, Olle Sköld, Isto Huvila   191

Minor Politics, Major Consequences
Epistemic Challenges of Metadata and the Contribution of Image Recognition
Beate Löffler, Tino Mager   221

The Diversity Paradox
Conflicting Demands on Metadata Production in Cultural Heritage Collections.
Anna Dahlgren, Karin Hansson   239

I   Field Research and Case Studies

Enabling Multiple Voices in the Museum: Challenges and Approaches
Paul Mulholland, Enrico Daga, Marilena Daquino, Lily Díaz-Kommonen, Aldo Gangemi, Tsvi Kulfik, Alan J. Wecker, Mark Maguire, Silvio Peroni and Sofia Pescarin   259

Biographical Notes   267

Introduction
The Politics of Metadata

Anna Dahlgren, Karin Hansson, Ramón Reichert and Amanda Wasielewski

A large proportion of our cultural heritage consists of images. While textual artefacts and literature can often be catalogued, studied and analysed within their own textual paradigm, the images that populate cultural heritage collections typically depend on text-based descriptors. Our interpretation and understanding of these images are therefore mediated by textual entries – so-called metadata. The practices and policies of tagging images in cultural heritage institutions are not only fundamental for searching and finding images of our past but also for understanding the present. Thus, the available metadata is the result, and also part, of negotiations between conflicting interests accumulated and transformed over time (Baca, 2016). We call this "the politics of metadata".

This special issue on the Politics of Metadata gathers together research from a wide range of disciplines in order to critically engage with the ideological and political dimensions of image metadata. The aim is to investigate an essential, but often overlooked, component of how we construct and interact with image collections and challenge assumptions of neutrality that tend to accompany the exercise of metadata creation – both when it is produced manually by humans and, increasingly, as it is produced through automation and machine-learning systems.

The transformation of image collections from files and boxes to digital interfaces has had implications for the way images are annotated and ordered. In particular, new issues arise in relation to the practices of, and policies for, creating metadata. The first generation of digitization in the 1990s sparked a lively debate around images and their credibility, which played out in the news media, political circles, and in relation to history writing (Mitchell, 1994; Ritchin, 1990). Although photographic manipulation is as old as the medium itself, the ease and availability of software that allowed not only professional image producers but anyone to "photoshop" images on their personal computers ushered in an era of digital distrust.[1] Yet, as pointed out by Rubinstein and Sluis, "In the past, concerns about manipulation of pixels caused people to doubt the veracity of the digital

---

1   The first recorded usage of "photoshop" as a verb, according to the OED, was in 1992. "Photoshop, v.," in OED Online (Oxford University Press), accessed 26 March 2020, http://www.oed.com/view/Entry/260649.

image; however, manipulation of metadata can have much more dramatic and far-reaching consequences and they indicate that the construction and design of metadata inflicts archiving and classification practices yet also the conditions of use" (2013). In other words, while many people worry about the consequences of digital image manipulation, the data we collect on our data, which is used to order and recall a vast array of digital material, can also be subject to biases and manipulations that are just as insidious and often more difficult to detect.

Metadata is increasingly important when image collections of cultural heritage institutions are published online. In this ever-growing body of visual material metadata situates individual images historically, geographically and socially (Baylis, 2014; Bunnik et al., 2016; Loukissas, 2017; Pollen, 2016). The actors and their agendas and interests, whether they are institutions (museums, archives, libraries, corporate image suppliers) or individuals (image producers, social media agents, researchers) affect the character of metadata (Schwartz, 1995; Schwartz and Cook, 2002). If, for example, nationality is an important founding rationale for a museum, their images will be tagged with national origin, which in itself is a historical construct that can be problematic (Rodini, 2018). Such interests may also vary over time. Whereas the gender of the image producer is of vital concern in memory institutions today the issue whether an image or artwork is produced by a woman or a man has not always historically been of interest for collections managers (Pierce, 2019). The fact that images today may be copied and redistributed digitally and circulate in different contexts makes the question of how images are equipped with metadata, when and by whom, central. Indeed, metadata not only enables us to find particular images or depictions but in fact steers how they are understood, interpreted and used. This is particularly pertinent for data-driven research using big data, where it is impossible to scrutinize each hit, each item in a collection. As the sheer volume of data generated in digital processes increases, metadata is becoming a key factor in the use and interpretation of images.

Metadata is data about data. Metadata describes, identifies, finds, analyses and administers images, and can be categorised in a variety of ways. There are three general types of metadata: administrative (used in managing and administering collections and information resources), structural (describing relationships of parts of resources to one another), and descriptive (describing the information resources). The type of metadata that is most relevant for users outside cultural heritage institutions – such as scholars, students, journalists, publishers and the general public – is descriptive metadata. From a pragmatic perspective, descriptive metadata is a tool to 'identify, authenticate, and describe collections and related trusted information sources' (Gilliland, 2016, pp. 11–12). In other words, it allows users to find and understand images in the collection (Riley, 2017). However, descriptive metadata is also often the most politically fraught area of metadata production, as it requires greater acts of interpretation and translation than administrative and structural metadata.

How do we begin to define the politics that influence and shape the creation of metadata in cultural heritage institutions today? The word "politics", from Greek *politiká* (literally, affairs of the cities), is a multifaceted term that has been defined in different ways, depending on geographical and historical context. In the context of the production, circulation and use of metadata we draw from Adrian Leftwich's definition of politics that focuses on how "people go about organizing the use, production or distribution of human, natural and other resources" (Leftwich, 2004). However, this does not mean that politics is merely about distribution of power without conflict. Politics can also be defined as the exercise of power, dialogue and negotiation or conflict between diverse interests; it can be overt or indirect, formally constituted and maintained or informally performed and contested. Politics are performed on a macrolevel, mesolevel and microlevel, and expressed in law and written policies, but politics are also defined by practice and use of language in the broadest sense (Fairclough, 2015). Among the contributions to this special issue are many different understandings of what the politics of metadata might entail, and we have purposely left the term open to broader interpretation. Several articles in this issue define politics in more concrete and pragmatic ways, as a reflection of *realpolitik* and specific public policies. Other articles, however, focus on larger power dynamics in society, moral issues inherent in historical power structures and how metadata can reflect changing values.

Descriptive metadata for images in cultural heritage collections is currently created in three major ways: by employed, professional cataloguers within the institution that governs the collection, by enlisting the help of the general public via crowdsourcing initiatives and purpose-built interfaces, or through automated systems that increasingly utilize machine-learning techniques.[2] However, machine-learning techniques used to create descriptive metadata are still dependent on human input when the system is trained. Thus all types of metadata production rely on the different human agents whether these are working directly with catalogue enrichment or indirectly through machine-learning development. The crucial question, then, is who these agents are. They could range from professional curators, archivists and cataloguers with very specific expertise on the material to support staff in LAM institutions (libraries, archives, museums) without particular subject knowledge, to amateur taggers who have a wide range of expertise and subject knowledge. Adding to the complexity of how material is furnished with metadata is the fact that the agents producing metadata are in many cases anonymous. This holds both for "professionally" produced metadata within libraries, archives and museums, and for amateurs who contribute to

---

2 See for example *The Vikus Viewer*, https://vikusviewer.fh-potsdam.de; *Buddhas at the Met*, https://shuvitran.github.io/MajorStudio1/Project2-qualitative/FrontEnd/, and *National Neighbors*, https://nga-neighbors.library.cmu.edu related to National Gallery of Art's project *Coding our Collection*.

crowdsourcing initiatives that are run by LAM institutions, or on social media platforms that showcase cultural heritage institutions' image collections. This is in stark contrast to contemporary online social media at large where a particular user's reputation and output history is often the determining factor in gauging the trustworthiness of the information produced. In metadata production, authentication is rather determined by the institution's name.

Given the high volume of data that needs to be tagged, metadata is increasingly being created through automated means rather than by individuals. While common machine-learning techniques for pattern recognition or face-recognition are already widespread in commercial platforms and interfaces, they have not yet been widely taken up by the cultural heritage sector. However, there is evidence of a growing interest (Bakker et al., 2020; Lincoln et al., 2020; Murphy and Villaspesa, 2020). This lag in uptake is not only an effect of limited budgets for publicly funded institutions but also has to do with an array of complex issues that are addressed by contributors to this special issue. The use of machine learning for mass indexing unstructured documents opens up new ways to make relationships between documents visible, among other things. Machine learning enables predictions about document classification or the extraction of knowledge from text passages, graphics or fields beyond simple pattern recognition. The increasing volume of machine-based data in digital forensic investigations is one of the most discussed challenges in the scientific field (Crawford and Paglen, 2019).

While automation makes the task of metadata creation faster and easier, it does not produce less biased results. As noted, machine learning, particularly the methods used for metadata creation, typically depends on human-produced data to train the system (Wieser et al., 2013). Owing to the prohibitive cost of employing experts, the humans involved in creating training data are often low-paid pieceworkers hired on platforms like Mechanical Turk, or volunteers from the general public. As Kate Crawford and Trevor Paglen have pointed out in relation to ImageNet, one of the most popular content-tagging training sets for machine-learning applications on image data, human biases are replicated within automated processes because datasets themselves are created by humans and are therefore not neutral (Crawford and Paglen, 2019). They argue that the "whole endeavor of collecting images, categorizing them, and labeling them is itself a form of politics, filled with questions about who gets to decide what images mean and what kinds of social and political work those representations perform" (Crawford and Paglen, 2019). In the case of cultural heritage datasets, this means that biases in historical categorization or cataloguing can be replicated under the guise of neutrality and objectivity when they indeed are not.

Underlying both human and machine-created metadata are assumptions regarding the objectivity of metadata labels and the equivalence between image and textual descriptor. As Brian Ballsun-Stanton writes, data scientists often see the transformation of raw data into metadata as a scientific enrichment process (Ballsun-Stanton 2010: 120). This results in a multilayered concept of data that is hierarchical, pyramidal and chronological. When conceptualized as a basic building block of knowledge, data is assumed to be a direct reference to reality and viewed as independent of the observer who creates it. The individual data is placed in a certain context in the interpretative-scientific refinement process using syntax rules for metadata and linked with additional information. When data is placed in a context of meaning, it changes register and is called "information" in the discourse of computer scientists. Information can then be used to make decisions. Individual pieces of information are then networked in complex argumentation and justification processes. Within this process, a metadata label that may have a subjective or variable status becomes ossified as a static and unitary fact. For example, terminology for race and ethnicity that are assumed to be neutral at a certain point in time may become outdated and even offensive later on. While this may not always be apparent on the surface, it becomes an underlying basis for organization and, even, knowledge production. The understanding of images is therefore linked concretely to textual data that would never normally be construed as fact, but which is nevertheless the basis for automated systems. This is precisely why a growing number of researchers have critiqued automated data analysis (Angwin et al., 2016; Benjamin 2019; Broussard 2018; Criado-Perez 2020, D'Ignazio and Klein, 2020; Eubanks 2018; Noble 2018; O'Neil, 2017).

The contributions to this special issue are organized according to the focus of their analysis, beginning with those that address issues pertinent to the understanding and categorization of individual collection items, to articles that deal with broader issues for collaboration and coherence between different actors in the cultural heritage sector. The first three articles, therefore, zoom in to analyse how particular images are understood via metadata within digital collections, the following four articles pull the focus out a bit wider to consider the challenges that arise at the institutional level of metadata production, and the final four articles zoom out further still to address intra-institutional aspects of the practices and policies of metadata.

In "Institutional Metadata and the Problem of Context", Jane Birkin addresses how the digitization of images and their presence on digital platforms erases or obfuscates their archival context. She argues that digitized images are often treated in isolation and given singular or simplistic keywords in lieu of more detailed descriptions and information about their archival context. Indeed, images have serial and hierarchical relationships to one another within the archive that add layers of meaning. Thus digitization, which aims to makes archives more open, accessible and transparent, actually hinders access to contextual information that might be readily apparent in a physical archive. As a result of this decontextualization, images become part of the commercialized online search economy and can be further decontextualized outside the framework of the institutional interface. In other words, in a push to make images more widely available, and thus exploitable, we lose some of their value when we lose the local archival context of these images.

In "One-Eyed Archive", Temi Odumosu and Mette Kia Krabbe Meyer approach the issue of metadata diversity as a question of representation, that is the diversity of the people who created historical collections and their metadata. They investigate the process of digitizing the Royal Danish Library's colonial photographic archive, and argue that the collection's one-sided point of view in favour of the colonizers might be revised so that colonial subjects documented by these photographs and other voices contribute to the metadata and therefore the understanding of the collection.

In her contribution "Man, Woman, Child", Rebecca Kahn provides an example of the ethical and political issues of such exploitation. Through a data-driven analysis of an ethnographic collection from the Pitt Rivers Museum at Oxford University, she shows how the opportunities and strong incentive to disseminate collection contents online to a broad audience can be marked by difficulties. It can be problematic to circulate sensitive material in museums and archives without its historical and institutional context, as historically produced records can contain unethical, outdated, or offensive attitudes and understandings of the work in collections. While these records are themselves an object of historical study, they may not be properly understood out of context.

In "Pioneers and Feminisms", Rachel Pierce highlights the historical issues of how feminism and women's movements are defined and argues that little attention has been paid to the technical infrastructure of two Swedish archives, KvinnSam and SKBL. In her investigation of these archives, which focus on women's history and the suffrage movement, Pierce discusses how, despite their superficial similarities, these two archives have very different approaches in their metadata production. She argues that in each case, the metadata creates conflicting interpretations about the women's suffrage movement and who should be included as protagonists in these movements. Through their availability online, these interpretations are given a new context in an institutional interface that differs from their context in the physical archive.

The article "Designing Digital Diagnostics", by Kathrin Friedrich addresses image archiving and communication systems for image data in the field of film-based diagnostics and the archiving of radiological images. From a media-theoretical perspective, she examines the development of heuristic norms such as the data format DICOM (Digital Imaging and Communication), which enables a basic (meta)data policy for radiological diagnostics and patient identification for technological and human actors. Friedrich concludes that the radiological diagnosis of metadata is involved in both a heuristic and clinical problem, since metadata is only made accessible through representation on graphical user interfaces. In this sense, doctors are also ordinary front-end users who receive metadata via interfaces but are not involved in their creation and design process.

In "Archiving the Leftovers of Science", Alina Volynskaya analyses the documentary artefacts of scientific study that are housed in digital scientific archives, using quantitative, distant reading methodologies applied to their metadata as well as close reading. In so doing, she addresses the representation of scientific knowledge and scientific practices and the basic characteristics of thematic metadata attached to those objects. The article examines the extent to which scientific knowledge is arranged and made available with the help of metadata, and how this affects the way scientific history is written and cultural memory established. In so doing, it not only examines the metadata sets for what they make visible, but also problematizes their political dimension or intervention by examining what remains hidden or is pushed into the background.

In "Europeana, EDM, and the Europeanisation of Cultural Heritage Institutions", Carlotta Capurro and Gertjan Plets discuss issues around the Europeana database and how it attempts to gather together disparate institutions under a singular European identity. They show how the identities of individual collecting institutions can be subsumed by systems like Europeana, which are designed to enable interoperability. Moreover, they argue that Europeana's metadata lacks specificity and therefore usability. They find that there are often conflicts or errors between automatically created data and institutional data, and that the information that survives in the pan-national system is often at a very basic level, owing to both copyright issues and the need to increase the level of compatibility globally. In sum, they identify a gap between *realpolitik* and an understanding of the historical past. The core political ideas of the European Union – "Unity in Diversity" – are therefore reflected in online interfaces for cultural heritage, such as Europeana.

In their contribution "Paradata in Documentation Standards and Recommendations for Digital Archaeological Visualisations", Lisa Börjesson, Zanna Friberg, Isto Huvila and Olle Sköld address the problem of the digitization of research data in the field of archaeology. They review a selection of standards and recommendations that are used for data processing in archaeological research and as a basis for archaeological visualizations. Against this background, they discuss the problems, processes and methods of standardizing, harmonizing and evaluating paradata and metadata. In other words, they describe the tension within standards to balance the need for coherence across the field with enough diversity to accommodate future needs. The purpose of their analysis is not to prove possible deficiencies in the coding of data, but to understand the contexts, decisions and assumptions in the use of paradata and metadata schemas, and to make the problems of presumption, standardization and construction of data creation processes visible.

In their article "Minor Politics, Major Consequences", Beate Löffler and Tino Mager discuss what they term 'minor politics' in the transition of analogue archives to digital platforms. These aspects may easily be overlooked but have vital consequences for retrievability, such as the intrinsic logic of the analogue archive, the role of the support staff in digitization projects and keywording practices. Based on their work with ArchiMediaL, which applies computer vision to automatically identify buildings in historical photographs, they show how automated image content recognition may compensate for weaknesses in textual metadata production. In fact, this more direct access to visual information may even highlight patterns, skew and biases resulting from these minor politics.

In "The Diversity Paradox", Anna Dahlgren and Karin Hansson address the question of diversity, meaning variety and heterogeneity, in metadata production. They investigate how metadata standards are implemented by information specialists on digital platforms and how the crowd is engaged in participatory metadata production. Dahlgren and Hansson point to the multifaceted implications of notions of diversity – and the contradictory demands that exists – for the cultural heritage institutions in relation to metadata production. They argue that diversity is not always a productive aim, as it can in fact hinder the distribution and interoperability of metadata. Likewise, participatory activities where heritage institutions reach out to the crowd do not automatically generate diversity.

Paul Mullholland et al., meanwhile, outline the recently launched research programme SPICE entering the field in a piece entitled "Enabling multiple voices in the museum". This project will focus on citizen curation methods to produce metadata which encompasses multiple subjective perspectives, including artist, museum curators and users alike, who can contribute and share their personal perspectives to museum collections.

In the call for this issue we outlined four tension points central to the production of metadata in a digital environment, which have been addressed in different ways by the contributors. First, the contributions to this issue focus on the relationships and systemic tensions between professional and amateur taggers, between metadata standards and folksonomies, between top–down and bottom–up practices of producing metadata (Cairns, 2013; Mayernik, 2020; Riley, 2017; Weller, 2007).

Second, several contributions testify to the challenges in creating metadata that is coherent and simultaneously reflects diverse perspectives. In order for images to be searchable, reliable and usable, collections need to create metadata standards for accuracy and uniformity (Zhang et al., 2019). Interoperability between institutions can be useful but this coherence risks erasing the specific local context of archives. At the same time, there is an increasing demand for descriptive metadata to be inclusive (i.e., to encourage participation and heterogeneity in representation). Given that these two objectives might contradict or come into conflict with one another, how can cultural heritage institutions strike a balance between them?

A third tension point evident in several contributions is between centrality and networks, which concerns the relationship between individual institutions' collections and international organizations, systems and platforms (Piotrowski, 2009). For example, there is a relationship between metadata production and its institutional, geographical settings. Should metadata standards be consolidated within a central position in order to preserve their connection to a particular local context or should they be developed and disseminated in a more diffuse way via networks? Networks require high interoperability which means that the particular and individual has to be downplayed and the lowest common denominator is the ideal.

Finally, there is the issue of anonymity and social identity in relation to metadata production. The vast majority of metadata is produced anonymously, just as the user's identity and reputation are becoming increasingly important in the online environment (Esteve, 2019). Related to this is the issue of automation and individuality in the creation of metadata, particularly given that machine-learning techniques are now frequently used to identify the contents of digital collections. As the examples presented in this issue prove, decisive differences exist between descriptive metadata produced by different agents in terms of content, structure and usability. Moreover, there are also differences between institutionally and publicly circulated metadata.

This special issue has its origin in the research project *The Politics of Metadata* led by Anna Dahlgren and Karin Hansson and funded by The Swedish Research Council 2019–2023 (2018–01068). The overall aim of the project has been to critically examine the policies and practices of tagging images in cultural heritage institutions' image collections online, to contribute to the development of sustainable image-archiving ecosystems which simultaneously meet the demands on high usability, professionality, diversity and participation. When *The Politics of Metadata* project was initiated in 2018, considerable scholarly attention had been given separately to: analogue image archives; cultural heritage institutions; the digital turn and crowdsourcing in a variety of disciplines. In contrast, this project addressed these three strands simultaneously, by combining the hermeneutic and critical traditions of the humanities with system analysis and participatory design methods from computer science, and we are therefore grateful to be able to explore this theme in a broader and interdisciplinary circle of colleagues across Europe in the context of the journal *Digital Culture & Society*.

References

Angwin J., Larson J., Mattu S., et al. (2016) 'Machine Bias: There's Software Used Across the Country to Predict Future Criminals. And it's Biased Against Blacks', In *ProPublica*. Available at: https://www.propublica.org/article/machine-bias-risk-assessments-in-criminal-sentencing (accessed 18 March 2017).

Baca, M. (ed.) (2016).*Introduction to Metadata*, 3rd edn. Los Angeles: Getty Publications.

Bakker, R., Rowan, K., Hu, L., Guan, B. and Liu, P. (2020) 'AI for Archives: Using Facial Recognition to Enhance Metadata'. FIU Library, Florida International University.

Baylis, G. (2014) 'A Few Too Many Photographs? Indexing Digital Histories', *History of Photography*, 38, 3–20. https://doi.org/10.1080/03087298.2013.828481.

Benjamin R. (2019) *Race After Technology: Abolitionist Tools for the New Jim Code*. Cambridge, UK: Polity.

Broussard M. (2018) *Artificial Unintelligence: How Computers Misunderstand the World*. Cambridge, MA: MIT Press.

Bunnik, A., Cawley, A., Mulqueen, M. and Zwitter, A. (eds) (2016) *Big Data Challenges: Society, Security, Innovation and Ethics*, Basingstoke: Palgrave Macmillan.

Cairns, S. (2013) 'Mutualizing Museum Knowledge: Folksonomies and the Changing Shape of Expertise', *Curator The Museum Journal* 56, 107–119. https://doi.org/10.1111/cura.12011.

Crawford, K. and Paglen, T. (2019) 'Excavating AI: The Politics of Images in Machine Learning Training Sets'. Available at: https://www.excavating.ai/.

Criado-Perez C. (2020) *Invisible Women: Exposing Data Bias in a World Designed for Men*. London: Vintage.

D'Ignazio, C. and Klein, L.F. (2020) *Data Feminism*. Cambridge, MA: MIT Press.

Eubanks V. (2018) *Automating Inequality: How High-Tech Tools Profile, Police, and Punish the Poor*. New York: Picador.

Esteve, Z., Asier Moneva, Fernando Miró Llinares (2019) 'Can Metadata be Used to Measure the Anonymity of Twitter Users? Results of a Confirmatory Factor Analysis', *International E-journal of Criminal Sciences*, 4(13), pp. 1–16.

Gilliland, A.J. (2016) Setting the Stage, in Murtha Baca (Ed.), *Introduction to Metadata*. Los Angeles: Getty Publications, pp. 1–20.

Lincoln, M., Weingart, S.B., Corrin, J. and Davis, E. (2020) CAMPI: Computer-Aided Metadata Generation for Photo Archives Initiative. Whitepaper on Successes and Failures in Computer Vision for Visual Digital Collections.

Loukissas, Y.A. (2017) 'Taking Big Data Apart: Local Readings of Composite Media Collections', *Information, Communication & Society*, 20, 651–564.

Margulies, S. (2017) Metadata and digital photography, in Peres, M.R. (ed.), *Focal Encyclopedia of Photography: Digital Imaging, Theory and Applications, History, and Science*. Amsterdam: Focal Press.

Mayernik, M. (2020) Metadata. ISKO *Encyclopedia of Knowledge Organization*. Available at: https://www.isko.org/cyclo/metadata.

Mitchell, W.J. (1994) *The Reconfigured Eye: Visual Truth in the Post-photographic Era*. MIT Press.

Murphy, O. and Villaspesa, E. (2020) The Museums + AI Network. London: Goldsmith University of London.

Noble, S. (2018) *Algorithms of Oppression: How Search Engines Reinforce Racism*. New York: New York University Press.

O'Neil C. (2017) *Weapons of Math Destruction: How Big Data Increases Inequality and Threatens Democracy*. London: Penguin Books.

Pierce, R. (2019) 'The Female Gaze? Postmodernism and the Search for Women in the Digitized Photographic Collections of Swedish Memory Institutions', *Open Information Science*, 3, 61–75. https://doi.org/10.1515/opis-2019-0005.

Piotrowski, P. (2009) 'Toward a Horizontal History of the European Avant-Garde', in *Europa! Europa? The Avant-Garde, Modernism and the Fate of a Continent*. Berlin: De Gruyter.

Pollen, A. (2016) The Rising Tide of Photographs. Not Drowning But Waving? Captures 1. Available at: http://revuecaptures.org

Riley, J. (2017) *Understanding Metadata. What is Metadata and What is it For?* NISO Primer Series. National Information Standards Organization (NISO), Baltimore.

Riley, J. (2009) 'Seeing Standards: A Visualization of the Metadata Universe'. Available at: http://jennriley.com/metadatamap/.

Ritchin, F. (1990) *In Our Own Image*. New York: Aperture.

Rodini, E. (2018) 'Mobile Things: On the Origins and the Meanings of Levantine Objects in Early Modern Venice: On the Origins and Meanings of Levantine Objects in Early Modern Venice', *Art History*, 41, 246–265. https://doi.org/10.1111/1467-8365.12332.

Rubinstein, D. and Sluis, K. (2013) 'Concerning the Undecidability of the Digital Image', *Photographies* 6, 151–158.

Schwartz, J.M., 1995. '"We make our tools and our tools make us". Lessons from Photographs for the Practice, Politics and Poetics of Diplomatics', *Archivaria*, 40, 42–46.

Schwartz, J.M. and Cook, T. (2002) 'Archives, Records, and Power: The Making of Modern Memory', *Archival Science*, 2, 1–19. https://doi.org/10.1007/BF02435628.

Society of American Archivists, n.d. Available at: https://www2.archivists.org/glossary/terms/d/data-structure-standard

Weller, K. (2007) 'Folksonomies and Ontologies: Two New Players in Indexing and Knowledge Representation', *Applying Web* (2), pp. 108–115.

Zhang, Junjie, Wu, Qi, Zhang, Jian, Shen, C., Lu, J. and Wu, Qiang (2019) 'Heritage Image Annotation via Collective Knowledge', *Pattern Recognition*, 93, 204–214. https://doi.org/10.1016/j.patcog.2019.04.017.

Institutional Metadata and the Problem of Context

Jane Birkin

Abstract

The traditional archive catalogue constitutes a form of structural and descriptive metadata that long precedes the internet; and the cataloguing of photographs is just one part of a process of archival administration. The application of keywords to images contrasts with archival prose description, which is based on the visual content of the image and is predominantly context-free; a remediation of the image itself. At the heart of this lies the notion that the single photograph is itself devoid of context; it is a discrete embodiment of shutter time and there is nothing certain either side of that. Thus, one can only speculate at its context, and institutional description techniques actively avoid such speculation. Yet context in the archive is ever-present and key to the function of images as objects of information and evidence. It is built through static relationships, through the situating of photographs in accordance with the concept of original order, and it is replicated through storage systems and hierarchical catalogue entries. Such orders, hierarchies and relationships are absent within sets of images that are brought together by keyword search, including through the websites of archival institutions that struggle to reconcile archival principles and identity with network culture. Images are transported to places where contextual information is at best difficult to access, especially for those unfamiliar with archival interfaces. In contrast to the controlled stasis of archival storage and interconnected recordkeeping systems, network storage is messy, unstable and poorly described. However, we must accept that context is not a prerequisite for many users, and for them the networking of archival images denotes a freedom; a democratisation of the archive. But in a media-driven society that is becoming more and more indifferent to the evidential value of documents of any kind, the context-free image is left predisposed to exploitation.

Keywords: archive, catalogue, context, description, digitisation, metadata, order, photograph

MS62/MB2/L5/166, "Leningrad". Copyright of the Special Collections Division, Hartley Library, University of Southampton.

Introduction

I have worked in a large university archive in the UK for more than fifteen years, most of these from a position of exhibition designer and maker. Through searching for and discovering objects — and making sense of them in an exhibition setting — I have a developed an understanding of how archive materials are structured and how order is preserved through catalogue and storage. I recognise the significance of context in giving meaning and power to objects that sit within this unique institutional structure, and how order and place can easily be lost through simple keyword searches of networked archives. Navigating relationships and hierarchies remotely through a computer interface that is designed to read metadata is possible, but it is difficult, especially without the guidance of an archive professional. At the same time, it is clear that not everyone is able to — or indeed should have to — visit physical archives and it would seem crucial that users working remotely should have similar opportunities to those in the reading room. Aspects of archival power, linked to the accessibility of archives, is most often understood in the context of material being purposely removed or hidden from view (with the attempt to destroy the records of the Stasi before the reunification of Germany often cited). However, Simon Fowler argues that poor web interface design is responsible for the invisibility — the silence — of archives, making it difficult not only for users to find material, but to know whether it exists — and with certain disadvantaged sections of the population most affected (2017: 59).

Whilst I identify the lack of contextual information in keyword search and retrieval as problematic; explain why this is so in terms of archival sense-making; and identify the ways in which institutions are trying to mitigate the effects for their users, I do not have any solutions as to how the problem might be properly solved as we move forward. It is hard to know what can be done, as cataloguing time is at a premium in underfunded institutions and applying metadata through schemas is less labour intensive — a somewhat de-skilled activity — and therefore saves money. It is, however, recognised that change is needed, especially when dealing with masses of born-digital material. Jane Winters and Andrew Prescott (2019:393) argue strongly that Google-style searching is not effective within large data sets. They give the example of the Wikileaks material, comprising "2,325,961 diplomatic and other US State Department records [...] which if printed would amount to some 30,000 volumes" (Assange 2015: 1). It is interesting that Winters and Prescott suggest something of an about-turn in retrieval methodologies when dealing with such large quantities of complex material, going back to a more tradition approach that acknowledges the importance of context (2019: 393). I want to look at the problem on a smaller scale — one that is perhaps more familiar to the user — and I take the example of the archived photographic image to examine the important role that context plays in our understanding of archives more broadly. I identify the photograph as inherently context-free, a discrete object that is predisposed to contextual misinterpretation, whether accidental or purposeful, and whether for political or artistic reasons (or both). This condition is reiterated by traditional archival image description, and the example of a description of a single archival image from the University of Southampton that I put forward below, entitled "Leningrad" (Figure 1), supports this idea: context commonly appears higher up in the hierarchy of descriptions, leaving the single image description, like the image itself, free of context. Thus, the photograph is of particular interest here, as it is an object that it is highly dependent for its veracity on the preservation of its particular place in the hierarchy of the archive and on its relationships with neighbouring materials.

Catalogue and context

Cultural institutions such as archives and museums have long relied on the functions of the catalogue to support the organisation, the visibility and the use of their collections; the catalogue constitutes a form of structural and descriptive metadata that precedes the internet. Cataloguing photographic images is just one part of a wider process of information management and archival administration. The textual layering of the catalogue needs be applied to images in order that they become usable archive objects that are situated amongst other archive objects, with their specificity of place preserved; they become documents and not simply visually interesting media that are out there in the world (cf Briet 1951; Gitelman 2014). Their inclusion in the archive and in the supporting catalogue presents them in a specific spatiotemporal zone; although there may be other photographs made from the same negative that are stored in different archives and places, their context will not be the same.

Whereas text-based archival material, correspondence for example, can be summarised or fully transcribed, the cataloguing of images (and other non-textual objects) is a different process altogether and requires different skills; it is a necessary but nonetheless problematic system of remediation. Jay David Bolter and Richard Grusin identify remediation as "a defining characteristic of new digital media" (2000: 45) but the traditional archival description of images before the advent of new media is a form of remediation that is as transformative as any in the digital realm. Translating images into words is a process that is by its very nature challenging. Entirely new problems arise when archive images are described via the application of digital descriptors, usually single word identifiers that struggle to define images at all. Descriptive metadata is just one part of an integrated system of institutional metadata, but it is the part that is visible and valuable to the user in terms of finding their images. It is applied to photographs in the form of a keyword, either spontaneously, as is common on social media platforms, or, at an institutional level, through a predetermined schema of thesaurus terms (although these two systems may converge, with institutions such as the Library of Congress uploading images to Flickr for signed-up users to tag, outside of any schema). These keywords link up images in unexpected ways, transporting them to distant corners of networks, where the contextual information that surrounds the image in its physical home is — at best — difficult to access. In contrast to the controlled stasis of archival storage and the interconnected recordkeeping systems of the catalogue, network storage is messy, unstable and badly described.

Context itself is a slippery thing; hard to pinpoint and all too easy to neglect. Jacques Derrida argues that context is never absolutely determinable, but what he does at least establish is that ambiguities in the field of communication can be "massively reduced by the limits of what is called a context" (1977: 2-3). In the archive institution, materials (photographs and other items) operate foremost as objects of information and evidence, or "veracity", which Michael Moss identifies as one of the four pillars of big data (2018: 259). As such, determining context is critical to the photograph's specificity of time and space, and to its successful communication and informational operability. Context exists at many levels and in many forms. A keyword may materialise as a broad contextual marker that reflects, rightly or wrongly, conditions outside of the discrete situation captured. Whilst single word descriptors might identify subject matter that is known and understandable to most people, designed to function within our shared systems of knowledge, they rarely apprise *actual* context. To further complicate things, single words are lacking in context themselves. They could be homophones or, because they not directly spoken but are written and then read, they could be homographs.

The cataloguing of archives by keyword has emerged for much the same reason that Melvil Dewey established his Dewey Decimal system of library classification: to support efficiency of time and labour. Whereas library material sits well inside this type of categorisation, as it is normally authored (and steered by publishers) to fit into subject categories, archive material is not organised or stored in this way. Instead, it is kept in the order in which it accumulated and was re-ordered and kept by the individual or organisation who passed it to the archive. This is known as developmental order and it varies enormously in the complexity of its arrangement; it defies categorisation; it does not fit within the constraints of simple subject identification. This may be a concept that is difficult for the user to grasp, as we are programmed to categorise and to search out categorizations, not just in our cultural interactions but in many aspects of our daily lives. Lev Manovich argues that humans are "categorizing machines", but he asks whether we can learn to think about culture without categories, arguing that we need to think about different types of relations and interactions, "especially since today we use interactive digital cultural media as opposed to historical static artifacts" (2018: 25-26). As Debra Ramsay remarks in her essay "Tensions in the Interface", where she examines the redesign of the website of The National Archives in the UK, archives are organised "through functional relationships rather than by subject", adding the cautionary note that this is an arrangement that "does not necessarily suit all researchers or users" (2108: 287). This is a glimpse into the difficulty of building a practical keyword search of diverse material for diverse users.

The context-free image

At the heart of the argument for accurate contextual information in regard to the photographic images lies the notion that the single photograph is *devoid* of context. Photographic images are objects that readily tell us about the scene in front of the camera at the moment of their making (notwithstanding the many and various arguments around manipulation that I will not be engaging with here). A photograph is at its heart a discrete embodiment of shutter time — whether long or extremely short — and there is no concrete evidence there to give us any information about what existed either side of that time. Although some would undoubtedly contest this particular reading, it fits with the much-cited view of the photograph's ability to freeze or fix time. When examining an individual photograph, the invisibility of contiguous time means that one can only speculate at its wider context. The traditional institutional cataloguing method of description of a single image employs a very particular writing form that does not speculate or attempt to give meaning outside of what is visible and recognisable; it reproduces in prose form the visual content of the image, replicating the time of the shutter opening and defining the scene as it is captured.

Image description comes from a time before the easy reproduction of photographic images and therefore evolved as a distinctive form of that had to be ready and able to stand in for the hidden image; to give as much information as possible in terms of visual content without straying outside. Bolton and Grusin argue with regards to remediation that "the new medium can remediate by trying to absorb the older medium entirely, so that the discontinuities between the two are minimized. The very act of remediation, however, ensures that the older medium cannot be entirely effaced; the new medium remains dependent on the older one in acknowledged or unacknowledged way" (2000: 47). Whilst image description certainly aims to minimise differences and discontinuities between text and image, the text is always dependent on the image and it clearly would not exist without it. There is no attempt to efface the original because the image and the text are different objects that are meant to be consumed in different ways and at different times. Although images may sometimes be rejected on the strength of a comprehensive catalogue description, the catalogue entry exists in order to open up access to the image itself.

The length of a description is variable, depending largely on the time available to the writer, but also on the nature of the material described. Image description is a type of administrative writing that is distinctive in terms of the poetics of grey literature, but that is another angle and not pertinent to the current argument, except that it coalesces with the idea of the unfamiliarity of the institutional form, in the midst of a world that seems to be over-saturated with images and with no need for description. For the benefit anyone unfamiliar with image description, the following is a fairly lengthy and comprehensive catalogue entry from the Mountbatten Archive, in the University of Southampton's Special Collections, and the image itself is reproduced above (Figure 1). The Mountbatten Archive contains some 50,000 photographs, and with many of them meticulously described. These descriptions are included in the Mountbatten Papers Database, where they are fully searchable. For example, the description below was found by searching with the keyword "street". The database also shows the sequencing of images in an album for example, so relationships are clearly identified, and there is a comprehensive guide to the structure of the database itself. However, this is a self-contained database for registered users, managed by Special Collections and with no discoverability through Google. The description is copyright of the Special Collections Division, Hartley Library, University of Southampton, MS62/MB2/L5/166:

> Black and white photograph of a building in Leningrad. It is a flat-roofed five storey building bordered by partially pictured buildings on either side. On the ground floor there are four large, rectangular apertures. Three are boarded-up shop fronts and the fourth is an opening into the building; the interior is in deep shadow. There are also two windows and a doorway. The central window on each of the third and fourth storeys

is a bay window; the roof of the fourth storey bay window provides a balcony for the window above. There are railings around the edge of the flat roof, between sections of wall. There are many antennas on the roof of this building and on the buildings on either side. The walls of the building are stained and flaking giving an impression of faded grandeur. The street in front is cobbled with tramlines along the centre. One man is standing in front of the building and another sitting. A woman and two children are walking out of the bottom left hand corner of the photograph.< "664. Leningrad" is printed on the bottom left hand corner of the photograph.

The discrete nature of the scene is underlined by the description of the figures "walking out of the bottom left hand corner of the photograph", as they are caught in that particular moment. And something else is flagged up by this description: the printed marks and annotations that appear on photographs, often on the back, may be lost through any digitisation process. This is vitally important information. It is analogue metadata that communicates information about the photograph and it has been put there by people who were close to it, perhaps in some way involved with its making or its early organisation. Ramsay regards all information presented to us via a computer interface as a filter of "the ideologies associated with the context of its production" (2018: 281). She also puts forward three interfaces of the archive: firstly, the archive itself; secondly, the catalogue; and thirdly, the archivist (2018: 286-87). At the top of Ramsay's list could be added the interface of the object; a photograph such as this one, with all the sensory signals and contextual markers that it offers and that help to form part of our broader understanding of it *as* object.

Hierarchies and interrelatedness

One might assume that such a long descriptive form as the one above is redundant today, in the already mentioned image-saturated world, and at a time when archive images are becoming subsumed into network culture and are viewable on our screens, discoverable by keyword. But many archive images remain invisible, as institutions struggle to come to terms with the labour involved in retrospective digitisation. High costs are incurred in the course of the digitisation process: the handling of often delicate objects; the photography and post-production processes such as colour calibration; and the cataloguing itself. The physical diversity of archive material means that all these constituent parts can differ for each object that is digitised, making it a very costly business altogether. Unless funding can be acquired for specific digitisation projects, it continues to be done in a piecemeal way, through a "digitise on demand" programme, meaning that whole archives, with their context inhered, are not being digitised. As Estelle Blaschke notes, "it is the client who will determine which pictures will be made 'visible'" (2009: 8). And, as Moss argues, "the reader approaches the content with all sorts of baggage and the experience is situated" (2018: 255). Researchers have their own contexts and the material they pick out and that may be subsequently digitised will not necessarily fit the needs of anyone else. This is fundamentally different to the way that the all-inclusive archive catalogue does not anticipate any particular future use of material but, as far as it is able, allows for all possible future uses. These are the traditional recordkeeping methodologies that can be traced back to the first formal guide to recording archives, *The Manual for Arrangement and Description of Archives: Drawn up by the Netherlands Association of Archivists*. This was authored by Muller, Feith and Fruin, published in 1898 and known as *Dutch Manual* (more on this below).

The single item description such as the "Leningrad" one above is anchored to some extent, as far as that the building described is placed in Leningrad, with cobbled roads, tramlines and so on, but object-level description is by nature devoid of any wider context, as it replicates the image itself in terms of its immediate embodiment of time. Context, however, is ever-present in the archive and discovering it is one of the pleasures of doing in-situ archival research. Context is built through serial (part-to-part) and hierarchical (part-to-whole) relationships; through the situating of photographs amongst other archive objects that are catalogued and stored in accordance with the concept of original order, that is, the order in which the material entered the archive from its previous owner. Importantly, context is preserved through static, hierarchical catalogue entries that do not attempt to define subjects or add meaning through their writing, but through their being together. Thus, knowledge is formed through what may be perceived as simple descriptive or transcriptive writing; a "copyist's medium", which, incidentally, is how art critics regarded photography itself in its early years, according to Allan Sekula (2003: 448).

Referencing a document from The UK National Archives — a guide to archives for non-archivists (2011) (now unavailable online, so there is no applicable URL) — Ramsay notes, "The meaning of archival records from the perspective of the archivist thus lies primarily in their interrelationships with other records and with the individuals or organisations that initiated them, rather than in the content of individual records." (Ramsay 2018: 286-287) This is especially relevant in relation to sets of photographic images. When seen together, a visual account of an event and a context for the temporally discrete photographic objects is built. Here I want to give an example from the Harry Price Collection in the University of London's Senate House Library. Price was a self-styled psychic detective, who specialised in investigating psychical phenomena through staged events that were planned and recorded meticulously. This is a collection that I repeatedly return to, because of the self-contained nature of the small events, described by the photographs and the resulting catalogue list of short descriptions. Below is a catalogue list of photographs recording an experiment with blindfolded reading:

HPG/1/12/9 Kuda Bux and his 'Eyeless' Sight 1935
Photographs of Kuda Bux and his experiments with 'eyeless sight', including the following:
i. Head and shoulders photograph of Kuda Bux, looking at the camera (n.d.) [1047] (Copyright: Tourist Library Photo)
ii. Studio head and shoulders photograph of Kuda Bux with hand on chin (n.d.) [486] (Copyright: Pollard Crowther)
iii. Photograph of Kuda Bux's eyes being bandaged prior to experiments (n.d.) [1340] (Copyright: Pollard Crowther)
iv. Photograph of Kuda Bux, head bandaged, reading a newspaper (n.d.) (2 copies: 1 backed with card) [1350A] (Copyright: Pollard Crowther)
v. Photograph of Kuda Bux standing with chalk, head bandaged (n.d.) [485] (Copyright: Pollard Crowther)
vi. Photograph of Kuda Bux, head bandaged, duplicating shorthand characters drawn on blackboard by Lucie Kaye (n.d.) [484]
vii. Upper body photograph of Kuda Bux standing holding the bandages removed from his eyes (n.d.) [79] (Copyright: Pollard Crowther)
viii. Upper body photograph of Kuda Bux, head bandaged and hand on head (n.d.) [487]
ix. Upper body photograph of Kuda Bux, head bandaged and hands clasped (n.d.) [488]
x. Upper body photograph of Kuda Bux, head bandaged and hand on head and other hand on book page (n.d.) [489] (Copyright: John Somerset Murray)
xi. Upper body photograph of Kuda Bux, head bandaged and hand on head and other hand on book page, different shot from photograph x above (n.d.) [490]
xii. Upper body photograph of Kuda Bux, head bandaged and hand near chin (n.d.) [491]
xiii. Upper body photograph of Kuda Bux, hand on head and other hand on book page (n.d.) [492]
xiv. Upper body photograph of Kuda Bux having his head unbandaged after experiments (n.d.) [78] (Copyright: John Somerset Murray)
xv. Head and shoulders photograph of Kuda Bux, head bandaged and hands clasped (n.d.) [78] (Copyright: John Somerset Murray)
xvi. Head and shoulders photograph of Kuda Bux, head bandaged and hand on head (n.d.) [77] (Copyright: John Somerset Murray)
1 folder

Wolfgang Ernst understands the archival mode of record management as "a non-narrative alternative to historiography, in the best tradition of early twentieth century avant-garde", and further argues that a collection of photographs "as accumulation" deconstructs narrative (2016: 12). The list above is not chronological and does not form a conventional narrative, although the storyline can be understood through a processing of the parts. Due to the way the photographs have been used and arranged in the past, a complex view of an event is constructed, with changes of camera angle and cuts in continuity that record and amplify the developmental thinking of the original owner. If we are to consider the archive as having a role in the preservation of memory and trace, the preservation and the visibility of order is critical.

Some of the most interesting archival photographs are not those in dedicated photographic collections, or those that have been separated out by their previous owners, but those that are preserved amongst correspondence and other documents. In their online guide to searching for photographs, The National Archives marks photographs such as these as, for example, "Photographs scattered among files"; "Numerous photographs scattered among papers"; or Photographs attached to data sheets" (https://www.nationalarchives.gov.uk/help-with-your-research/research-guides/photographs/#3-how-to-search-for-photographs [accessed 15-01-2021]). Still, the same deconstruction of narrative takes place and needs to be carefully considered. All this demands more time and thought from the researcher, but it is entirely necessary to the understanding of archive material outside of its own moment of inscription.

As already mentioned, Ramsay sees the catalogue as the second interface of archival research, the first being the archive itself (2018: 287). Indeed, Nina Lager Vestberg describes how the filing cabinets and boxes that house the photographic archives of the Conway and the Warburg Libraries in London act as a finding aid and a repository at one and the same time (2013: 476). She acknowledges that a computerised index system allows searching and locating, but that browsing a physical archive in this way allows one to *find*, to think through an archive (2013: 487). But these are fairly small collections that are open access and can be browsed; the physical archive is not normally such an easily accessible interface. Large archives are mostly removed from public view, with reading room and strong room kept as separate spaces with different environmental and security requirements. The standalone archive catalogue (sometimes known as the paper catalogue, even though it is often deposited online as a PDF) is a document, a finding aid, that is able to stand in for the physical archive. It presents context in a succinct and accessible way, as it replicates the organisation and therefore the relationships of the storage itself.

Inside the catalogue, as in the strongroom itself, specificity of context decreases and as we move from a particular archive of an organisation or individual (fonds) to the single object, an image for example. In their publication *ISAD(G): General International Standard Archival Description*, the International Council on Archives (ICA) notes: "The fonds forms the broadest level of description; the parts form subsequent levels, whose description is often only meaningful when seen in the context of the description of the whole of the fonds" — hence the discrete nature of the "Leningrad" description. The ICA gives the following guidance on description "from the general to the specific":

Purpose:
To represent the context and the hierarchical structure of the fonds and its parts.
Rule:

At the fonds level give information for the fonds as a whole. At the next and subsequent levels give information for the parts being described. Present the resulting descriptions in a hierarchical part-to-whole relationship proceeding from the broadest (fonds) to the more specific. (2000: 12)

Archival standards adopted by the ICA can be traced back to the *Dutch Manual*: in their introduction, the authors explain the importance of their publication in terms of "making archivists aware that the boundaries and structure of an archive need to be respected and that the components of which an archive consists can only be comprehended within their original context." (2003 [1898]: xvi-xvii) The manual places more emphasis on arrangement than description and encourages the creation of an inventory matching the original order of the archive and replicating its storage (Horsman et al 2003: 262). Thus, the *Dutch Manual* makes it abundantly clear that context and order are wholly interdependent, reliant on original order and related recordkeeping techniques; and that the catalogue, the archive and its storage are firmly bound together. The placing of a document inside a file, inside a box, arranged on a shelf amongst related boxes, establishes a physical archival hierarchy, an embodiment of the cataloguing process.

Order and hierarchy such as found in the archive are absent within sets of images that are brought together because they share the same keyword; images are decontextualised and their meaning lost or fragmented by such semantic assemblages. Ernst argues that "repositories are no longer final destinations but turn into frequently accessed sites. Archives become cybernetic systems. The aesthetics of fixed order is being replaced by permanent reconfigurability." (2013: 99) He makes the pertinent point that the archive institution is a "read-only memory"; that archival order cannot be changed at will: "Just like in computing, a rewriting of the code in the operating system would make the whole function collapse." He identifies photographs as especially compromised through any reordering, where "the tight coupling of symbolic evidence [...] is being replaced by a loose archival coupling", which he terms (via social psychologist Fritz Heider) as "mediatic" (2016: 10-12).

Alexander Galloway (2020a) argues that the word "metadata" is a monstrosity (a Greek prefix to a Latin root), and Daniel Rubinstein and Katrina Sluis suggest that the simple definition of "data about data" is not extremely helpful because "it does not clarify metadata's place as mediators between humans and computers" (2013: 152). Jisc (an academic organisation based in the UK that provides advice and digital services to higher education) nevertheless defines metadata as 'structured information about information' and explains how institutional metadata breaks down into a number of different categories, all playing very different roles in the ecology of the image (or other object) and in providing contextual information for the user and for the archive itself. As well as the descriptive element that we usually think of in terms of images, metadata can record the numbers and types of user accessing certain material; the physical state and conservation of material; and what is known as 'structural' metadata, facilitating relationships between digital resources. (See https://www.jisc.ac.uk/guides/metadata/describing-metadata [accessed 15-01-2021]). It must be noted that such information has long been gathered and kept — and still is — outside of networks; archives continue to perform a very physical form of metadata collection, such as the creation of extensive conservation documentation and the keeping of user logbooks and paper request slips to record the use of collection. User data, whether collected digitally or physically, is extremely influential, in that it can impact the acquisitions policies of archives and libraries. Meanwhile, our engagement with images on social media platforms creates useful data for Facebook, Instagram and the like; this is the metadata that Rubinstein and Sluis describe as 'a valuable by-product of interaction with the image' (2013: 151). It is not only valuable in terms of the efficacy of our search results, it is highly monetarized data.

In the archive or image collection, metadata is generally applied through the use of schemas, which afford the addition of keywords to an image or object via a limited vocabulary of pre-defined thesaurus terms. Thesaurus sets are available from organisations such as Getty, who provide subject-focussed lists of terminologies. These can be adapted and built on, but they are limited vocabularies by name and by nature; limitations exist in order to preserve interoperability across different collections and institutions within the culture of keyword-based searching. However, Ramsay recognises the deep flaws in the frequently hyped concept of interoperability: "The interface's seamless interlinking of different kinds of records from different sources in turn undermines the structures of archival description and, by doing so, threatens the foundational principles of the archive itself." (2018: 296) Nonetheless, the application of keywords to describe photographs is becoming increasingly routine; professional archivists' time is at a premium, especially in those archives that are part of underfunded public institutions. The use of schemas is extremely cost-effective and time-efficient when compared to other description methods. As recognised cautiously above, it increases interoperability between institutions, as common thesaurus sets are downloaded and used, and it undoubtedly brings images to us, even if they are not always the ones we expect.

Even though archival hierarchies may be fragmented through the process of keyword searching, hierarchies indeed proliferate through web organisation, with data about data about data and so on in an ever changing and near endless chain. As Galloway observes, "it's metadata all the way down." However, as he argues, these hierarchies are held up artificially; structure is added by computer scientists; no "media-infrastructural mechanism exists to distinguish between data and metadata." (2020b). If we point this up the chain once again, then the archive object (already identified as an interface) is itself a form of metadata, as it comprises information about information; it is an object that tells us about other objects, which in turn reciprocate. But these archival structures are not imposed, they are natural, diachronic, and ultimately static. Galloway's assertion that the "meta" part carries with it the meaning "among', or "in the middle of" (ibid.) is also wholly appropriate to this setting of the word.

Navigating knowledge

The guidelines in relation to the use of metadata schemas are in fact close to those put forward by the ICA for standard archival description, in that they demand operation within a hierarchical system, moving from fonds to single object. Differences materialise in the operational strategies of schemas as well as in the settings in which they are used. The use of schemas discourages the description of single objects and description ends at group level (a further time-saving strategy). Of course, this is something that is often found in the standalone archive catalogue, which might end with a broad description of a box or a file of objects. The difference is that when users are working inside the archive search room, although they may have to go through a box or a file to find a specific document or image, if it is there, then it can be found — with the added bonus that other objects of interest may be found as well. In the case of the networked search, the user may not know whether the object they are looking for even exists, never mind whether or not there is other related material that may shed light on its meaning. What is also apparent is that problems such as this are exacerbated as the online user, often working remotely, is denied the knowledge and expertise of the archivist. Ramsay's third interface of archival research is the archivist, as they "perform the essential function of assisting users and researchers in navigating archival description and finding aids and in guiding them to the records they require" (2018: 287). Archives can be unwelcoming places, surrounded by security protocol and strict regulations on use of material; not everyone wants to — or indeed is able to — visit an archive in person.

Various "help" initiatives are built in to the websites of large institutions such as The National Archives in the UK. For example, a search returning the image described as `Coal-mining or underground life'. Men descending in two level cage (document reference: COAL 13/24), has a box bottom left which asks, "Need more context?" (https://discovery.nationalarchives.gov.uk/details/r/C2056184 [Accessed 15-01-21]), with a link to the catalogue description for the whole of COAL 13:

> Reference: COAL 13
> Title: The Cobb Photographs
> Description: This series contains a set of slides which were nearly all taken at the collieries of the former Barber Walker and Co (mostly at Moorgreen and Brinsley) around Eastwood, Nottinghamshire between 1907 and 1914. The slides were taken by the Rev F W Cobb, Rector of Eastwood, Nottinghamshire from 1907 to 1917. The set is entitled *From Pit to Fireplace* and would appear to have been used to illustrate a talk on the history of coal mining.

> COAL 13/116 consists of a complete album of contact prints, prepared from the original slides for viewing.
> Copies of the slides are also available from The National Archives' Image Library.

This is an exceptionally useful and user-friendly feature, but the problem is, as Ernst states, many users are bypassing archive systems altogether:

> More and more, archives find themselves both inside and outside the "Web 2.0" or "social Web" economy. [...] As a result, new challenges arise: what if the public will prefer to use Google rather than institutional Internet portals to get access and information on national, academic and cultural memory? In other words, will the World Wide Web, Web 2.0 and the emerging Realtime Net replace the traditional guardians of memory such as archives, libraries and museums, just as Internet radio and IPTV (Internet Protocol Television) are replacing the traditional broadcasting media? (2016: 15-16)

And as Jane Winters and Andrew Prescott argue, the Google search has familiarised us to simple keyword searching of online resources, but "googling" is especially problematic when searching within the vast quantities of born-digital archive material: "It is particularly unsuited for establishing the scope of a dataset or digital archive, as it encourages researchers to look for what they know to be there rather than to seek the unknown or to identify gaps or absences." Moreover, as already mentioned, they argue that "it is already evident that we need to move from a search-oriented approach to one that reflects classic archival methods, with an emphasis on hierarchy and context". (2019: 393)

There are two very different problems connected to the extension and subsumption of archives into networks: Firstly, for archives: they may be minded to commercialise their web interfaces in terms of functional and aesthetic design in order to meet the expectations of general web users, and this, Ramsay argues, "reveals the penetration of interface culture with its overtones of capitalist ideology into archives'" (2018: 292). Daniel Rubinstein argues that "An untagged image is worthless, as it is invisible to search engines and so cannot enter the economy of the search industry, whereas a tagged image can be discovered by web crawlers and returned as a search result." (2010, p.198). It is clear that the economies of the search industry and the moral integrity of the archive are two things that are hard to reconcile. Secondly, there are difficulties with archives websites for general public users (as opposed to academic researchers) and Ramsay sees the question of "what constitutes a 'record' in the digital age and how the term is understood by users with no experience of archives at all" as fundamental to the design of archival interfaces (2018: 294). Although dedicated archive websites are at pains to preserve and flag up relationships between archival materials, if the user has never visited an archive and does not understand the complexity of archival systems, these relationships will be meaningless, and keyword searches will return for them a range of results that are similarly discombobulated as those that would be thrown up by a Google search. According to Ramsay academic researchers are now in the minority at The National Archives, with those interested in family history now making up a large proportion of users, spurred on by such things as the popular BBC TV programme *Who Do You Think You Are?* (2018: 298). Moss claims that libraries and archives have in the past been reluctant to allow commercial indexing of their content that would feed into search engines was because they feared getting too many requests for material. The result of this, Moss argues, "has been to leave the market wide open for organisations, such as Ancestry and FindmyPast, even if they are simply supplying content from the archives." (2018: 260-261) The UK National Archives website now has a specific guide for those researching family history (https://www.nationalarchives.gov.uk/help-with-your-research/research-guides/?research-category=family-history [accessed 15-01-21]).

It must be acknowledged that putting a word into a search box is only the first step in a research project, and time and tenacity on the part of the user is required to take it further. However, I find the websites of many large archive institutions mind-bogglingly difficult and extremely frustrating, although I unable to say whether this is in fact a direct result of my knowledge of physical archives and their structures and the expectations that I have because of this. Navigating these sites is like getting lost in a complex road system, only to be brought back to the same place over and over again. Whilst it might be quite straightforward to access a digitised image, it is far more difficult to access the catalogue list in which it exists and to find out how and where it lies in relation to other images and documents. The UK National Archives website is an exception to this; perhaps this is proof that the web redesign that Ramsay observed by attending meetings with archivists and web designers between October 2014 and March 2015, and which forms the basis of her chapter, was on the whole a successful one. Shedding light on the difficulty of the task and the danger of the loss of identity of the institution, Ramsay argues that the "push-and-pull between archival principles and interface culture goes to the heart of what it means to be an archive in the digital world." (2018: 295-296) This applies as much to smaller, less digitised archives as to the vast one that she worked with; all archives now exist in the digital world and however much they choose to engage with it, they have to live with the expectations and disappointments it affords.

Conclusion: When context is not a thing

Winters and Prescott argue that our addiction to Google-style searching has resulted in us becoming not only less aware, but also less interested in the interrelationships on which traditional archive systems are built (2019: 400). Accordingly, and notwithstanding the attempts of organisations to render their online material traceable and transparent, sometimes the answer to the question "Need more context?" that is posed on the UK National Archives website is simply "No". For some users, the context-free nature of the photographic image is exactly what makes it attractive and useful, hence the success of sites selling stock images, found quickly through keyword searches and used liberally on company and institutional websites. Artists and designers can grab images (film and sound material) from an ever-growing range of network spaces. They are able to create new contexts through re- and juxta-positioning of such material, and this is a valid way of working: de-contextualised images, for example, can be striking in their perplexity and their disconnect, and this was the case long before material was available online. But although appropriating images from any source can be productive, I suggest that it is more interesting — and safer — to be aware of their cultural or political connotations; it is best to know your context before you obliterate it, even if you do not wish to immediately share this information with your audience. Ernst describes how working with digitised archives can indeed result new creative insights, based on chance retrieval, but he strongly argues that that 'Such operations are possible in computational space without destroying the material and symbolic order of the existing archive' (2016: 11). In this sense, the material archive (and the catalogue) acts as a solid back-up for the many archive images that travel unabated through networks.

In her essay "In Defense of the Poor Image", artist and writer Hito Steyerl presents digital images as being "liberated from the vaults of cinemas and archives and thrust into digital uncertainty" (2012: 32). She presents a certain positivity, arguing that these images are transformed by people who care about them, and that they are opened up to a wider audience (ibid: 41). On the other hand, Michael Moss, a Professor of Archival Science, deems the mass release of digitised content from archives that happened in the 1990s (specifically census data, so once again he is writing mostly with regard to genealogists) in a more negative light, arguing, "The walls that surrounded the archival fortress were besieged" (2018: 261). The language of freedom — the breaking down of walls and the escape from slavery and chains — is recurrent in relation to the uploading of archival images to the internet, whether through purposeful release or accidental escape.

The networking of archival images represents a lightness of movement, a freedom from the chains of institutions that are often perceived to be heavy on power and control. Yet, even in 2002, Ernst argued that "values such as identity and meaning dissolve in a network of links which decide, more relentlessly than ever, what counts as context" (2002: 481). Are we now, more and more, becoming a media-driven society — post-veracity? — that is not overly concerned about the evidential value of documents of any kind; one where ambiguities in the field of communication (Derrida 1977: 2-3) are welcomed; one in which narratives are built that do not exist, from material that grows increasingly independent of its original context and that fluctuates in its identity and meaning from one day to the next? So, whilst it is important that images and data remain open for reuse, the photographic image, by its very nature a temporally discrete and context-free object, is predisposed to both premeditated and speculative manipulations of context.

References

Assange, Julian (2015): Introduction to the Verso collection: The Wikileaks Files: The World According to the US Empire, London and New York: Verso.

Blaschke, Estelle (2009): "From the Picture Archive to the Image Bank: Commercializing the Visual through Photography. The Bettmann Archive and Corbis." In: Études photographiques 24 November 2009, pp. 1-11.

Bolter, Jay David & Grusin, Richard (2000) Remediation: Understanding New Media, Cambridge, MA: MIT Press.

Briet, Suzanne (1951) What is Documentation? (Translated and edited by Ronald E. Day, Laurent Martinet and Hermina G.B. Anghelescu), Paris: Éditions Documentaires.

Cobb Photographs, National Archives, Kew.

Derrida, Jacques (1977) Limited Inc, Evanston, Illinois: Northwestern University Press.

Ernst, Wolfgang (2002) "Archive in Transition." In: B. Von Bismark/H.-P. Feldmann/H.U. Obrist, D. Stoller/ U. Wuggenig (eds.), Interarchive, Köln: Verlag der Buchhandlung, pp. 475-484.

Ernst, Wolfgang (2013) Digital Memory and the Archive. Edited and with an introduction by Jussi Parikka. Minneapolis: University of Minnesota.

Ernst, W. (2016) "Radically De-historicising the Archive. Decolonising Archival Memory from the Supremacy of Historical Discourse." In: Decolonising Archives, L'Internationale Online, 2 February 2016, pp. 9-16.

Fowler, S. (2107). "Inappropriate Expectations." In D. Thomas, S. Fowler & V. Johnson. The Silence of the Archive (pp. 41-63). London: Facet Publishing.

Galloway, Alexander R. (2020a) "Metadata as a Problem for Thinking." Available at http://cultureandcommunication.org/galloway/metadata-as-a-problem-for-thinking [accessed 11-09-20]

Galloway, Alexander R. (2020b) "Metadata=Data." Available at http://cultureandcommunication.org/galloway/metadata-data [accessed 11-09-20]

Gitelman, Lisa (2014) Paper Knowledge: Towards a Media History of Documents, Durham and London: Duke University Press.

Harry Price Archive, Archives and Manuscripts, Senate House Library, University of London.

Horsman, Peter/Ketelaar, Eric/Thomassen, Theo (2003) "New Respect for Old Order: The Context of the Dutch Manual." In: The American Archivist 66/2, pp.249-270.

International Council on Archives (2000) ISAD(G): General International Standard Archival Description (2nd edition), Ottawa: International Council on Archives.

Ketelaar, Eric (1996) "Archival Theory and the Dutch Manual." In: Archivaria 41, pp. 31-40.

Manovich, Lev (2018) "Can We Think Without Categories?" In: Digital Culture and Society 4/1, pp. 17-27.

Moss, Michael (2018) "Memory Institutions and Digital Disruption?" In: Andrew Hoskins (ed.), Digital Memory Studies: Media Pasts in Transition, New York: Routledge, pp. 253-297.

Mountbatten Papers, Special Collections Division, University of Southampton.

Muller, S./ Feith, J.A./ Fruin, R. (2003) Manual for the arrangement and description of archives, drawn up by direction of the Netherlands Association of Archivists (translation of the second edition by Arthur H. Leavitt), Chicago: Society of American Archivists.

Ramsay, Debra (2018) "Tensions in the Interface." In: Andrew Hoskins (Ed.), Digital Memory Studies: Media Pasts in Transition, New York: Routledge, pp. 253-279.

Rubinstein, Daniel (2010) "Encyclopaedia: Tag, Tagging." In: Philosophy of Photography, 1, pp. 197-200.

Rubinstein, Daniel/Sluis, Katrina (2013) "Concerning the Undecidability of the Digital Image." In: Photographies, 6:1, 151-158

Sekula, Allan (2003) "Reading an Archive: Photography Between Labour and Capital." In: Liz Wells (ed.), The Photography Reader, London: Routledge, pp. 443-452.

Steyerl, Hito (2012) The Wretched of the Screen, Berlin: Sternberg Press.

Vestberg, Nina Lager (2013) "Ordering, Searching, Finding." In: Journal of Visual Culture 12, pp. 472-489.

Winters, Jane/Prescott, Andrew (2019) "Negotiating the Born-Digital: A Problem of Search." In: Archives and Manuscripts 47/3 pp. 391-403.

One-Eyed Archive
Metadata Reflections on the USVI Photographic Collections at The Royal Danish Library

Mette Kia Krabbe Meyer, Temi Odumosu

Abstract

During 2016, the Royal Danish Library digitized more than 200.000 pages from the library's, collections all of which related to the former colonies in the Caribbean. This included books and other printed matter, but also sheet music, manuscripts, personal documents, photographs and drawings. Images were published in Digital Collections, the library's platform for digitized materials, and were accompanied by limited metadata, thereby posing challenges in terms of accessibility and important historical contextualisation. This essay therefore reflects on the gaps and the silences that haunt indexing and descriptive practices in the migration online. Mette Kia Krabbe Meyer is Senior Research Fellow at the Royal Danish Library and has been project-managing the digitisation. Temi Odumosu is Senior Lecturer in Cultural Studies at Malmö University and has worked intensively with the collection as user and collaborator in the project What Lies Unspoken. *As the Library embarks on initiatives to address the limited metadata associated with its digital collections, the authors come together to unfold key questions about approaches and process. They describe the characteristics of Digital Collections and the metadata currently provided, and ask what is left out and why; thereby engaging cultural biases that uneasily mirror the colonial project. The authors also explore how more inclusive user involvement, particularly in the United States Virgin Islands (USVI), could shift language and epistemology. The leading inquiry question is: In the one-eyed colonial archive, what is it possible for metadata to do?*

Keywords: Colonialism, photography, Denmark, US Virgin Islands, Royal Danish Library, metadata, archives, description, keywords, participation, open access, crowdsourcing, Caribbean, visual culture

Old and New Ground

In 2015 Danish cultural heritage collections prepared for an important commemorative moment in Denmark: the centennial of "transfer day", marking the official sale of the former Danish West Indies (St. Croix, St. Thomas, and St. John) to the United States on 31 March 1917. Public discourse during this period was polarised and uncomfortable, as the limited and somewhat nostalgic attention previously paid to these histories in Denmark was exposed. Moreover, the mainstream discussion was unable to sufficiently grapple with the enormity of colonial reverberations: reconciling the actuality of slavery and its remembrance; political and economic entanglements with other Danish colonial settlements; traumatic effects on Caribbean people, their identity and culture; acknowledging and accepting participation in colonial violence; and, also apology and healing. Meanwhile, arts and cultural heritage institutions embarked on a process of consolidation that involved identifying collections evidencing these histories, and also digitising the material for greater access. In the context of postcolonial relations, digitisation also served as a symbolic gesture of return, or rather historical redress (Agostinho 2019a). The weathered, fraying and burnished documents, the fragile mirrored daguerreotype plates, and the dust-infused maps were all digitally converted and joined databases as JPEG and TIFF files. This dematerialisation process was generally understood as a practical way to reach out, share and visualise materials that were subject to strict protocols and often kept in storage, also rarely used in exhibitions.

Open-accessing Danish colonial archives and collections as digital data had several effects. The 'scandal and excess' that characterised slavery and its archival footprint, was now available for consultation and witnessing outside the walls of institutions (Hartman 2008). This effort provided a scaled overview of Danish colonial endeavour, but it also registered ongoing African-descendant and Indigenous presence, and role, in the shaping of Denmark (and Danish families); further revealing how they too were agents of change in emancipation from slavery. Open access also meant that a wider range of artists, researchers and other interested stakeholders now had the possibility of engaging with this material on their own terms. At the same time, institutions were somewhat absolved from accountability with regards to guidelines for general use of material, since many Danish collections have made a commitment to creative commons licensing for historical material.

Ill. 1: Installation view of What Lies Unspoken: Sounding the Colonial Archive designed by Temi Odumosu for the exhibition Blind Spots: Images of the Danish West Indies Colony (2017-2018). Photo: Brian Berg.

Writing together as cultural practitioners with research and curatorial roles during the 2017 commemorations, we use this reflective paper to engage with what informs current praxis, and therefore address the ongoing possibilities for oversight and symbolic violence in Danish collections cataloguing and metadata. During the year of commemoration, we both worked with unfolding the context and the reaction to the material. Mette Kia Krabbe Meyer (MKKM) co-curated the exhibition *Blind Spots: Images of the Danish West Indies Colony* together with Senior Lecturer Mathias Danbolt, and Research Librarian and Curator of Photography Sarah Giersing. Confronting the notion of images as neutral windows to the world, the exhibition focused on the lopsidedness of the images in public collections, which were created by Danish colonial actors, at home and abroad. It analysed the exclusions, the embellishments, the condescending typologies, and the power-over expressed in Danish colonial imagery; all in an effort to contribute a Nordic perspective to the critical work being done internationally on colonial visual cultures. Having researched and written about similar material in a British context, Temi Odumosu (TO) designed an experimental sound installation called *What Lies Unspoken: Sounding the Colonial Archive,* which was developed collaboratively with Statens Museum for Kunst (SMK), with curator Henrik Holm as internal project lead (Ill.1). This double collections intervention at the library and SMK, involved a participatory process of gathering diverse people to critically respond to the physical artefacts in workshop settings, their voices being recorded and later edited into sonic compositions, as an alternative interpretive layer in the exhibition spaces (See Krabbe Meyer 2019; Odumosu 2019). Both manifestations are still available online, to some extent, but most users will meet the colonial material in their usual virtual state, which is without interpretation and with basic metadata. Having experienced the colonial collections in various unique manifestations, we wanted to think together, and return to unanswered questions about their condition online in the Digital Collections. We will describe and contextualise the digitisation process, in order to unfold what haunts indexing and classification systems as they migrate online.

Ill. 2: Participant in 2018 CHANT Summer School photographing the current site represented in a 20th century postcard Children's Home Frederiksted, St. Croix, D.W.I, from the library collection, with photographer David Berg. Photo: Mette Kia Krabbe Meyer. Original postcard in The Royal Danish Library. http://www5.kb.dk/images/billed/2010/okt/billeder/object301944/en/

Thinking about digital rights and responsibilities in an information society is tentative work, and the proposed goal when considering the library collections is ultimately to produce a more open and inclusive digital collection; one that can both articulate and resignify its colonial inheritances. The 2017 commemoration disturbed habits and produced openings (possibilities) for change that we want to hold on to, therefore our discussion articulates some of what we heard in a patchwork of critical responses that came from different kinds of meetings in the process of commemorative work: with independent artists and researchers who used the collections on and offline; in recorded workshops with artists, historians, students, and curators during the *What Lies Unspoken* project; with visitors to the *Blind Spots* exhibition; and on USVI with participants in the 2018 Archive Summer School at Crucian Heritage and Nature Tourism CHANT, run by Frandelle Gerard, which MKKM held together with Mathias Danbolt, artist Katrine Dirckinck-Holmfeld and photographer David Berg (who also volunteered in the library when visiting Denmark) (Ill.2). These encounters were eye-opening, intensive, and sometimes challenging, and they were not always planned as spaces for considering collections online specifically. However, the layering of perspectives in this way has been profoundly important for understanding the affects and effects of Danish colonial collections, when they appear in different contexts. That said, it is important to highlight that the lopsided nature of the archive also mirrors who is tasked with doing the work of curation and transforming possibilities. We do recognise that resource extraction can also happen when seeking collaboratively to open up a collection, which has been closed to any significant reconsideration for much of its history. Specifically, a lot of affective labour (energy, good will, critical concern, enthusiasm, and love) has paved the way for shifting awareness and catalysing a reevaluation of institutional practices. We hope to honour this work with our words, and in our attempt to envision expanding Digital Collections to become more meaningful for the many, rather than the few. Finally, we must insist that this text is not a forging of new concepts, but rather a moment for careful assessment and pause. We consider this going over trodden ground as an ethical act of threshing, in the sense that we write with purpose to clarify, to sift, and to nuance, in preparation for future initiatives (Tuck et. al. 2014).

Digitisation as a means to set "our" cultural heritage free

As a National Library with Legal Deposit Law and Special Collections dating back to the beginning of colonialism The Royal Danish Library holds substantial source material evidencing this history. The current scope is vast, in terms of time, content, and media: encompassing a 1494 German edition of Christopher Columbus's conquest letter to the King of Spain, all the way to recent media documentation of the artist monument *I AM Queen Mary* (2018), co-produced by Jeannette Ehlers and LaVaughn Belle. Back in 2015, when organisations were preparing for

"Transfer Day" commemorations, the National Archives had already scanned and made available written sources associated with the political and administrative history of Denmark's colonial rule in the Caribbean. These documents have long been considered an important part of Danish cultural heritage, and in 1997 they were included alongside all of the archives of Danish overseas trading companies in UNESCO's Memory of the World Register. To contextualise their newly digitised Caribbean material, the National Archives developed a bespoke website in English and Danish, where the material could be explored in thematically curated sections, and searched through a simple catalogue interface. With much more limited resources, the library wished to follow their lead and digitize and make available its collections too. The main focus at the time was the historical collection, consisting of manuscripts, books, periodicals, but also images in the form of postcards, photographs and drawings. In terms of content this included scientific material pertaining to the study of the Caribbean landscape, as well as details about the colonial structure, such as trade and military operations. Also, fictional works (novels, plays, poetry), as well as documents illuminating personal experience and living conditions. It is fair to say that the collections represent the Danish colonial worldview, as it was intentionally recorded for posterity, and in so doing also includes (or rather entangles) Afro-Caribbean and Indigenous subjectivities, experiences and modes of knowledge production.

Positivist formulations of digitised cultural heritage have characterised the effort to transform collections into big data, as a herculean feat of unprecedented sharing. All over the world museums, archives and libraries promote the digital replicants of their collections as opportunities to come closer to those things that are ordinarily out of reach, or difficult to see properly behind glass vitrines. In Denmark, digitisation has long been hailed as a form of soft cultural diplomacy that bridges the gap between institutions and new audiences, through the rhetoric of collective ownership (Sanderhoff 2014; Valtysson 2017). The desire to reach users where they are, can be seen as a byproduct of an evolving experience economy in Danish cultural industries, where visitors are encouraged to engage on their own terms (often framed as participation), rather than being educated by specialists and institutional gatekeepers. For context, it is important to highlight that since the 2000's Danish heritage institutions have been subject to a slow assault on specialisation, where a new governmental focus was placed on accessibility. In his 2002 New Years Eve speech Prime Minister Anders Fogh Rasmussen criticized specialists from "statslige råd og nævn og institutioner" for diminishing the rights of citizens to decide for themselves (Rasmussen 2002). Since then, the cultural sector has experienced financial cutbacks, whilst at the same time receiving extra pressure to be more content-driven, since institutional relevance and success are increasingly measured by the quantity of material available (rather than the depth of knowledge about them). Added to this, technological developments that lowered the cost of scanning, also contributed to the cherishing of digitisation as the tool for speeding up public engagement, relegating bespoke knowledge and detail to the domain of academic articles and hefty catalogues. In such a climate digitised material from libraries, museums, and archives, are introduced to users doubly as gifts, but also as shared cultural property that can be accessed anytime, generally used for any purpose, and stored on personal devices. A notable example from the Royal Danish Library collection are the open-access catalogues of the department store Daells Varehus, which have been digitized for their cult value as widely known and beloved examples of Danish vernacular culture.

For 2017 commemorative work, digitisation certainly provided the means through which a more transparent negotiation of the library's colonial collections could unfold, especially in the space of visual culture. However, because the resurfacing of challenging histories is not usually the intended outcome of such a process, the materials were treated in the same way as all other collections, following digital collections standards with only basic metadata and no contextual framing. One of the key aims of the *Blind Spots* exhibition was to counter the nostalgia involved in looking back at the sepia past, which has (to some extent) been facilitated by a longstanding practice of using images as an illustrative backdrop to history; an easy way to show how things used to be for Danes, rather than everyone else included in the space of colonial imagery. Formulations of Danish heritage have shifted over time, but a narrative of innocent colonialism has characterised Danish storytelling about the country's role as a small-time colonial power that was less brutal than other European nations, and also the first to legally abolish the Slave Trade in 1792 (Andersen 2014; Danbolt & Wilson 2018; Olwig 2003; Simonsen 2016). When the islands were sold in 1917, the populations living there became American overnight, which means that there has been a limited immigrant community with Caribbean-Danish background to challenge the dominant understandings of this history with their embodied presence: that direct awareness of "we are here because you were there" prevalent in other European post-colonial contexts. The nostalgia for a lost paradise, and the celebration of courageous Danes who opposed slavery, has therefore endured, and come with consequences for the way Danish colonialism is represented, explained, and treated. In this context digitisation is not a simple scan and release of data, but a process of *implication*, a graphic exposure to documents that evidence the seen and unseen of the colonial world, and therefore a haunting (Gordon 2008); for institutions and users (Agostinho et al. 2019b, 2020). This is why the library's Digital Collections have become a point of focus for this discussion, since we consider it a space of possibility, but also an information resource that is troubled by gaps, absences and silences.

Who owns cultural heritage?

The characterisation of the Royal Danish Library's colonial collections as an open cultural commons is somewhat misleading, given their mixed acquisition history. The library collections were not like those of the National Archives, which were transferred from the islands to Denmark, specifically to be archived as heritage, when the US took over (Bastian 2003; 2001). There is no inherited "colonial collection" as such, although the digitisation process (and the 2017 commemorative context) have facilitated a specific categorisation of this material under "Dansk Vestindien" in order to make materials easier to find. Collections from and about the Caribbean, including prior to Danish rule and after, have come by legal deposit (handing over of printed material from printers), donations from private entities, and purchase on auctions. This means that the colonial "views" the library has are uneven to begin with, and the collections themselves represent formulations of private property that are inherently colonial. Nowhere is this better demonstrated than in the photographic collections, where questions of power and ownership reach all the way back to the taking of photographs. The thousands of anonymised Afro-Caribbean people who appear in albums and on commercial postcards made from photographs, show extractive representational practices that disconnected subjects from familial ties, making questions of rights and consent impossible to answer.

A daguerreotype in the collections illustrates these asymmetries of power clearly (Ill.3). Taken in 1847, the double portrait of Charlotte Hodge and Louise Bauditz (an Afro-Caribbean servant and the child she was nurturing) has been kept in the library as former property of the German Bauditz family of St. Croix. Questions of rights here are complex. Research in local parish records suggests that Hodge was free at the time of the photograph, a widower, and a mother who had lost at least seven of her eight children.[1] But this was also a year before emancipation, and though she may have been legally free, the extent of her freedoms under an ongoing colonial regime are difficult to ascertain; especially where she may have worked among fellow servants counted as enslaved property. Photography in these situations was generally a privilege for white colonial families who were recording (and fashioning) their existence away from Europe (Langford 2001). In many colonial contexts, native maids and wetnurses appear in family photography, particularly due to their closeness to children (Wood 2013; González-Stephan and Good 2016; Hirsch 1999; Stoler 2002). Also, in the early days of the medium, nannies were called on as supporting figures and "props" for children, who needed to be kept still to produce clear portraits. It was not uncommon for

---

1   A short biographical summary entitled 'Who was Charlotte Eliza Hodge of St Criox?' was written in June 2017 by USVI historian George Tyson, and is available to researchers upon request.

some of these women to be veiled or cloaked, to obscure their identities as "hidden mothers" (Nagler 2013). The ambiguities surrounding how and why such women appear in these photographs thus tend to result in a default reading of their role as marginal, and any rights are assigned/assumed to the dominant family (Hirsch, 1997). But, these images depict multiple subjectivities, with gazes that often address the viewer directly, and therefore need to be recognised. The 'labor of imagination' involved in making connections between what is visible and invisible in photographs, is the ethical work involved in facing colonial histories (Smith 2013, 98; Azoulay 2008).

Ill. 3: Record in Kunstindeks Danmark of daguerreotype depicting Charlotte Hodge and Louisa Bauditz, 1847. The Royal Danish Library. https://www.kulturarv.dk/kid/ VisVaerk.do?vaerkId=480073

 Dobbeltportræt af Louisa MacPherson Bauditz med sin amme Charlotte Hodge

Kunstner:
Titel: Dobbeltportræt af Louisa MacPherson Bauditz med sin amme Charlotte Hodge
Datering: ca 1847
Værktype: Daguerreotypi
Nettomål: lysmål: 71 x 55 mm
Signatur/betegnelse: Ikke bet.
Museum: Det Nationale Fotomuseum, Det Kongelige Bibliotek, inv. nr. 2007-65/10
Erhvervelse: [Blank], 2007

Perhaps Charlotte Hodge considered it an honour to be photographed alongside the children she cared for; perhaps it was an infringement on personal boundaries that she had to swallow; or perhaps she simply accepted that being photographed was a part of her role attending to a wealthy colonial family. We do not know. Even with historical hindsight, engaging her presence as a willing photographic subject is tentative work. For example, a second, slightly damaged, daguerreotype shows Hodge in another group portrait, once more with Louise on her lap and the two other Bauditz boys on either side of them. What can we realistically infer from her repeated presence in the family frame? There are other ethical considerations. Since the library's collections bridge public and private interests, the broader issue of image circulation is also critical. For Hodge to become part of 1840's white Danish family photography is a situation we cannot change, but what about uses of her image in the present day? During 2017, the photograph was used as a poster and promotional eye-catcher for the library's *Blind Spots* exhibition. This was done intentionally, in order to visualise and give space to Hodge's story, as an example of the many nameless ones that had not been told. However, reflecting back on this choice it is important to ask: Who truly "owns" the portrait within which Charlotte Hodge features? If Hodge had or has living descendants, should they be involved and recognised in the library's stewarding of this portrait?[2] And importantly, how should the Royal Danish Library explain, and allow use of, this image? In an official legal response to such questions, the library may refer to personal rights having expired, making digital use and reproduction freely available, without needing to seek permission. But this does not neutralise the underlying frictions, nor the brutalising historical and material conditions that permanently bind the library's collections to slavery and colonialism. Thus, the library is left to contend with ethical issues, leaving the safe harbour of legality to engage in more delicate conversations about fairness (Dalgleish 2011; Odumosu 2020); or what Marika Cifor theorises as 'emotional justice' (Cifor 2016).

In the exhibition *Blind Spots* Charlotte Hodge's personal story was explained in the accompanying label text, which also addressed the power exercised in taking the photograph. In the sound intervention *What Lies Unspoken*, participants reacted strongly, and spoke of their ambivalence when faced with beauty in the context of horror. They found it difficult to ascertain the extent of Hodge's freedoms and agency, and also asked questions about intimacy, privilege, and self-fashioning. Both text and sound intervention are still available on the library website, and are included in learning materials for students on questions of ownership, digitisation and ethics. All these critical engagements have added meaning and context to

---

2   This is a question that haunts engagement with photography in so many colonial contexts, such as the Zealy Daguerreotypes of elder Renty and seven other enslaved Africans photographed for a race biology project by Louis Agassiz (Barbash et al. 2020).

the Daguerreotype, as it continues to exist as historical evidence in the collection. However, when viewed online the double portrait appears with minimal metadata that belies all the efforts to resignify the image.

More than 10 years ago the portrait was added to Kunstindeks Danmark (the central register of artworks owned by Danish state-owned and state-subsidised museums), along with the large collection of daguerreotypes held by the library. This means that engagement with the digital record happens in the index and not the library's Digital Collections. In the public record there is no official naming of those portrayed. The names of the Hodge and Bauditz are instead included in a constructed title that was likely created in the absence of an official one, when added to Kunstindeks Danmark. Since the name of the photographer is unknown, the public record only includes the year of creation and acquisition, object material and name of institution. No information is provided about the history of the image, nor the history of the persons depicted, and as a user one is unable to contribute to or adapt the record. It is this standardised way of referencing and organising collections that allow for silencing and erasure on the basis of ownership, which is another way of establishing rights - to exist, to decide, to belong.

Historically the catalogue has been the source of information for librarians mainly; protocols, filing cards, registers have been managed by library staff for centuries, but with Digital Collections new possibilities have been created. In the following we will describe and discuss the advantages and risks involved in opening the catalogue to the public. The USVI-collection may be the collection where it makes most sense, but is at the same time a delicate place to experiment.

Applying metadata

When the library chose to digitise collections back in 2015, it was for a range of reasons concerned with accessibility for the public good: making collections available for artists, researchers and the broader public interested in understanding and entering into a dialogue about the colonial past. Online access was especially crucial for reaching an international audience, and also allowing the material to become part of the global discourse on colonialism. In practice, however, the conversion of materials into data has been a largely technical process without curation or contextualisation. The financial and time investment has been used primarily for taking materials out of storage, then out of envelopes and boxes, and then putting them into a scanner etc. To some extent it was anticipated that images could "speak for themselves", and be deciphered without added description. This meant that there were very few resources for adding metadata to the materials whether that was existing metadata or metadata added in the process of digitisation. 2017 commemorative work revealed how important descriptive practices are in situating the collections, historically and in the present day. Not only to develop research and knowledge, but also to revisit the frames of reference that guide professional practices and transfer meanings to users. As Saidiya Hartman crucially explains in the context of titles given to (and imposed on) photography, 'the caption produces what appears. It subsumes the image to the text' (Hartman 2019, 20). If we thought about metadata as an extended form of captioning collections representing colonial events, then what kind of words should we use, and why?

Ill. 4: Screen view of Digital Collections under the catalogue title Vestindien. The Royal Danish Library. http://www5.kb.dk/images/billed/2010/okt/billeder/ subject5259/en?view=masonry

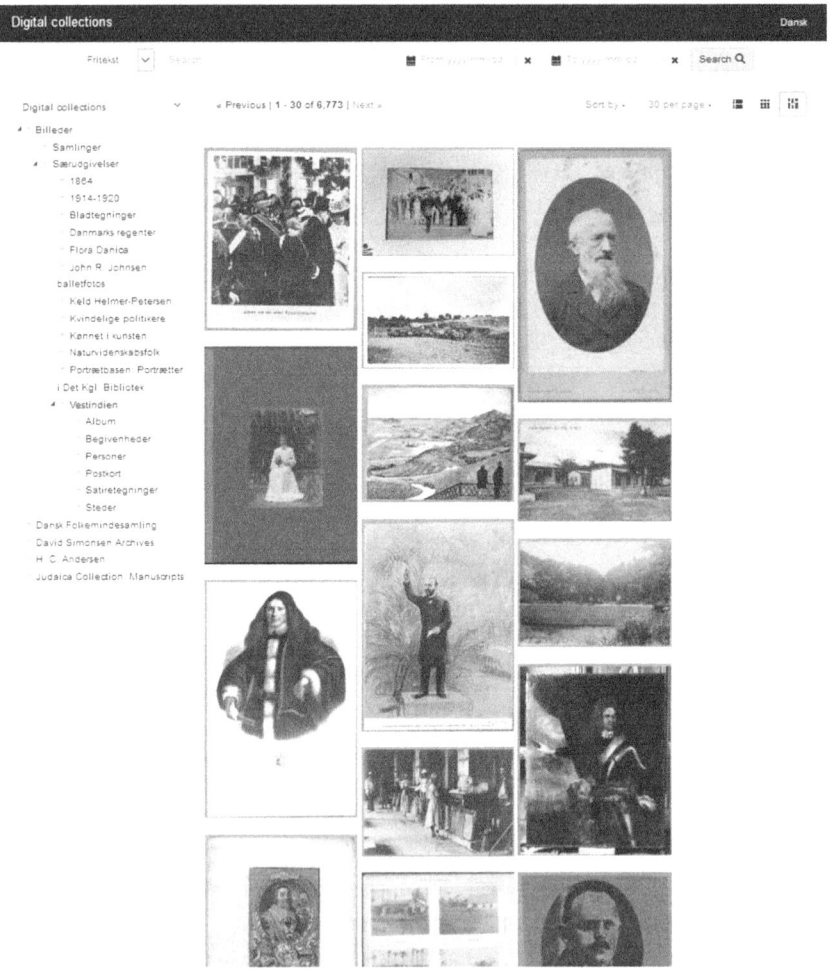

In the library, as with most collections, digitisation begins with locating physical materials. In line with colonial notions of ownership and processes of land acquisition, the topographical collection already had a section titled "Danish West

Indies". Materials such as maps and landscape prints were taken out for scanning, along with a number of portraits, photograph albums and other images found through research. Collections were then sent to the Digitization Department and originals and files returned to Special Collections, where metadata were assigned by Research Librarians in the Canto database. USVI materials would then be published into Digital Collections, not Kunstindeks Danmark, and follow the template and standards of this platform (Ill.4). The template used only allows for basic information to be included in each record, and within this there are hierarchies. For example, information about the creator of an image is paramount, since copyright law requires this to be available when the image is published. Information about location, the place the photographs were taken, as well as the date of exposure (which seldom appears within the image itself), are also regarded as basic or primary metadata. In online collections there is also a field for names of recognised subjects, such as those represented in material. Very often, the older catalogues also contained other more detailed information, such as size, condition, acquisition numbers, provenance, as well as any hand-written annotation, both by original image producers and viewers, or later, by librarians. All these details are part of an ecology of information that have been critical for researchers, since they situate colonial collections within layered historical contexts. They also explain how practices of imperial prospecting and/or management, are also an institutional inheritance (Carby and Vermeulen, 2015). However the drive to digitise has exposed a gap between the information that constitutes a complete digital record, and what is required to give critical insight into the historical importance and cultural relevance of these collections.

The Royal Danish Library does not have a written catalogue of the USVI collection. Materials have therefore been recorded in the acquisition protocol, very often with little information. And, in terms of organisation, the library's collections are sorted according to already established headlines in the archives. There are some keywords that feature in the protocol, but these are often simple terms, pointing to the main subjects or objects in the images. No thesaurus or other standard lists, such as Denmark's "Saglig registrant for kulturhistoriske Museer", were used as a guideline, as they did, for example, in Europeana Collections 1914-1918 project, where more nuanced terms such as "foreign policy" or "principle of neutrality" expressed the political dimensions of WWI remembrance. Of critical importance to address is the fact that words such as slave trade, slavery, imperial, or imperialism are not associated keywords for the USVI material in the Royal Danish Library; even though they are standard terms in the metadata *Thesaurus for Graphic Materials*, instituted by the Library of Congress. Most keywords concern what the image literally shows, rather than what it represents or conveys about the situation; content rather than meaning (Schwartz, 2002). This is in line with the general interest in communicating the "material in itself" and not the context it was made or understood in.

However, rather than making the collections uniform or neutral, the keywords used (or not used) reveal institutional blind spots and reify old knowledge structures, making them complicit in the violences embedded in the material. When the library does not use the Digital Collections to explain the contexts out of which its primary collections emerged, it also reproduces the nostalgic idea of colonialism (and colonial history) as abstract, free-floating, detached from the present, easy or simple, and lacking substance. Certainly, there is a need to develop metadata by considering how users approach collections, either with questions, curiosities, or more invested engagements with the material. Recent activist work in library and archival information sciences is reviewing descriptive practices within a social justice framework, and taking a stand about how we conduct this work more inclusively and carefully. For example, the *Archives for Black Lives Matter in Philadephia* anti-racist description resource, emphasises the importance of developing an anti-oppressive mindset in the development of metadata; and foregrounds the 'emotional ties' that stakeholder communities have to collections (Antracoli et al. 2020). Furthermore, they encourage the use of 'accurate and strong language' (words articulating forms of violence) to represent collections more faithfully, and at the same time signal to users what is at stake when they engage with this material.

There are many words missing in the library's USVI digital collection. For example, there is no reference to important terms, such as: colonial, colonialism, slavery, Transatlantic Slave Trade, or enslavement. There are also no racial, ethnic or cultural identifiers such as: Black, Indigenous, Afro-Caribbean, Creole, or even white. Without many of these words, any other keywords such as "sugar" or "worker" lose their historical intensity, as a way to cite inequitable contact. The template for digital records does, however, include information about the "placing" of objects within the collection. These markers are added in order to maintain a link between digital files and the original materials. In this context a photograph may appear as part of the digital collection bearing the term "Folkeliv". This is an old Danish word describing a genre of images (paintings or photographs) representing everyday life situations, which would not be used today. The genre also became a cataloguing term that allowed for the organisation of some collections thematically. However, in the digital collection, it has survived as one of those so-called "universal" terms that basically indicates where the original is located in collections storage. The presence of such terms in the frontend user experience online, implies continuity between (for example) a street scene in Copenhagen, Inuit fishing in Angmagsalik, and a market scene on St. Croix. This issue, and the term, was a key topic of discussion during workshops that took place during the *What Lies Unspoken* project, whose aim was to register the affects and effects of the library's collections. Participants noted how this term worked to frame images of Afro-Caribbean people into benign types and memories (like the "cries" compendia of 19th century street life), whilst undermining the harsh labour realities behind these images. Also, the term failed to register the imaginative tropicalisation at play in the staging of certain images for a distant audience (Thompson 2006). The migration of original metadata has been clunky in this regard, with indexing terms such as "Folkeliv" silencing specificities and structural conditions. These administrative terms are institutional leftovers, but also hauntings that produce divergent meanings for different users on and offline. In this sense, the "then" and the "now" of the collections, continue to constitute each other; meaning that they maintain colonial equivalences by reproducing centres and peripheries of power. If the collections themselves are an index for Danish colonial entanglements, then the indexing practices the library uses, also signal what and how knowledge is being constructed.

Public preferences move in

Alongside advances in cultural heritage digitisation, crowdsourcing has become popular as a means to outsource cataloguing labour to enthusiastic volunteers and general members of the public (Ridge 2017). This goes hand-in-hand with the opening of collections as a way to enhance the rhetoric of shared ownership. 15 years ago, institutions such as New York Public Library, Power House Museum in Australia, and others were frontrunners in introducing crowdsourcing technologies, which are now commonplace (See Chan 2007). Levels of engagement with these systems of data acquisition are varied. For example, users have been invited to add basic keywords in the manner of a familiar hashtag on social media, sometimes as part of folksonomy projects (Peters 2009). They have also entered into deeper classificatory and identification systems; scrolling through protocols and tapping in numbers or letters, to confirm or deny automatic translation of letters, or recognition of elements in images. In crowdsourcing, metadata is built through augmentation, in the sense that users are co-opted as a second eye, whilst also adding their own preferences; responding to what they literally see, or what is absent and they would like to be included. These work-sharing practices may not fundamentally change the institutional outlook on their collections, but at the very least crowdsourcing does propose a different way to invest in the caretaking of public culture.

Several Danish cultural institutions have made it possible for users to add keywords to digital collections, and also to identify locations by citing images geographically (for example in early street photography). Generally, however, institutions have remained conservative in their use of crowdsourcing as a method. And in fact, some scepticism was expressed, both within institutions and by users of systems, towards platforms which allowed for other metadata beyond the basic names, places, and years (Jongma and Dijkshoorn 2016). This is understandable due to the fact that this approach comes with major risks in terms of accuracy, consistency, abuse, and bias (Ibid; Bates and Rowley 2011). There are also very limited resources to review public responses on a regular basis. From an institutional perspective crowdsourcing is doubly a meeting with and mode of feedback from invisible publics; a demonstrable form of outreach framed as "playlabour" (Agostino, 2015). But it's exploitative dimensions in hours of free unregulated work, has also been critiqued, and this is of special concern when we are speaking about caretaking colonial heritage. Fundamentally there is an issue of power, and the role that different actors play in cultural and historical production. However, opening up Digital Collections to users does make it possible for them to engage with and influence collections. If authority is not shared with users, collections will continue to act in monologue, as a one-way communication system.

There are many examples of participatory approaches to augmenting collections information through user influence, and they range in scale, boldness, and levels of resource investment. For example, inviting a "Wikipedian in residence" in order to develop wiki-pages on collections, which can then be maintained collaboratively and autonomously outside the institution, and meet a general web-browsing public. Such an approach has been taken by many institutions internationally, such as the British Museum, Smithsonian Institution, and the Swedish National Heritage Board. In Denmark, the City Museum of Copenhagen took an innovative and direct approach through their former project *The WALL (Væggen)*, which physically entered public space as a mobile interactive unit, and a website, allowing users to add their own metadata, but also photographs and memories into the collection (Sandahl et al 2011). This initiative capitalised on the situated nature of the city's collections and encouraged residents to take ownership and participate in storytelling about their urban environment, by mapping 'social lines' and 'paths of desire' (Ibid.). Another approach to transforming digital records has recently caught our attention, and is important to mention here. The "Critical Catalog" project initiated by researchers at Syracuse University Information School in New York, offers a provocative fabulation that disturbs the hidden hierarchies in library catalogues (Clarke and Schoonmaker 2020). Here they use the library catalogue as 'design material for social justice', and enter the records to shift metadata and indexes so that they privilege marginalised content (Ibid, 1). For example a query for "science fiction" would first bring results by Octavia Butler, rather than established white, male authors, who maintain prominence in such catalogues due to their organisation around chronology and disciplinary canons. The project also altered the machine-readable side of fixed date data, so that all examples of 'white normativity' in the catalogue are linked to the year when the first slave ship entered the US, in Virginia, in 1619 (Ibid, 4 & 9). Although conceived as a "what if" design speculation, the experiment presents a radical decentering of norms and perspectives from behind the scenes, pointing to ingrained structural biases, and the ways in which cataloguing shapes user experience.

Notes from imperfect data interactions

Many inspiring examples demonstrate that it is possible for each library collection, and maybe even each document, to have its own context of communication, and that the digital collection could be remodelled as a forum for user interaction and influence. Furthermore, Danish cataloguers, whose collections substantiate colonialism and its legacies, could begin to come together and formulate a broader and more critically situated set of keyword or indexing terms that carefully set the tone for public engagement; thereby taking accountability for collections and the stories housed there. In this sense the catalogue does not "lose" anything, but rather encompasses established data and alternative forms of referencing, such as user reactions, and other forms of inclusive description. Opening up to these possibilities for the USVI materials is especially important because access to physical collections is restricted in Denmark, and impossible for people in the Virgin Islands. Whilst the Royal Danish Library Digital Collections cannot fully substitute being with original materials, it is an already established platform with the potential for addressing unfinished histories and collaboratively revising descriptive practices in an ethical way. With this in mind we return to some of the important reflections that emerged from external stakeholders during 2017 commemorative work, and in continued interactions afterwards.

During workshops in both Denmark and the USVI, a primary issue noted in discussions about the Digital Collections was the issue of language barriers, since much of the metadata is written in Danish. When digitisation began, the original idea was to provide initial metadata in Danish but with the hope for multiple choice translation software that would be installed in the catalogue. However, given the time required for implementation and the ongoing issue of resources, this has not yet happened; which has thus produced another barrier to user engagement that will now need to be addressed manually, so to speak. The issue of translation is not necessarily unique to collections in a Danish context, but when viewed critically through (post) colonial entanglements with the USVI, and accompanying attempts at historical redress, this enclosure of language continues to present the sources of the past from a dominating standpoint.

Decentering the Danish tropicalisation of the USVI, and the similar approach to colonial collections, has been an important shift in perspective when considering the meaningfulness of collections in different contexts. One of the practical ways in which people from the USVI engaged with the library's digital material was by using their experiences of the lived environment as a starting point. For instance people expressed looking for the street in which they live, or browsing through the material to see if they could recognise places. When volunteer David Berg posted images from the collections on his Facebook account, he noted that often people would respond wanting to know if there were images of their house or from their neighbourhood in the collection. This is a familiar response also with Danish users. In this case institutions that utilise crowdsourcing benefit from this situated knowledge of place, and make it possible to identify and map locations not cited in the archive, or currently unknown to institutions. This option is available, for example, in the Copenhagen digital database Kbhbilleder.dk. Considering USVI relations to space and place is important to underscore. In Danish colonial histories, the habitual focus has been on privileging topographical (over)views, as well as historic buildings and architecture that housed Danish administration, or, were the homes of Danish colonists.

Ill. 5: Katrine Dirckinck-Holmfeld at 2018 CHANT Summer School, showing students an image of a 20th century postcard titled Hospitalsgade i Frederikssted, from the library collection. Photo: Mette Kia Krabbe Meyer. Original photograph in The Royal Danish Library. http://www5.kb.dk/images/billed/2010/okt/billeder/ object278054/da/

Within the last decades however USVIers have conducted research to find and contextualise the dwellings of enslaved people and the Afro-Caribbean population more generally, as well as the materials used to produce these buildings. The library's image collection is useful in this regard, since it holds many representations of houses that the Afro-Carribean population lived in, and also documents local building techniques such as shingles or embellished woodworks. Crucian artist La Vaughn Belle has explored these structural embellishments as examples of Black creativity and freedom-claiming in her work *Constructed Manumissions* (2017). At CHANT Frandelle Gerard is practically educating young men to become woodmasters, and to assist in the reconstruction of old houses that have been weathered by time and recent hurricanes. As part of the 2018 CHANT summer school, photographs by Danish apothecary Alfred Paludan-Müller, from around 1900, were used to try to locate houses and obtain knowledge about construction, as a way of bridging present to the past. Today the Digital Collections bear no traces of this outreach activity, which has been critical for developing situated knowledge about the collections overall, as well as nuancing understanding of how Caribbean landscapes evolved, and were constructed, within (and in spite of) the confines of colonialism. Furthermore, the enthusiasm witnessed around this outreach work, physically citing and marking space in the USVI, suggests that georeferencing capabilities in digital records, might encourage more local interaction with images of buildings represented in the collections.

Ill. 6: David Berg. Hospital Street, 2018. Digital photograph. Courtesy of the artist..

Closely connected to the interest in specific buildings and streets, is the interest in historical moments. At the CHANT, artist Katrine Dirckinck-Holmfeld drew attention to a postcard in the collection, featuring a building on Hospitalsgade in Frederiksted, St. Croix (Ill.5+6) In Digital Collections the image is accompanied with basic metadata, and a singular keyword "house" (even though on close inspection a child stands in the background of the image). Looking at the writing on the backside of the postcard it appears that this was the place where labour rights campaigner Hamilton Jackson (1884-1946) gave speeches during his efforts to galvanise resistance to colonial rule in 1915-1916. All this information is lost to international users, but also to Danish speakers, who are not given any contextual information in the catalogue. The importance of this place and the presences invoked there, go unreferenced in the Digital Collection, simply because the current cataloguing processes leave little room for the records to grow and evolve as information resources; living (rather than dead) archives (Caswell and Cifor 2019).

Another example is a postcard with the title *Queen Marys indsejling i Frederikssted* / Queen Mary's arrival in Frederiksted, which represents a faded harbour scene with a scattered crowd of people, and is marked in pen with a black star, likely by the postcard's writer, to signal the presence of two army officers. The postcard was found recently by researchers looking for information about Queen Mary Thomas, one of the key freedom fighters leading the 1878 labour revolt on St. Croix, known locally as the Fireburn. However, the image does not depict Queen Mary, but rather her son Hezekiah Smith who (according to the postcard writer) had fled arrest to America, but was now returning to St. Croix. In their US Virgin Islands history resource online, The National Archives provides a more detailed account of Hezekiah Smith's troubling story, and multiple criminal convictions, describing him as the last convict from the "Danish West Indies" who was eventually pardoned by King Christian X. Contextualised, the library's photograph takes on further meaning, and its production and mislabeling is better explained. What could more rigorous metadata and cross referencing between digital resources have done to shed light on these important historical moments? Discussions about these and other materials in the Digital Collections continue to confirm that Danish colonial narrations are filled with errors, slippages, and practices of misidentification; that they are shifting, rather than fixed and stable, sources of history.

Finding people in the collections is also fraught with problems inherited from the colonial administrative mindset. This was a frustration aired by researchers as well as more casual users of Digital Collections. In the example with the return of Hezekiah Smith, the library subsequently added his name to the collection record, so that the image could be found in searches for historical persons. In the Digital Collections it is mostly white men who are featured in the category "persons". This is a result of the fact that historical sources focusing on them were used for selection, and because the portrait collection itself has the same preference towards white males; as such they have become prototypical of self-determined subjectivity. Cataloguing has absorbed these biases. For example, the initial searches for images of Hamilton Jackson were difficult because they had been placed in a section of the catalogue containing "unidentifiable" people. Many discussions over the course of commemorative work were particularly concerned with this erasure of important Afro-Caribbean presences from the cataloguing structure, and with the ways cataloguing continues to perpetuate these erasures. Colonial portraitures are, of course, varied and multimodal, as the image and citation of Hezekiah Smith's arrival points to. There are numerous images of Afro-Caribbean families, some nannies, maids and servants, coal workers, field workers, and everyday pedestrians, mixed up with Danish merchants, military officers, and colonial families. However, many Afro-Caribbean people who appear in the photographs were not named in the accompanying records. This anonymisation transferred to island postcards, where some of the same people figure as island-types with assigned labels such as "a happy worker". There are examples of people who had their names added to the physical material, by people who knew them. Charlotte Hodge is one example, where her name is written on the backside of the photograph, likely by the Bauditz family. Due to this her identity is known in Kunstindeks Danmark (here her name is added in the title due to lack of field for depicted persons). For others, such as Sarah, the maid in Paludan-Müllers photo album, her name was not entered in the record in the field "person" in Digital Collections but only appears in the scanned image, from the handwriting in the album (Ill.7). An open-end catalogue might include the possibility of adding names written on the materials to the record thereby making them searchable and visible.

Ill. 7: Record in Digital Collections showing photograph labeled "Sarah i Baldragt (stuepige)" in Alfred Paludan-Müllers album, ca. 1900. The Royal Danish Library. http://www5.kb.dk/images/billed/2010/okt/billeder/object300079/da/

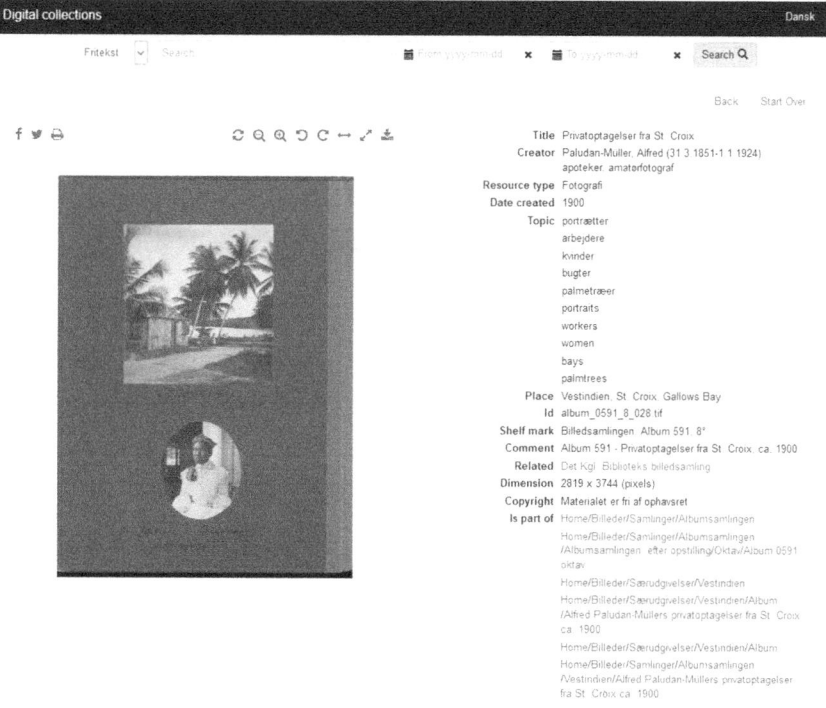

There is much about the library's colonial collections that is difficult to put words to. This was a feeling and tension that characterised engagements with this material in the *What Lies Unspoken* project, but was also expressed in so many different interactions during commemorative work. For visual artist Jeannette Ehlers, the portrait of Sarah, dressed in what is called a "brides dress" in the album, caused many emotions. The direct gaze of Sarah addressing the viewer, the photographer, and perhaps even her employer who set-up the situation, was particularly arresting. This confronting but ambiguous gaze led the artist to create *Black is a Beautiful Word. I & I* (2019). The work layers video portraits of Black women seated in the same pose as Sarah, slowly fading in and out of view. These still-moving-images of quietly breathing women with an intent gaze, are accompanied by a spoken monologue addressed to Sarah, and written by Trinidadian-American writer & activist Lesley-Ann Brown (Campt 2017).[3] The work begins with the important assertion that: "you are a possible me in the past, I am a possible you in the present".

Artistic practice and engagement with the collection has unfolded photographic situations in ways that poetically extend what can be addressed by descriptive records and single keywords. At the same time artistic interventions also pose their own questions about language, and the values invested in keyword terms. For example, the term "housemaid", which not only defines a colonial working situation, but has also become a stereotype for how Afro-Caribbean women are assumed to appear in this material; meaning that the cataloguing confines subjects to the limitations of its colonial shorthand. When David Berg worked as a volunteer in the collection this issue also came up regarding some of the street scenes. Houses in the collection had been named "workers" housing but Berg insisted that Crucians today would not make such distinctions, and more likely search simply for homes. He also pointed to the fact that "family life" (for instance) was a phrase not currently used in Digital Collections, but which might appeal as a local search term. Many of the discussions challenged the library in its proscribing of collections based on outdated terms of reference, and called for more open catalogues, and critical considerations in labelling and descriptive practices.

Conclusion, or, unfolding terms of reference

Writing in 2020 we are at a distance from the year of commemoration. 2017 moved quickly with a plethora of activities, exhibitions, media, talks, debates, and concerts. The energy and dynamism of the moment offered new perspectives and experiences, as well as revived old problems that were difficult to fully process in the moment. Once the year ended, for a short while it seemed as if the familiar pattern of "out of sight, out of mind" returned to the Danish cultural domain. But

---

3   Ehlers's work is now part of the Royal Danish Library collection, and joins other contemporary reformulations of colonial materials in the Library's Digital Collections, such as La Vaughn Belle's *Photomontage Series* (2016).

things are shifting slowly. Now with space and time for reflection, in a different but still urgent context, the need to address colonial legacies and structural racism is challenging all stakeholders working in the public domain. 2020 has demonstrated that anti-blackness is a collective, common, environmental issue concerning general conditions which must be changed (Sharpe 2016). In this situation the Digital Collections may seem like a strange place to begin, but it is also a structure that produces knowledge, an evident object of study and a critical site for tangible change. There are many questions that emerge when attention is focussed on templates, documents, and terms of reference in an online catalogue, but the key ones in a Danish context seem to be these: Who and what appears, and why? What kinds of information and descriptive practices would adequately reflect the nature and tenor of colonial collections? And how will this work be done, inclusively?

In this paper we have taken the experiences we gained during the year of commemoration and the time following, and reflected upon the digitization of the USVI collections in The Royal Danish Library. As we stated at the beginning our mission was not to outline new methodologies (although some ideas have appeared), but instead to soberly take stock of choices already made, and to give voice to source criticism and ethical issues, which are sometimes left out of Danish digitization discussions. We look back at a digitisation drive, with its accompanying rhetoric of sharing and openness, but which in reality has left few resources for developing metadata, allows limited exchange with users, and currently provides no formal possibilities for adding new information to the Digital Collections. In short, stories cannot be fully told. This streamlining of digitisation, with a focus on machine-reading processes and the provision of digital images, has had epistemic consequences. For example, central metadata, such as acquisition numbers that make it possible to trace the size of smaller collections donated to the library, and thus to know more about the provenance of an item, were not initially added.[4] Written texts, notations and markings visible on the physical collections (such as postcard greetings or notes in photo albums), were also not added. Furthermore, the descriptive handling of the images themselves has remained on the surface denotative level, reproducing a distancing effect from historical context and social meanings that undermines the very purpose of institutions tasked with the responsibility of cultural stewardship.

Producing an open catalogue online, as a conscientious space for purposeful information sharing and user interaction, requires resources. Not simply financial,

---

[4] During 2020, some students working at the library, who were sent home during covid-19, helped to begin making additions to the Digital Collections, such as adding acquisition numbers and English keywords. An overall change of the name of the collection from "Dansk Vestindien" to "Vestindien" was also made, although this will continue to be reconsidered.

but also in terms of diversity of expertise. More importantly there needs to be a will to reach out, and transform habits of being. By this we mean truly collaborative approaches to developing healthy digital resources, both in terms of learning from international colleagues who share similar challenges with their collections, but also including (and empowering) Afro-Caribbean stakeholders in the behind the scenes processes; moving forward, the USVI collection needs an international advisory panel. We also mean that a major change in mindset is required for understanding colonial collections as living entities that are emotionally charged, and the role of librarians and cataloguers as caretakers and witnesses (Caswell and Cifor 2016; Odumosu 2019). In this sense a poethic sensibility is required to consider a range of approaches to the task at hand. The question of opening up to crowd-sourcing possibilities still needs careful consideration, although we can identify key areas where this would be useful. For example, reading and transcribing written information on collections like the handwritten postcards. Also, providing USVI users the possibility of adding local knowledge to the records, whether in the form of georeferencing, or adding relevant names and events. However, alongside specific initiatives we consider the broader task to be the development of a critical digital catalogue, with a clear agenda for countering a long history of racialisation, nostalgia, and tropicalisation. For this we need words (a lexicon) to describe what the collections attest to: slavery, colonialism, dehumanisation; but also a framework for managing transformations in discourse, so that the catalogue can carefully adapt to the sensibilities of this historical moment. These are some ways we consider the process of turning an old monolith into a living information resource.

References

Agostino, Cristiano. 2015. "Museum Crowdsourcing as Playful Labour". *ICOFOM Study Series*. 43(a): 23-37.

Agostinho, Daniela. 2019a. "Archival Encounters: Rethinking Access and Care in Digital Colonial Archives". *Archival Science*. 19(2): 141–165.

Agostinho, Daniela et al. 2019b. *Archives that Matter. Infrastructures for Sharing Unshared Histories. Nordisk Tidsskrift for Informationsvidenskab og Kulturformidling*. 8 (2).

Agostinho, Daniela et al. 2020. *Uncertain Archives: Critical Keywords for Big Data*. MIT Press.

Andersen, Astrid Nonbo. 2014. "'We Have Reconquered the Islands': Figurations in Public Memories of Slavery and Colonialism in Denmark 1948– 2012." *International Journal of Politics, Culture, and Society*. 26(1): 57– 76.

Antracoli, Alexis A., Annalise Berdini, Kelly Bolding, Faith Charlton, Amanda Ferrara, Valencia Johnson, and Katy Rawdon. 2020. *Archives for Black Lives in*

Philadelphia: *Anti-Racist Description Resources*. Published online October 2020. https://archivesforblacklives.files.wordpress.com/2020/11/ardr_202010.pdf

Azoulay, Ariella. 2008. *The Civil Contract of Photography*. New York: Zone Books.

Barbash, Ilisa, Rogers, Molly and Willis, Deborah. Eds. 2020. *To Make Their Own Way in the World: The Enduring Legacy of the Zealy Daguerreotypes*. NY: Aperture/Peabody Museum Press.

Bastian, Jeannette A. 2003. *Owning Memory: How a Caribbean Community Lost Its Archives and Found Its History*. Westport, CT: Libraries Unlimited.

Bastian, Jeannette. 2001. "A Question of Custody: The Colonial Archives of the United States Virgin Islands". *The American Archivist*. 64(1): 96–114.

Bates, Jo and Jennifer Rowley. 2011. "Social reproduction and exclusion in subject indexing: A comparison of public library OPACs and LibraryThing folksonomy". *Journal of Documentation*. 67(3): 431-448.

Carby, Hazel V, and Heather V. Vermeulen. 2015. *Prospects of Empire: Slavery and ecology in eighteenth-century Atlantic Britain*. New Haven, CT: Yale University Library.

Caswell, Michelle, and Marika Cifor. 2016. "From Human Rights to Feminist Ethics: Radical Empathy in the Archives". *Archivaria*. 81: 23-43.

Caswell, Michelle, and Marika Cifor. 2019. "Neither a Beginning Nor an End: Applying an ethics of care to digital archival collections". *The Routledge International Handbook of New Digital Practices in Galleries, Libraries, Archives, Museums and Heritage Sites*. Eds. Lewi, Hannah, Wally Smith, Dirk vom Lehn, and Steven Cooke. Abbington, UK; New York: Routledge.

Chan, Sebastian. 2007. "Tagging and Searching – Serendipity and museum collection databases". *Museums and the Web 2007: Proceedings*. Eds. Trant, J. and D. Bearman. Toronto: Archives & Museum Informatics. Consulted online October 01, 2020. http://www.archimuse.com/mw2007/papers/chan/chan.html.

Cifor, Marika. 2016. "Affecting Relations: Introducing Affect Theory to Archival Discourse." Archival Science 16(1): 7-31.

Clarke, Rachel Ivy and Sayward Schoonmaker. 2020. "The Critical Catalog: Library Information Systems, Tricksterism, and Social Justice". Proceedings of the 2020 CHI Conference on Human Factors in Computing Systems (CHI '20). Association for Computing Machinery, New York, NY, USA, 1–13. DOI:https://doi.org/10.1145/3313831.3376307

Daells Varehus catalogues. Consulted online January 21, 2021. http://www5.kb.dk/pamphlets/dasmaa/2008/feb/daellsvarehus/subject7/da/

Danbolt, Mathias, Giersing, Sarah, and Meyer, Mette Kia Krabbe: *Blind Spots. Images of the Danish West Indies colony*. Consulted online January 23, 2021. http://oplev.kb.dk/danish-westindies

Danbolt, Mathias & Wilson, Michael K. 2018. "En monumental udfordring for dansk historieskrivning". Kunstkritikk.no. Consulted online January 21, 2021.

http://www.kunstkritikk.no/kommentar/en-monumental-udfordring-for-dansk-historieskrivning/

The Danish West-Indies - Sources of History (Danish National Archives). Consulted online January 21, 2021. www.virgin-islands-history.org/

González-Stephan, Beatriz, and Carl Good. 2016. "The Dark Side of Photography: Techno-Aesthetics, Bodies, and the Residues of Coloniality in Nineteenth-Century Latin America." *Discourse*. 38.1: 22-45.

Gordon, Avery F. 2008. *Ghostly Matters: Haunting and the sociological imagination*. Minneapolis: University of Minnesota Press.

Hartman, Saidiya V. 2008. "Venus in Two Acts". Small Axe: A Journal of Criticism 26:1–14.

Hartman, Saidiya. 2019. *Wayward Lives, Beautiful Experiments*. New York; London: W.W. Norton.

Hirsch, Marianne. 1997. *Family Frames: Photography, narrative, and postmemory*. Cambridge: Harvard University Press.

Hirsch, Marianne. Ed. 1999. *The Familial Gaze*. Hanover: University Press of New England.

Jongma, Lizzy, and Chris Dijkshoorn. 2016. "Accurator: Enriching collections with expert knowledge from the crowd". *MW2016: Museums and the Web 2016*. Consulted online October 01, 2020. https://mw2016.museumsandtheweb.com/paper/accurator-enriching-collections-with-expert-knowledge-from-the-crowd/

Meyer, Mette Kia Krabbe. 2019. "Contested Paradise: Exhibiting Images from the Former Danish West Indies". *Curatorial Challenges: Interdisciplinary Perspectives on Contemporary Curating*. Eds. Hansen, Malene V, Anne F. Henningsen, and Anne Gregersen. Abingdon, Oxon; New York, NY: Routledge. 199-210.

Meyer, Mette Kia Krabbe, Smed, Sine Jensen & Sauerland, Nina: "Blinde vinkler: Undervisningsmateriale til billedkunst-, dansk- og historieundervisningen 9. og 10. klasse samt gymnasieskolen". 2019. http://www5.kb.dk/da/dia/undervisning/Vestindien/vestindien_materiale.html

Langford, Martha. 2001. *Suspended Conversations: The Afterlife of Memory in Photographic Albums*. Montreal: McGill-Queen's University Press.

Mirzoeff, Nicholas. 2012. *The Right to Look: A Counterhistory of Visuality*. Durham, North Carolina: Duke University Press.

Nagler, Linda Fregni. 2013. *The Hidden Mother*. London; Monaco: MACK and Nouveau Musée National de Monaco.

Odumosu, Temi. 2019. "What Lies Unspoken". *Third Text*. 33(4-5): 615–629.

Odumosu, Temi. 2020. "The Crying Child: On Colonial Archives, Digitization, and Ethics of Care in the Cultural Commons". *Current Anthropology*. 61(22). Consulted online October 01, 2020. https://www.journals.uchicago.edu/doi/10.1086/710062

Olwig, Karen Fog. 2003. "Narrating Deglobalization: Danish Perceptions of a Lost Empire." *Global Networks*. 3(3): 207-222.

Peters, Isabella. 2009. *Folksonomies. Indexing and Retrieval in Web 2.0*, De Gruyter Saur.

Queen Marys indsejling i Frederikssted. Consulted online January 23, 2021. *http://www5.kb.dk/images/billed/2010/okt/billeder/object279776/da/*

Rasmussen, Anders Fogh. 2002. Nytårstale. https://www.regeringen.dk/statsministerens-nytaarstale/anders-fogh-rasmussens-nytaarstale-1-januar-2002/

Ridge, Mia. Ed. 2017. *Crowdsourcing our Cultural Heritage.* London: Routledge.

Sandahl, Jette, et al. 2011. Taking the Museum to the Streets. *Museums and the Web 2011: Proceedings.* Eds. Trant, J. and D. Bearman. Toronto: Archives & Museum Informatics. Consulted online October 01, 2020. http://conference.archimuse.com/mw2011/papers/taking_the_museum_to_the_streets

Sanderhoff, Merete. Ed. 2014. *Sharing is Caring: Openness and sharing in the cultural heritage sector.* Copenhagen: Statens Museum for Kunst.

Schwartz, Joan. 2002. "Coming to Terms with Photographs: Descriptive Standards, Linguistic "Othering," and the Margins of Archivy". *Archivaria* 54:142–171.

Sharpe, Christina. 2016. *In the Wake: On Blackness and Being.* London: Duke University Press.

Simonsen, Gunvor. 2016. "Introduction: The historiography of slavery in the Danish-Norwegian West Indies, c. 1950 - 2016". *Scandinavian Journal of History.* Vol 41: 475-493

Smith, Shawn Michelle. 2013. *At the Edge of Sight: Photography and the unseen.* North Carolina: Duke University Press.

Stoler, Ann Laura. 2002. *Carnal Knowledge and Imperial Power: Race and the Intimate in Colonial Rule.* Berkley, CA: University of California Press.

Thompson, Krista A. 2006. *An Eye for the Tropics: Tourism, photography, and framing the Caribbean picturesque.* Durham: Duke University Press.

Trouillot, Michel-Rolph. 2015. *Silencing the past: power and the production of history.* Boston: Beacon Press.

Tuck, Eve, Mistinguette Smith, Allison M. Guess, Tavia Benjamin, and Brian K. Jones. 2014. "Geotheorizing Black/Land Contestations and Contingent Collaborations". *Departures in Critical Qualitative Research.* 3 (1): 52-74.

Valtysson, Bjarki. 2017. "From policy to platform: the digitization of Danish Cultural Heritage". *International Journal of Cultural Policy.* 23(5): 545-561.

Wood, Marcus. 2013. *Black Milk: Imagining Slavery in the Visual Cultures of Brazil and America.* Oxford: Oxford University Press.

Man, Woman, Child
Ethical Aspects of Metadata at the Pitt Rivers Museum

Rebecca Kahn

Abstract

This paper is concerned with the ethical aspects of museum metadata. These are not always immediately evident when working with the metadata related to museum objects, although, I will argue, they are embedded in the object, accumulated at each phase of its journey into the institution; and continue to accumulate while it is part of a collection. This takes place against a backdrop of new development and possibilities afforded by digital technologies for building connections between and across heritage collections online, which can result in these complicated metadata potentially entering the data ecosystem. This eventuality, I will argue, has ethical and technical implications which need to be considered and understood through the theoretical lenses of critical data studies, museum informatics and the growing calls from museum scholars and others to decolonisation of museum collections. Using a small collection of drawings from the Pitt Rivers Museum of Anthropology and World Archaeology at the University of Oxford, I will demonstrate how difficult museum metadata can be buried deep in museum documentation, and how this data, once brought to the surface by digitisation, can expose the trauma of a collection's origins. I will go on to ask whether the current models used to share heritage data online are appropriate mechanisms for materials with such sensitive histories, and ask how best to handle them in the increasingly digital future.

Keywords: Museum data, Museum digitisation, Ethnographic data, Data decolonisation, Anthropological museums, Museum big data, Critical data studies

Introduction

This paper considers the problematic ethical issues embedded in museum objects, their digital records and, consequently, their metadata. This complex metadata is accumulated throughout the object's life, are stored in a variety of locations, are transmitted when the records are digitised, and spread across the web when digital records are connected to others, either by means of semantic web technologies or in shared repositories.

Managing complexity in cultural heritage collections data management is an emerging field, and in this regard, this paper takes an impetus from the collections as data approach, which originated among libraries, but is equally pertinent to museum collections. This approach reframes all digital objects in a collection as computationally processable data, rather than as individual, discrete objects (Padilla et al. 2019). By viewing a collection in this way, it becomes possible to step back, and view the full composite nature of a collection, the connections within it and what it links to (Padilla 2017). This approach forces us to examine collections within broader social, ethical and informational contexts, which I will illustrate by examining a subset of collections data from the Pitt Rivers Museum at Oxford University[1]. The collection consists of 1,600 drawings made by children in North America and Britain and their associated records, which were collected by one pioneering female anthropologist between 1923 and 1925. This collection was created during a historical period when attitudes towards ownership, recognition and consent were different to today, and this paper will show how these attitudes have been embedded in a set of object metadata that can be read as deeply political, revealing relationships of power, identity and consent which continue to be controversial in museums today. At the same time, these relationships also require that we question whether an approach that sees heterogenous, complicated museum data as a source for mass computational processes is always appropriate. The paper will consider the ethical and technical challenges of making this information visible online despite a growing research context in which searching for digital content is increasingly taken to mean 'just Google it'.

The Pitt Rivers Museum

While the drawings which form the case study will be described in detail in the later sections of this paper, at the outset it is important to describe the intellectual, historical and institutional context in which these drawings were collected, and documented.

The Pitt Rivers Museum (PRM) is a museum of archaeological and anthropological collections, founded in 1884 with an initial collection of about 22,000

---

1   The author would like to thank the organizers of the original data sprint, Dr Anne Luther, Krystelle Denis and Alex Horak. I am also indebted to my fellow workshop attendees, Meghan O'Brien Backhouse and Marenka Thompson-Odlum of the Pitt Rivers Museum, Ilias Kyriazis of the Deutsche Nationalbibliothek and Jules Sauer from Sciences Po, Paris, for the initial collaborative work on the provenance records in the Pitt Rivers Museum database.

archaeological and ethnographic objects collected between the 1850s and early 1880s by General Augustus Henry Lane Fox Pitt-Rivers (1827-1900) an officer in the British Army and part-time archaeologist and anthropologist. Today, it holds roughly 312,000 objects of archaeological and anthropological origins from around the world, as well as extensive photographic and manuscript collections. A fraction of these objects are displayed in the main court, upper gallery and lower gallery of the museum in Oxford. These rooms are, in many ways, a fulfilment of the fantasy of a traditional museum - glass cases are closely packed together across the main court and filled with spectacular objects. One of the hallmarks of the PRM is that the materials are not displayed chronologically, as in many other museums, but typologically, by how they were used. Thus, a case displaying money might contain cowrie shells collected in the Punjab in the 1890s, an Italian postage stamp used as currency during WWI and a compressed brick of tea used as currency in Tibet and collected in 1935. This arrangement is not only visually exciting - it can also be read as an expression of the PRM's historical role in the development of western, specifically British, anthropology as a discipline in the late 19th century. At the time, the field was notable for the close networks of anthropologists, ethnologists, scholars, colonial administrators, collectors and curators who helped to shape the discipline. These early social anthropologists focused on topics that can be loosely defined as the 'phenomena of culture', such systems of kinship, ritual and religious practices (Ingold, 1985) and took the evolutionistic view that non-Europeans are undeveloped in comparison with Europeans, whose society was sophisticated, rational and advanced (Soukup, 2014).

These interrelated networks of individuals, who worked, studied and travelled together shaped the museum through the materials they collected (Gosden 2009) and were members of the same scholarly societies and academic elites who frequently crossed paths over the course of their research and teaching (Larson et al, 2007:213). This network of associations is significant, for a few reasons: Firstly, the shared anthropological backgrounds of many of the collectors and curators resulted in unusually high-quality documentation for many of the objects, which, as we will see later, is important in a study of the museum's metadata. Alison Petch, writing in 2003, attributes this to the fact that the PRM was able to attract high-calibre staff who stayed at the museum for a long time and who had a very keen interest in the processes and techniques of documentation itself (110). Secondly, this network of early anthropologists and the high quality of the documentation they produced can be seen as bolstering the legitimacy of a museum which was a beneficiary of the reach of the British Empire (Hicks, 2013). The act of collection is never neutral, and if the ethnographic project of a museum - namely to collect, classify and display material culture is to be legitimate, it must prove that this has been done in a systematic and intentional fashion, rather than a fetishistic or souvenir-driven one, which would de-legitimise the project (MacDonald and Silverstone 2006, Pearce 1992). At the PRM this has resulted in many richly described objects, with in-depth records, which, as we will see later, are also replete with accumulated significance. As Dan Hicks, currently curator of World Archaeology at the PRM points out, anthropology museums represent a unique index of Victorian colonial history, and often became vehicles for the militarist vision of white European supremacy that characterises that period (Hicks, 2020: 30). While the intertwined histories of several of the collectors and curators who contributed to the acquisition and documentation of materials at the PRM have been a subject of in-depth study (Petch 2003, 2014) until recently scant attention had been paid to the colonial contexts in which many of these objects were collected (Hicks, 2020: 73), and the associated questions of power, permission and consent that this raise. These issues, and how they manifest in the metadata of the PRM collection will be explored further in the theory section of this paper.

The ethics of children's data

The use of children's figurative drawings as a source for anthropological research has a long history. Canonical early 20th century anthropologists such as Margaret Mead, Meyer Fortes, Gregory Bateson and Cora duBois all collected drawings by children during their fieldwork in Papua New Guinea, the African Gold Coast, Bali and Indonesia. This work is marked by particular attitudes to their subjects, which were prevalent at the time - they were interested in the development of society and culture, and since children were understood as unformed adults who were still learning these things, Mead and those who followed her deduced that by researching children, they were able to investigate the processes through which children acquire culture, not the society and culture itself (Soukup: 553). The prevailing perspective also paralleled the relatively crude art produced by children with that of 'primitive' art made by other racial groups, and so the study of children's art was seen as a way of gaining insight into the so-called primitive minds of the societies they were studying (Unger-Heitsch, 2001; Gamradt & Staples, 1994). Indeed, much of the early 20th century anthropology which used children's drawings as a source can be characterised by its positioning of children as 'simple, or less complicated' than their adult counterparts, thus justifying the researcher's view of them as valid subjects, without the need to ask their permission (Phillips, 2014). This framing is important when we consider the works which make up the case study, and how they were described and documented. In contrast, researchers today understand that children, rather than being simple versions of adults, have their own agency, are capable of understanding the concept of consent, and of giving it (Niell, 2005; Mitchell, 2006). Drawing on the UN Convention on the Rights of the Child, there is a growing acceptance among researchers that children have the right to be 'properly researched' that the traditional ethical frameworks for offline data collection, analysis and regulation should be extended into the digital world and that tighter data privacy controls for children's data should be enforced (Berman & Albright, 2017). In the context of the PRM collection, this sensitivity to protecting the identity of children means that very few of the drawings are available via the museum's online collection database, and no identifying information is made public[2].

Theoretical Background

Theoretically, this paper draws on several schools of thought which could be loosely grouped under the umbrella of digital humanities approaches, since they are all concerned, to one extent or another, with what Christine Borgman characterises as data scholarship in those fields which are concerned with the study of human culture and the human record (Borgman 2015). Humanities scholars rely heavily on artefacts – texts, maps, archival sources, images and objects which, until fairly recently, only existed in physical forms. Using these sources required visiting museums, archives and libraries, and making use of finding aids such as catalogues and indexes to locate these artefacts, and provide contextual information about them. These aids were (and still are) the products of the processes of acquisition, classification, retention and conservation, enacted by librarians, archivists and museum curators, who made certain choices about what to include and exclude, giving shape to the collections under their care (Bowker 1997; Star 1999). The result is collections that are not neutral agglomerations of facts, but rather sets of information that can be read as having an agenda of their own. This idea of the constructed agenda is highlighted by Langdon Winner, who argued that it was possible for artefacts to have their own sets of politics, distinct from those of the social and or economic systems in which they are embedded (Winner 1980). He presented two possibilities for this – firstly artefacts which have been designed in ways which enable a means of establishing certain patterns of power or authority, or, secondly, technologies which are inherently political in and of themselves. This second type displays or contains properties which are unavoidably linked to certain institutionalised patterns of power and authority (134). In this paper, I will show that museum records are of this second type, as are the knowledge management systems, ranging from paper catalogues, to digital databases and semantic data models which we use to which we use to organise them. These institutionalised power relations have made these systems a topic of study for scholars of museums and critical data studies, who pivot these technologies from representing one type of power or authority to being representative of multiple authoritative voices, then engagement with their latent politics is essential.

---

2   In the case of the image illustrating this paper, it is accessible only because no associated surname cannot be found, thereby making it impossible to identify the child.

Defining Politics

In their introduction to the special issue of this journal which dealt with Big Data, Mark Coté, Paolo Gerbaudo and Jennifer Pybus argued that Big Data is political in the same way in which identity, the body, gender, sexuality, race and ethnicity are political - that is, as sites of struggle over meaning, interpretations, and categorisations of lived experience (2016: 5). These conditions, I would argue, are no different for metadata, and it is from Coté, Gerbaudo and Pybus' assertion that I draw a working definition of the politics of museum metadata as the politics of struggle. In a museological context, this can be seen through the practice of recording all information about an object in its metadata, which is generally defined as data about data and scholars generally agree that it has been in existence for as long as humans have tried to organise information (Baca, 2016, Gartner, 2016). While in the past this may have been the preserve of catalogues and librarians, metadata is increasingly gaining attention and becoming more visible as the mass digitisation of what we read, how we communicate and where we search for information has become reliant on, and a source of, different kinds of metadata. Tags, descriptions, keywords, and search terms are all forms of metadata, which we both use and produce constantly. Many scholars of Big Data have made the point that data is never truly neutral or raw (Iliades & Russo, 2016; Graham, 2015; Gitelman, 2013; boyd & Crawford, 2012,) but has been shaped and influenced by those who collected it. This is not news to information professionals such as librarians, curators and archivists who have been selecting, appraising, including and excluding certain elements of the data related to the objects in their care for much of recorded history. As Gartner points out, no metadata can ever be said to be neutral, rather it should be understood as a human creation, which bears the imprints of the progenitors who made the initial decisions of what data to include or exclude and presents a subjective view of their world outlook (41). In museums, these imprints are embedded during the making of metadata, or, as Turner (2020) specifies, in the record keeping, data collection and digitisation that makes up a significant aspect of contemporary museum documentation practice (4). The choices made by the individuals who facilitate the collection, classification and organisation of knowledge in cultural heritage collections are codified in records; when records are digitised, the choices become part of the data of the collection which, in turn is encoded into the metadata (Beltrame and Jungen 2013, Beltrame 2016, Geismar and Mohns 2011; Geismar 2018). The resulting collections, argues José van Dijck are a view of reality which is far from being either comprehensive or objective, but consists, rather of 'value-laden piles of code that are multivalent and should be approached as multi-interpretable data' (2014: 202). These analyses of metadata highlight its ideological potential, and it's capacity to express a particular view of the world, a capacity which makes it inherently political. In museums metadata not only a tool for describing and creating meaning and interpretations of information objects – it also controls the classifications and categorisation of the lives of the individuals connected to the objects – rendering it inherently and entirely political. As Iliades and Russo argue 'Data, along with its sciences and infrastructures, are informed by specific histories, ideologies, and philosophies that tend to remain hidden' (p2). As this paper will go on to show, the ideology of museum data challenges us to expose these histories but also to consider and manage the ethical considerations of the data with care.

Objects, Biographies and Museum Metadata

Since the late 1980s, the agentive turn in social studies has embedded the notion that material objects have social lives and biographies, through which we can trace their creation, movement, uses, possible commodification and, in the case of museum objects, reification into collections (Kopytoff 1986; Appadurai 1988). Museum scholars were quick to take up this perspective, and apply it to their own context (Pearce 1994; Hoskins 2006; Dudley 2012; Geismar 2018). They argued that the process of collecting is an inherently selective one, and that the decisions regarding which objects to include and which to exclude creates narratives within the collections, through which we can read as much about the people who made the collections and documentation as the objects themselves (Enright, Hellinga, and Leigh 1989; Turner 2017). When these narratives are layered on top of each other, we arrive at an understanding of museums as sites of complex narratives and multiple voices, which tell us a great deal about the institutions themselves (Gosden and Marshall 1999; Alberti 2005). This holds true for museum records as well, where the biographies of the records reflect the subjective decisions of the people who created them.

The computerised collections management systems used in museums today have centralised the role of metadata, as the source of all internal knowledge about an object (Navarrete and Mackenzie Owen 2016; Cairns, 2013). Within a collection, it is the metadata that makes the object findable, allows connections to be made to other objects which share certain attributes, and ultimately enables it to be shared online in useful ways. In institutions that have been collecting for centuries, and where documentation may be messy or idiosyncratic at best, these records offer the best mechanism for the internal discovery of objects (Griffiths 2010). Increasing numbers of cultural heritage institutions are publishing their collections online, using various different digital tools and platforms, and with a variety of different access and usage restrictions. However, the advent of digital technology has not removed all the constraints to providing access to these metadata records. In fact, some restrictions have had to be added in order to manage these large collections of heterogenous data online (Freire et al. 2018; Anderson and Blanke 2012). For example, the proliferation of different descriptive vocabularies used in individual institutions has made interoperability difficult, resulting in the need to use shared ontologies and data models such as Dublin Core and CIDOC-CRM which facilitate interoperability, but also risk losing contextual detail. However, there are significant drawbacks to this approach, as few of the models make allowance for contextualising metadata, which is crucial for the verifiability and quality management of the data (Sikos and Philp 2020), as well as maintaining the attribution record (Bechhofer et al. 2010). Thus, in order to manage the volume of resources, and support the interoperability required across data collections and between different ontologies, a paradoxical situation has arisen - in order for links to be made across data collections, a mass of interoperable data is required. However, in order to be interoperable, this data has to be pared down to an essential minimum, rendering it less useful for the kinds of enquiries humanities researchers might undertake. This risks putting data into the ecosystem without added context, which is crucial to its ethical use. In museum collections, this contextualising metadata is often entered as free text, rather than controlled terminology. Free text fields are difficult to manage in automatic search and linking technologies, due to a lack of controlled vocabularies, and so often this information is not readily available. As the case study will show, this has resulted in a chicken and egg scenario: contextual data is essential to providing users with a deeper understanding of the biographies of the collection, but it is created and stored in ways which make it difficult to access. If the data is too precarious to be shared, does that mean that we need to find better approaches to sharing it, or should it not be shared at all? These questions are increasingly being asked by museum professionals, particularly those who work with collections which have their roots in histories of oppression and colonialism, and for whom the question of how to decolonise and share data are preeminent, and are, I will show, central to considering how to manage the metadata of the Pitt Rivers collection which forms the basis of the case study.

Decolonising Data

Over recent years, there has been an increasing discussion among museum scholars and professionals about the need to decolonise their collections (Boast 2011; Boast and Enote 2013; Srinivasan et al. 2009; Nakata et al. 2008). In many cases, these discussions focus on the display and documentation of individual objects and collections, but this impulse also has implications for data infrastructures. Led by institutions in Canada, New Zealand and Australia, digital infrastructures have been developed which seek to find a balance between the desire for digital accessibility, the need for cultural accountability and legal and cultural restrictions on who may or may not have access to certain cultural materials (Brown and Nicholas 2012). The Pitt Rivers is no exception: access to their collections online is mediated by a cultural warning which alerts users to the fact that some records were created using scientific research models and language that is now considered outdated and offensive, and that some of the records contain information or photographs of objects associated with ritual or ceremonial activity that cannot be made public due to prohibitions in Indigenous communities relating to the age, gender, initiation and ceremonial status or clan of the viewer. These restrictions are crucial to the ethical management of museum data. But in the context of sharing large sets of museum metadata online, for example via a SPARQL endpoint or a data dump, the practical realities of managing these restrictions can be a challenge. In a recent sample of materials taken from Europeana, the European linked cultural heritage data aggregator, several examples of ethnographic materials which include images of human remains were found, despite restrictions on the display of these objects being implemented in the supplying institution (see Kahn and Simon, forthcoming).

The Pitt Rivers is also taking more concrete steps towards decolonising its collections. Pressure is on European museums, as sites of display of items which were stolen and looted from colonial societies, to push further than the dominant modes of reflexivity and self-awareness, in order to 'open up and excavate our institutions, dig up our ongoing pasts, with all the archaeological tools that can be brought to hand, sometimes a teaspoon and tooth-brush, other times a pick-axe or a jack-hammer' (Hicks 2020: 19). At the PRM this excavation has taken the form of several research projects, some of which have sought to revisit the way the museum displays and uses outdated racialised language in its records and others which are working to develop plans for the restitution of certain objects from their collections to communities in Nigeria, Kenya and South Africa. It was within this context that the PRM made their database available to researchers for the workshop described in the next section. These efforts are admirable, and go much further than many other European museums are. However, as I hope to show in the remainder of this paper, the ethical complexity of museum metadata can often be buried very deeply in a database, and require significant digging to be brought to light. These excavations may reveal significant narratives, but the question of how to manage these complex, even explosive data artefacts in an increasingly digital context remains vexing.

The need to balance on the one hand technical requirements for access and on the other, the need for sensitive treatment of museum data becomes more urgent as data scientists are increasingly turning to heritage collections as sources of structured training data for machine learning and artificial intelligence (AI) algorithms. The attraction of using data pre-collected and curated by archivists and librarians is easy to see. However, this approach presents its own risks - the topic of managing data bias in cultural heritage collections is also in its infancy. Thanks to the recent work of scholars in the field of library studies (Reidsma 2019; Coleman 2020; Padilla 2020) and machine learning and AI (Buolamwini & Gebru, 2018, Jo & Gebru, 2019) there is a growing understanding that the work of curators, archivists and librarians has value for the development of automated discovery and interconnection systems. However, these scholars are also quick to point out that heritage collections are not neutral, and that both legacy collections and incoming data need to be reviewed routinely for evidence of inherited or inherent bias must be considered before wholesale ingestion of large heritage datasets takes place.

Methodology: Behind the scenes in the museum database

The data used in this case study was extracted, cleaned and examined as part of a four- day workshop entitled 'Activating Museum Data for Research, Scholarship and Public Engagement' held between September 30th and October 3rd, 2019. Hosted by the Department of Modern Art History at the Technical University of Berlin and funded by a grant from the Volkswagen Stiftung, the workshop was held in conjunction with the Pitt Rivers Museum at Oxford University and Sciences Po Media Lab Paris, with the intention of instigating collaboration between scholars with an interest in exploring the data of cultural materials and initiating new tools for exploring and visualising data from cultural collections. The workshop was designed as a data-sprint - an approach outlined by Venturini et al (2018) which facilitates bringing participants from a broad variety of backgrounds together to work on a dataset for a limited period of time in order to develop potential research questions from it. The method is ideally suited to working intensively on a large amount of data, while at the same time eschewing the ideal of exhaustivity which is often associated with big data explorations. Implicit in the model is the understanding that participants will only manage to treat a limited amount of digital material and that results will be, at best imperfect. These constraints are considered as a methodological challenge, rather than a weakness (2).

This 'quick and dirty' approach was particularly apt for the event, since we were working with the objects database of the Pitt Rivers Museum, a set of records for over 300,000 artefacts. The database was created in the 1990s, when the museum began to digitise their accession book entries for all the objects in the collection. During this process, individual entries were created for each object listed in the Museum's accession books, and as the objects were retrieved, examined and catalogued as part of the day-to-day collections department work, these entries were added to. In the in-house version of the database, used by PRM staff, volunteers and visiting researchers, there are 52 information fields for each object record, containing a range of descriptive, administrative, and technical metadata. For the purposes of the data sprint some of these fields were removed, including confidential data, data related to where the objects are stored, conservation processes, and whether any hazardous substances were included with the object (the PRM collection includes several objects containing lead, poisonous plant matter, and poison tipped arrows and darts). What remained were roughly 31 fields-worth of data, totalling about 120MB. Before being given access, all participants had to sign a non-disclosure agreement, in which we agreed not to share the data without prior permission from the PRM. We were also warned about the language used to describe some of the objects in the collection. This warning is standard for any researcher who tries to access the PRM's collections online, and is described above. With these considerations in mind, workshop participants set out to identify and discuss possible areas of investigation, and then to work with the data we had to hand.

The public-facing interface of the Pitt Rivers Museum Collections Online, showing the record and thumbnail image for one of the drawings (accession number 1994.15.98). Image courtesy of the Pitt Rivers Museum, Creative Commons CC BY-NC-ND 4.0

The process of identifying questions was initially approached as a collective exercise. Questions around provenance, descriptive language, missing data and the physical display of certain objects were all discussed as possible topics. Individuals then coalesced into working groups around the questions they were most interested in. The group in which I found myself decided to tackle the issue of missing provenance in many of the records, and in particular the overwhelming absence of the names of creators for many of the objects in the collection. The group felt that looking into the provenance of these objects would be a good way to try and uncover some of the narratives that might be latent in the collection. These stories would, we hoped, be able to tell us about the objects themselves and about the documentation practices at the Pitt Rivers at the time they were accessioned. For the purposes of this exercise, we focussed on the fields which described where and when an object was collected and by whom, who made them, and the source community or cultural group from whom the object was collected. We also found ourselves frequently cross-referencing these with the information in the *Primary Documentation* field. This field consists of descriptive details about the individual objects, entered as free text strings by collectors, curators and cataloguers who have worked with the collection over the years.

Named Makers

The first step in finding out how many of the objects in the PRM's collection had a named maker required us to do some basic sorting of the data. In order to reduce the dataset to a more manageable size, it was necessary to remove all records which had no maker recorded, either as blank entries or the term 'unknown' or a variation of that. This left us with about 5% of the collection, roughly 12,500 objects which had an explicitly named maker. Once this subset had been established, it was possible to use Open Refine's text facet function to sort out those makers who were most likely to be individuals, from those which were not. The PRM collections include a significant number of trade objects made by named companies, such as guns, buttons, beads and candles, and for which the name of the manufacturer is listed in the 'Maker' column. On the other hand, the faceted search also revealed objects with maker entries such as 'Unnamed French prisoners of war' (PRM object 1945.2.3). We decided to leave these entries in, since they showed evidence of an attempt to provide an identity to the maker.

For the next step, we decided to look at who had collected the objects, in the hope of finding a discernible correlation between individual collectors and the practice of naming a maker, and in particular the gender politics of collecting practices. Were female collectors more or less likely to name the makers than male collectors? Could we ascertain a point in time when male collectors start naming the makers of objects, and when female collectors began to show evidence of the practice? And would we be able to identify when (historically) and where (regionally) female anthropologists were active in the field? Exploring these questions required us to sort collectors by gender, including codes for male, female, unknown or both, since many of the field collectors were recorded as husband and wife teams. Through this process we were able to identify 535 individual field collectors. The most prolific was George Phillip Elphick, a historian of church bells, who also named himself as the maker of several thousand casts of bells, and to whom we were able to attribute 2629 objects. However, fairly close on his heels was Beatrice Blackwood, a legendary figure in the history of the Museum and the history of British anthropology. She collected 2233 objects with named makers. The next most prolific collector, Henry Balfour, only named the makers of 485 objects, while Gigi Crocker Jones, another early female anthropologist and collector, was the fourth most prolific with 248 named makers among her acquisitions. These statistics struck us as intriguing. Firstly, the large gap between the first two collectors and the subsequent two is notable. The almost even gender split, with two women and two men in the group seemed worthy of deeper exploration as well.

It is at this point that the narrative of this paper requires a shift in gears. The data sprint group went on to continue our explorations of the male and female collectors who named the sources of their objects, and to visualise and compare where and when these individuals collected, using a set of different visualisation tools. These collaborative results will, it is hoped, form the basis of a joint publication in the future. However, for the remainder of this article, I will go on to describe research I undertook on my own into the materials collected by Beatrice Blackwood.

Beatrice Blackwood: pioneer product of her time

An anthropologist and field collector, Beatrice Blackwood (1889-1975) was an early British anthropologist who worked at the Pitt Rivers from the late 1930s until shortly before her death in 1975, and effectively ran the museum from the early 1940s onwards. She studied anthropology at Oxford in 1916, and between 1923 and 1928 conducted field work in North America, during which time she collected objects for the museum (Larson, 2011). Of the roughly 5000 objects listed in the database which were collected by Blackwood, during the workshop we were able to identify 2233 objects which included an individual name in the creator field. We were immediately struck by the large number of children's drawings in this subset, many of which seemed to have been collected from a variety of cultural groups in North America, and noted these objects as worthy of further exploration. However, due to the time constraints of the data sprint, and the knowledge that our efforts would never be exhaustive, the focus of the workshop group shifted to broader questions of gender and collecting practices. However, the children's drawings stayed in my mind, and in 2020, after receiving permission from the PRM to continue working with the data, I undertook to find out more about these drawings, and where they had been collected.

I began by creating a subset of the 1626 drawings collected by Blackwood. Again using a faceted search to cluster entries in the 'Region' field which have similar features, I was able to determine that they had been collected in the United States (specifically Alabama, Arizona, San Francisco, Tennessee, Kentucky, North Carolina, Minnesota, New Mexico and South Dakota), Canadian British Columbia, Buckinghamshire, Wimbledon, and other unspecified parts of Britain, and were made and collected between 1923 and 1927. Most of these records provide a full name and surname for the creators in the 'Maker' field, some only provide initials. The 'Description' field gives more detail on the drawings, most of which are figurative, with at least two people in them. Some provide explanation of what the scene contains - for example, one is described as a 'Drawing by schoolchild of three figures. The drawing is in pencil and green colouring pencil' (Pitt Rivers Collection, Object no: 1994.15.98, see Fig 1 for illustration). In others, several dozen drawings will have the same description, such as 'Drawing by a child of three figures'.

What stands out, however, is the information entered into the 'Cultural Group' field. Blackwood recorded the drawings as being made by children who were documented as 'African American', 'Chinese', 'Navajo', 'Zuni', 'Chippewa', 'Ojibwa', 'Mexican American', 'Sioux', 'Kwakwa☐ ka☐ ☐wakw', 'European British' and, in some cases, simply 'American'. On sorting the results by *Region* it became evident that many of the drawings had been collected on what were, at the time, called 'Indian Reservations' (now known as First Nations Reserves) and at residential schools for Indigenous Americans and Canadians. Others had less detailed descriptions, such as the 99 drawings made by children described as 'African American' which were recorded as being collected in 'Alabama Montgomery', or over 400 drawings made by children whose *Cultural Group* field records them as 'Chinese' and were collected in 'California, San Francisco'. In total, I was able to locate 29 different schools listed in the *Region* field, and by their names was able to tell that twelve of these were residential schools – institutions which were established by the American and Canadian governments for the purpose of educating Indigenous children. However, not all of the drawings had specific details about the schools recorded in these fields, and so I realised that it would be necessary to cross reference the records I had found with the information in the *PrimaryDocumentation* field, since I suspected that more information might be located there. This was possible by searching for individual records using the accession number, but crucially, it had to be done using the data supplied by the PRM as part of the data sprint, rather than using the PRM's Collections online web portal, since much of free text in the *Primary Documentation* files is not available on the web because it contains identifying information.

Reading the Drawings

Reading the *Primary Documentation* files, it became evident that Blackwood attached detailed notes to some of the drawings, describing the figures, the children who made them and how the drawings were collected. In this note, attached to a drawing collected at the school attached to Fisk University, (a historically Black university which was founded in the 1860s to educate freed slaves after the Civil War) we find out about her collecting process, intentions and anthropological approach:

'These children were told to draw 'a man, a woman and a child', what the thing that looks like a cross between a centipede and a beetle is, I can't imagine... these drawings which were given to me this morning, are by the children in the school here where the students get their teaching practice. Unfortunately the teachers only got them from the very smallest children, I am trying to get the next grade too... I'll get some more from Tuskegee, they will make and interesting comparison, especially as I can get Indian children's drawings next year, and possibly also Chinese.../ Yours ever / Beatrice Blackwood' (Pitt Rivers collection, Object no: 1994.15.846)

Blackwood also annotated many of the drawings with details about where they were collected. For example, in the drawings made by children at Vest Community Centre, Kentucky, Blackwood notes:

'Drawings by Children of the Vest Community Centre, Kentucky. This school has been going for two years, many of the children had a little very inadequate teaching before this in low-grade county schools. They have never had drawing lessons. Some of them, particularly the bigger boys were ashamed of their efforts and said they couldn't draw. Two big boys got up and went off home when I explained what I wanted done. They do that whenever anything doesn't please them, and the teacher can't do anything about it. Attendance very irregular especially in winter, except for some of the children who live at the school.' (Pitt Rivers Collection, Object no: 1994.15.1474)

In another example, collected at the US Indian Boarding School, Chinle, Arizona, we find Blackwood's note which reads:

'Chin Lee [sic] is 80 miles from the railroad in the heart of the Navajo Reservation. The children all come from the reservation and have not been in contact with white people much except in school. Their drawings are typically Navajo in most cases. They have a drawing period in school but have never been taught to draw people. The boys said they couldn't draw a man without a picture to copy from, and mightn't they draw horses instead!' (Pitt Rivers Collections, Object no: 1994.15.98)

Some drawings done by children at the Calhoun School for African American children in Alabama include the annotation 'N.S' after their names. Blackwood's notes reveal that this stands for Night School, and that:

'Night School' children are those who have no money to pay for their board so they work at a trade all day and are paid for it a little more than they need for their board, this is accumulated for them till they have enough to enter the day school. Meanwhile they study and have classes from 7-9 every evening after their day's work. So they are far behind other children of their age.' (Pitt Rivers Database, primary documentation, Museum object number 1994.15.929)

Other records reveal annotations on individual drawings. On one, a note states that the child '...had the bright idea of putting the second eye outside the face!

I haven't seen that done before!' (Pitt Rivers Database, Museum object number 1994.15.960). These notes, although inaccessible to most users, reveal the richness of this collection, in ways which were not immediately evident from the basic records. They also reveal the multi-layered politics embedded in these metadata records, the most obvious of which is the traumatic histories behind the Residential Schools.

Residential Schools

In both the USA and Canada, residential schools were established to force assimilation and 'civilisation' on the children who attended them, in a long-term attempt to destroy Indigenous cultures in North America. Indeed, in 1920 the Canadian deputy minister of Indian Affairs predicted that in a century, thanks to the work of these schools, Indigenous people would cease to exist as an identifiable cultural group in Canada, thanks to this genocidal policy (Nagy and Kaur Sehdev, 2012). They were sites of physical, sexual and emotional abuse, as well as illness and malnutrition (Reynaud, 2014; Lightfoot, 2015). Many communities consider the schools to be the sites of explicit Indigenous genocide and cultural loss (Davis 2001; D. B. MacDonald and Hudson 2012). Although in 2018 Canadian Prime Minister Harper made a public apology on behalf of Canadians for the Residential School system, this history continues to be a source of pain. The history of these institutions and their long-term impacts on Indigenous communities is also increasingly being investigated as part of a complex web of structural inequality and violence which have long-lasting social, political and personal implications for the communities affected (Gone, 2017, Walsh & Lopes, 2009). As Metis scholar Marie Battiste writes, the school systems was were part of a broader 'cognitive imperialism', through which settler knowledge systems, by means of systemic and structural power, were positioned as exclusively legitimate, while Indigenous knowledge systems were deemed parochial and pushed to the margins of institutionalised education (Battiste, 1998, Nagy & Kaur Sehdev, 2012) In the context of the children's drawings at the PRM, it is important to consider these social and political contexts, as they manifest in the metadata.

Conclusions

If metadata is political because it is both ideological and a site of struggle, then the descriptive metadata attached to the drawings reveals an array of political issues which must be considered in the context of digitisation and sharing this data. First, there are the Blackwood's own professional intentions, as evidenced in her notes, about comparing the work of children from different cultural groups she was collecting from. Secondly, we have to consider Blackwood herself, an exceptional woman working in what was, at the time, an overwhelmingly male field. Thirdly, and perhaps most significantly, we have to consider the political struggles of the communities from whom she was collecting, and finally, there is the politics of the subjects whose work she was collecting - namely children.

Blackwood's choice of sources reveals an interest in communities who were distinctly marginal - located in remote rural settlements such as Kentucky, on Indigenous reservations or in communities of outsiders, such as immigrants. From her notes, it is clear that the social context in which the children lived was as significant, as the details of the drawings. However, the ethical questions about this context were less of a concern to her, although they are extremely significant today. If the drawings were made as part of a school exercise, we need to consider whether the children were informed about the objectives of what they were being instructed to do. Did they know what the drawings were to be used for, or give their permission to have them collected, and their names and ages recorded? In some ways, this information is what makes them exceptional - as Turner notes, it was uncommon for collectors of this period to attribute work to individual makers, since they prioritised 'pure facts' over individual experiences, resulting in a practice of field collecting which strove to remove any subjective voices of individual creators and leading to an overall absence of Indigenous voices in museum collection documentation (665). It seems evident that Blackwood did not take this view – naming the children and noting their ages marks them out as individuals and served a particular anthropological purpose. And while it is probably fair to say that by choosing to collect works created in an educational context meant that the children had little choice but to agree to produce what was asked of them, Blackwood's notes also show us that, in some cases, the drawing exercise did generate individual responses from children, and those too were considered worthy of recording. At the same time, however, it is this detail which makes the images impossible to show to the general public. Contemporary sensitivities to the privacy of the children, even applied retrospectively, requires access to be limited for reasons of data privacy.

Secondly, the story the metadata tells us about the intellectual and social backdrop against which they were created may preclude it from ever being made public. Andrea Walsh, a Canadian anthropologist who has worked extensively on the art created by survivors of the residential school system explains that, sometimes, it is necessary to remove these works from the public view for good (Watts, 2017). While the PRM is careful to ensure that no identifying information about the makers of the drawings is available via their online collections database, thinking about the drawings raises the question of how to think about not only this data, but the many petabytes of collections data like it around the world, particularly in light of the demands for access to increasingly large amounts of museum metadata. How can data curators balance the appeal of these large-scale sources of curated, computational information, which form the basis of the collections as data approach, with the need for granular attention to the ethics of individual objects? Making such detailed exceptions is almost impossible to manage automatically or algorithmically, but it is difficult to imagine how, in an increasingly digital future, researchers and institutions might manoeuvre around these explosively powerful objects, buried deep in a collection's records.

What began as an exploration into the PRM database with the intention of discovering which collectors named makers revealed an unexpected set of data with many layers of power dynamics, from Blackwood's interest in marginal communities, to her co-option of institutionalised authority as part of her collecting modus, to the powerlessness of her subjects, the children who did the drawings and were embedded in those systems. All of these realities were transferred into the collections of the Pitt Rivers museum through Blackwood's careful recording of the descriptions, names of the children, and the notes she included in the primary documentation.

The question which faces museum staff and researchers now is how to manage this digital information, and this paper represents only an early, tentative attempt to outline the challenges to hand. The data's politics should not deter us from working with it – that would be unhelpful. Without a doubt, certain aspects of the collection make it impossible to imagine adding it to a linked data collection or aggregated repository without making significant redactions, which would render it less than useful. However, it can also tell us a great deal about life in these communities – the drawings reveal how the children saw themselves and the world around them, and the supplementary information adds to the picture of these worlds. Excavating these kinds of data and considering how to manage them is a significant contemporary concern for museum professionals. Finding technical solutions to the ethical problems is essential if museum professionals and data scientists are to be able to preserve, store and manage this data and the stories it tells with discretion and respect.

Works Cited

Alberti, Samuel (2005): 'Objects and the Museum.' In: *Isis* 96/4, pp. 559–71.
Anderson, Sheila, and Blanke, Tobias (2012): 'Taking the Long View: From e-Science Humanities to Humanities Digital Ecosystems.' In: Historical Social Research/ Historische Sozialforschung, 37/3, pp.147–64.
Appadurai, Arjun (1988): The Social Life of Things: Commodities in Cultural Perspective, Cambridge: Cambridge University Press.
Baca, Murtha (2016): 'Introduction to Metadata'. Getty Research Institute, Los Angeles, 20 July 2016. http://www.getty.edu/publications/intrometadata.
Battiste, Marie, (1998): 'Enabling the Autumn Seed: Toward a Decolonized Approach to Aboriginal Knowledge, Language, and Education.' In: Canadian Journal of Native Education 22/1, pp:16-27.

Bechhofer, Sean, Ainsworth, John, Bhagat, Jiten, Buchan, Iain, Couch, Philip, Cruickshank, Don, De Roure, David (2010): 'Why Linked Data Is Not Enough for Scientists,' *2010 IEEE Sixth International Conference on e-Science*, Brisbane, Queensland, pp.300-307, doi: 10.1109/eScience.2010.21.

Beltrame, Tiziana Nicoletta, (2016): 'Creating New Connections: Objects, People, and Digital Data at the Musée Du Quai Branly' In: Anuac 4/2, pp.106–29.

Beltrame, Tiziana Nicoletta and Jungen Christine, (2013): 'Cataloguing, Indexing and Encoding.' In: Revue d'anthropologie Des Connaissances 7/4, https://doi.org 10.3917/rac.021.a.

Berman, Gabrielle and Albright, Kerry, (2017): 'Children and the Data Cycle: Rights and Ethics in a Big Data World', no. 2017-05, UNICEF Office of Research; https://www.unicef-irc.org/publications/907/

Boast, Robin, (2011): 'Neocolonial Collaboration: Museum as Contact Zone Revisited,' In: Museum Anthropology 34/1, pp.56–70. https://doi.org/10.1111/ j.1548-1379.2010.01107.x.

Boast, Robin and Enote, Jim, (2013): 'Virtual Repatriation: It Is Neither Virtual Nor Repatriation,' In P.F. Biehl and C. Prescott (eds), Heritage in the Context of Globalization: Europe and the Americas, New York: Springer Science + Business Media.

Borgman, Christine, (2015): Big Data, Little Data, No Data: Scholarship in the Networked World, Cambridge, Massachusetts: The MIT Press.

Bowker, Geoffrey, (1997): 'Lest We Remember: Organizational Forgetting and the Production of Knowledge.' In: Accounting, Management and Information Technologies 7/3: pp. 113–38.

boyd, danah, and Crawford, Kate (2012) 'Critical Questions For Big Data: Provocations for a Cultural, Technological, and Scholarly Phenomenon.' In: Information, Communication & Society 15/5, pp.662–79. https://doi.org/10.1080/1369 118X.2012.678878.

Brown, Deidre, and George, Nicholas (2012). 'Protecting Indigenous Cultural Property in the Age of Digital Democracy: Institutional and Communal Responses to Canadian First Nations and Māori Heritage Concerns.' In: Journal of Material Culture 17/3, pp.307–24. https://doi.org/10.1177/1359183512454065.

Buolamwini, Joy, and Gebru, Timnit (2018): 'Gender Shades: Intersectional Accuracy Disparities in Commercial Gender Classification' In: Proceedings of Machine Learning Research Conference on Fairness, Accountability, and Transparency 81/1.

Cairns, Susan (2013) 'Mutualizing Museum Knowledge: Folksonomies and the Changing Shape of Expertise.' In: Curator: The Museum Journal, 56/1.

Coleman, Catherine Nicole (2020) 'Managing Bias When Library Collections Become Data.' In: International Journal of Librarianship 5/1, pp. 8–19. https:// doi.org/ 10.23974/ijol.2020.vol5.1.162.

Coté, Mark; Gerbaudo, Paolo; Pybus, Jennifer (2016): 'Introduction. Politics of Big Data.' In: Digital Culture & Society, 2, pp. 5–15. https://doi.org/10.25969/

mediarep/947 Davis, Julie (2001): 'American Indian Boarding School Experiences: Recent Studies from Native Perspectives on JSTOR.' IN: OAH Magazine of History 15/2, pp.20–22.

Dijck, Jose van (2014): 'Datafication, Dataism and Dataveillance: Big Data between Scientific Paradigm and Ideology.' In: Surveillance & Society 12/2 pp.197–208. https://doi.org/10.24908/ss.v12i2.4776.

Dudley, Sandra H. (2012) Museum Objects: Experiencing the Properties of Things. Leicester Readers in Museum Studies. London, New York: Routledge.

Enright, Brian, Hellinga, Lotte and Leigh, Beryl (1989): Selection for Survival: A Review of Acquisition and Retention Policies. London.: British Library.

Freire, Nuno; Meijers, Enno; Voorburg, René and Isaac, Antoine (2018): 'Aggregation of Cultural Heritage Datasets through the Web of Data.' In: Proceedings of the 14th International Conference on Semantic Systems 10th – 13th of September 2018 Vienna, Austria, 120–26. https://doi.org/ 10.1016/j.procs.2018.09.012.

Gamradt, Jan, and Staples, Carolyn (1994): 'My School and Me: Children's Drawings in Postmodern Educational Research and Evaluation.' In: Visual Arts Research, 20/1, pp. 36–49.

Gartner, Richard (2016): 'Metadata: Shaping Knowledge from Antiquity to the Semantic Web' Springer International Publishing. https://doi.org/10.1007/978-3-319-40893-4.

Geismar, Haidy (2018) Museum Object Lessons for the Digital Age, London: UCL Press.

Geismar, Haidy, and Mohns, William (2011) 'Social Relationships and Digital Relationships: Rethinking the Database at the Vanuatu Cultural Centre.' In: Journal of the Royal Anthropological Institute, 17/1, pp. 133–55.

Gitelman, Lisa (2013): 'Raw Data Is an Oxymoron' Boston: MIT Press, https://doi.org/0262518287.

Gone, JP (2017) 'It Felt Like Violence: Indigenous Knowledge Traditions and the Postcolonial Ethics of Academic Enquiry and Community Engagement.' In: American Journal of Community Psychology 60/3-4, pp.353-360. doi: 10.1002/ajcp.12183.

Gosden, Chris and Marshall, Yvonne (1999): 'The Cultural Biography of Objects.' In: World Archaeology 31/2, pp.169–78.

Gosden, Chris 'The Relational Museum', January 16, 2009 (https://materialworldblog.com/2009/01/the- relational-museum).

Graham, B. (2015) 'Open and Closed Systems: New Media Art in Museums and Galleries.' In: In *Museum Media*, Henning, M (ed.) The International Handbooks of Museum Studies, Wiley & Sons.

Griffiths, Antony (2010) 'Collections Online: The Experience of the British Museum.' In: *Master Drawings*, 48/3, pp. 356–67.

Hicks, Dan (2020) The Brutish Museums: the Benin Bronzes, Colonial Violence and Cultural Restitution, London, Pluto Press.

Hicks, Dan (2013): 'Characterizing the World Archaeology Collections of the Pitt Rivers Museum.' In: Dan Hicks/Alice Stevenson (eds), World Archaeology at the Pitt Rivers Museum: a characterization, Oxford: Archaeopress, pp. 1-15.

Hoskins, Janet (2006): 'Agency, Biography and Objects.' In: Christopher Tilley/Webb Keane/Susanne Küchler/Michael Rowlands/Patricia Spyer (eds) Handbook of Material Culture, Sage, pp.74–84.

Iliades, Andrew and Russo, Federica (2016): 'Critical Data Studies: an introduction.' In: Big Data and Society, 3/2, pp.1-7.

Ingold, Tim (1985) 'Who Studies Humanity? The Scope of Anthropology.' In Anthropology Today 6/1, pp 15-16.

Jo, Eun Seo, and Gebru, Timnit (2019): 'Lessons from Archives: Strategies for Collecting Sociocultural Data in Machine Learning' ArXiv:1912.10389, December 2019 https://doi.org/10.1145/3351095.3372829.

Kahn, Rebecca and Simon, Rainer (2019): 'Famine and Feast: The Problem of Sources for Linked Data Creation'; Conference Proceedings of Graph Technologies in the Humanities 2019/2020, University of Vienna.

Kopytoff, Igor (1986) 'The Cultural Biography of Things: Commoditization as Process.' In: Appadurai, Arjun (ed) The Social Life of Things: Commodities in Cultural Perspective Cambridge: Cambridge University Press, pp.70–73.

Larson, Frances; Petch Alison and Zeitlyn, David (2007): 'Social Networks and the Creation of the Pitt Rivers Museum.' In: Journal of Material Culture 12/3, pp.211–39.

Lightfoot, Sheryl (2015): 'Settler State Apologies to Indigenous Peoples: A Normative Framework and Comparative Assessment.' In: Native American and Indigenous Studies, 2/1 pp.15-39.

MacDonald, David and Hudson, Graham (2012): 'The Genocide Question and Indian Residential Schools in Canada.' In: Canadian Journal of Political Science / Revue Canadienne de Science Politique 45/2, pp.427–49.

MacDonald, Sharon, and Silverstone, Roger (2006): 'Rewriting the Museums' Fictions: Taxonomies, Stories and Readers.' In: Cultural Studies 4/2 https://doi.org/10.1080/09502389000490141.

Mitchell, Lisa (2006): 'Child-Centred? Thinking Critically About Children's Drawings as a Visual Research Method.' In: Visual Anthropology Review 22/1, pp.60-73.

Nagy, Rosemary and Kaur Sehdev, Robinder (2012): 'Residential Schools and Decolonisation.' In: Canadian Journal of Law and Society / Revue Canadienne Droit et Societe, 27/1, pp. 67-73. doi: 10.3138/cjls.27.1.067

Nakata, Martin; Nakata, Vicky; Gardiner, Gabrielle; McKeough, Jill; Byrne, Alex and Jason Gibson (2008): 'Indigenous Digital Collections: An Early Look at the Organisation and Culture Interface.' In: Australian Academic & Research Libraries 39/4 pp.: 223-36.

Navarrete, Trilce, and Mackenzie Owen, John (2016): 'The Museum as Information Space: Metadata and Documentation'. In Borowiecki, Karol Jan; Forbes,

Neil and Fresa, Antonella (eds) Cultural Heritage in a Changing World, pp. 111–23. Springer International Publishing. https://doi.org/10.1007/978-3-319-29544-2_7.

Neill, Sarah (2005): 'Research with children: a critical review of the guidelines.' In: Journal of Child Health Care 9/1, pp:46-58.

Padilla, Thomas (2020): 'Responsible Operations: Data Science, Machine Learning, and AI in Libraries'. OCLC. 4 May 2020. https://www.oclc.org/research/publications/2019/oclcresearch-responsible-operations-data-science-machine-learning-ai.html.

Padilla, Thomas (2017): 'On a Collections as Data Imperative' https://labs.loc.gov/static/labs/work/reports/tpadilla_OnaCollectionsasDataImperative_final.pdf.

Padilla, Thomas; Allen, Laurie; Frost, Hannah; Potvin, Sarah; Russey Roke, Elizabeth and Varner, Stewart (2019): 'Final Report --- Always Already Computational: Collections as Data', https://doi.org/10.5281/zenodo.3152935.

Pearce, Susan M. (1992): Museums, Objects and Collections: A Cultural Study. Leicester, Leicester University Press.

Pearce, Susan (1994): Interpreting Objects and Collections: Leicester Readers in Museum Studies. New York & London: Routledge.

Petch, Alison (2003): 'Documentation in the Pitt Rivers Museum: The Contribution of Sir Francis Knowles (1886-1953).' In Journal of Museum Ethnography, 15, pp.109–14.

Phillips, Louise (2014): 'Research with Children.' In: Midgley, Davies, Oliver, & Danaher, P.A (eds.), The Echoes of Voice in Education Research Ethics. Rotterdam, Sense Publishers.

Reidsma, Matthew (2019): Masked by Trust: Bias in Library Discovery, Library Juice Press.

Reynaud, Anne-Marie (2014): 'Dealing with Difficult Emotions: Anger at the Truth and Reconciliation Commission of Canada.' In: Anthropologica 56/2, pp. 369-382.

Sikos, Leslie F., and Philp, Dean (2020): 'Provenance-Aware Knowledge Representation: A Survey of Data Models and Contextualized Knowledge Graphs.' In: Data Science and Engineering, May. https://doi.org/10.1007/s41019-020-00118-0.

Soukup, Martin (2014): 'Photography and Drawing in Anthropology.' In: Slovenský národopis, 62/4, pp.534-546.

Srinivasan, Ramesh; Boast, Robin; Becvar, Katherine M and Furner, Jonathan (2009): 'Blobgects: Digital Museum Catalogs and Diverse User Communities.' In: Journal of the American Society for Information Science and Technology 60/4, pp.666–78. https://doi.org/10.1002/asi.21027.

Star, Susan Leigh (1999): 'The Ethnography of Infrastructure.' In: American Behavioural Scientist 43/3, pp.377–91.

Turner, Hannah (2020) 'Cataloguing Culture - Legacies of Colonialism in Museum Documentation' Vancouver, UBC Press.

Turner, Hannah (2017): 'Organizing Knowledge in Museums: A Review of Concepts and Concerns.' In: Knowledge Organization 44/7 pp.472–84. https://doi.org/ 10.5771/0943-7444-2017-7-472.

Turner, Hannah (2016) *Critical Histories of Museum Catalogues*, Museum Anthropology, 39(2).

Unger-Heitsch, Helga (2001): 'Intercultural Perception and Social Change As Seen In Human Figure Drawings by School Children in Jordan.' In: Zeitschrift für Ethnologie, 126/2, pp.269-291.

Venturini, Tommaso, Munk, Aanders, & Meunier, Axel (2018): 'Data-Sprint: a Public Approach to Digital Research.' In: C. Lury, P. Clough, M. Michael, R. Fensham, S. Lammes, A. Last, & E. Uprichard, (eds.) Routledge Handbook of Interdisciplinary Research Methods,

Walsh, Andrea and Lopes, Dominic McIver (2009): 'Objects of Appropriation.' In: James O. Young Conrad G. Brunk (eds), The Ethics of Cultural Appropriation, Blackwell.

Watts, Richard, (2017) 'Ideafest: The Dark Echoes of Residential Schools'. Times Colonist. Accessed 11 January 2021. http://www.timescolonist.com/life/islander/ideafest-the-dark-echoes-of-residential-schools-1.10973355.

Winner, Langdon (1980): 'Do Artifacts Have Politics?' In: Daedalus 109/1, pp.121–36.

Pioneers and Feminisms
The Swedish Suffrage Movement as Archival Boundary Object

Rachel Pierce

Abstract

Feminist historiography is rife with debates about the nature and boundaries of women's movements. Arguments over who to call an activist or a feminist sit at the heart of these definitional debates, which provide the groundwork for how scholars understand contemporary feminisms. Given the heated nature of ongoing disputes over the complicated identity politics of feminism and its archives, it is surprising that scholars have afforded so little attention to the technical infrastructure that defines and provides access to digitized primary source material, which is increasingly the foundation for contemporary historical research. Metadata plays an outsized role in these definitions, especially for photographic material that cannot be made word-searchable but is favored by digitizers because of its popularity.

This article uses qualitative content analysis to examine how two digital archives define the Swedish suffrage movement – a historically contested concept, here understood through the theory of Susan Leigh Star as a "boundary object" subject to "interpretive flexibility". The study uses keywords attached to photographic material from the the National Resource Library for Gender Studies (KvinnSam) and metadata within the related Swedish Women's Biographical Lexicon platform for women's biographies. The findings indicate that the hierarchies of archival organization do not disappear with individual document digitization and description. Instead, the silences built into physical archives are redefined in digital collections, obscuring the tensions between individual and movement feminisms, as well as the contested nature of movement boundaries.

Keywords: Archives, Women's history, Photograph, Identity politics, Suffrage, Descriptive metadata

The historiographical path of the suffrage movement as an object of study has influenced and been influenced by the multiple and fluid histories of women's rights and feminist activism. This relationship is both fraught and enormously productive, disagreements fuelling further research and vice versa. The challenge for cultural heritage institutions is to represent their collections in a way that makes the keyword structure and practices for applying keywords transparent and productive of new interpretation. Keywords and digitised documents should be understood as processual, reflective and constitutive of the definitional process that has been ongoing since the birth of women's history. These archives should, in the words of Eichhorn, "recognize the past as a way of reinvigorating a beleaguered present and [...] recognize the future as always already implicated by the pull of the past" (2013: 30).

A friction exists between the historical distance typically required for a traditionally sustainable and academically useful descriptive practice and the need to reflect the needs of a current community of activists whose identity is based in a history of struggle documented and thus legitimated by archival materials. The ability to find documents across collections and outside the strictures structures of hierarchical collection organization is tantalizing for academics interested in challenging an older "great men make history" approach to the archives (Bishop 2017). With extensive metadata, Geoffrey Yeo has argued that digital archives could be rearranged and remade to deconstruct *fond* hierarchies – the archival organization practices that structure collections around donating organizations and historical individuals – and place formerly invisible groups at the centre of history (Yeo 2015).

And yet, as media theorist Kate Eichhorn notes, the theoretical and activist debates about identity politics and labels "have rendered earlier feminist approaches to cataloguing inadequately equipped to address contemporary feminist challenges" (2013: 140-141). One of the threats to sustainable archives documenting social movements is politically charged disagreement over the meaning of these movements, a fight that intersects with disagreements within the cultural heritage sector about how to correct historical classification practices that marginalize some voices while normalizing others (Drabinski 2013). These disagreements often revolve around conflicted relationships to past activism. However, much of this scholarship has focused on the era of social justice DIY archives, with little attention to materials preceding the late 1960s (Bastian & Flinn 2020; Eichhorn 2013). This article aims to expand this focus, whose literal short-sightedness is challenged by the numerous library, archival, and museum (LAM) projects and displays currently commemorating the 100th anniversary of women's right to vote, which often explicitly aim to place the fight for suffrage within the context of a century of feminist struggle.

The article conducts a qualitative content analysis of the linked subject headings and keywords that describe and establish hyperlinked relationships between the 110 KvinnSam photographs and 97 SKBL entries tagged with a

"Suffrage" keyword in the Swedish women's suffrage movement in the collections of the Swedish National Resource Library for Gender Studies (KvinnSam) and the Swedish Women's Biographical Lexicon (SKBL). KvinnSam holds the country's largest digitized collection of photographs documenting the suffrage movement, while SKBL is a scholarly project that reuses some of KvinnSam's digitized portraits to illustrate Swedish women's history through biographical sketches of "pioneers." These two digital archives demonstrate how cultural heritage institutions organized around gender use metadata to collectively define – consciously or not – the relationships between the politics of individual actors and the politics of social movements and between past and present feminisms.

As in other countries, the Swedish suffrage movement has undergone a historiographic re-evaluation in recent years, which has destabilized an international paradigm of suffrage movements as nationally bound, white, and middle-class (Blom 2012; Sneider 2015). As a result, this article will examine the Swedish suffrage movement as a boundary object as elaborated by Susan Leigh Star (2010) using an intersectional understanding of the history of feminism as implicated in the systems of raced, heteronormative, and classed inequality that are built into the archive. This approach requires an examination of what is in the metadata alongside the silences in these classification systems as applied. An investigation of metadata attached to photographs is especially needed because these terms are the only entry points for documents lacking machine-readable text; photographic metadata reveals the importance of metadata systems for setting the boundaries of objects like "suffrage movement", thus structuring access to information online.[1] This data provides a good way of investigating how digitizers might best use metadata to foreground the archival invisibility of non-normative groups, the politicization of the past, and the perils of (a)historical description.

Archiving feminists, archiving feminism: a literature review

This article builds on research from four distinct fields: women's and gender history, the digital humanities, media studies, and archival studies. The current disjuncture between these fields obstructs the development of a politically and historically grounded understanding of metadata practices. Historians, especially feminist historians, have only intermittently engaged in theoretical discussions of the archive and digitization while simultaneously becoming ever more dependent on these sources for research (Enoch & Bessette 2013; Strandgaard Jensen 2020). Meanwhile, the digital humanities and media studies are slowly acknowledging

---

1   Indeed, KvinnSam has only applied keywords to and created a search function for its photographic collection, while other primary documents are accessed via general web searches or in chronological order on a webpage with links.

the political implications of digital materials and tools (Allington, Broillette, & Golumbia 2016; D'Ignazio & Klein 2020; Noble 2018). A solid grasp of debates within historical scholarship is integral if the fields most concerned with digitization are to understand the meaning of archival documents – physical and digital – as constructed and contingent and thus political.

Describing something as wide-ranging and fuzzy as the suffrage movement is inherently a political project. Tensions over assimilation and difference sit at the heart of feminist politics. Balancing arguments about women's unique historical position with arguments about the meaning of equality has both facilitated productive, flexible activism and incited harmful division (Hemmings 2011). These disputes are longstanding because activists and scholars have at times associated formal membership in a few key movement organizations with a right to speak about and for women and feminism, collapsing the boundaries between individual identity, collective activism, and ideology. Scholarship on feminisms and intersectionality has aimed to open up this conversation to counteract its historically exclusionary tendencies, which have allowed privileged groups with greater resources (whiter, wealthier, educated, married, urban, Western) to dominate the historical narrative (Hemmings 2011; see also the intersectionality subsection in McCann & Kim 2017).

These conversations about tactics, naming, and belonging transfer to and politicize archival collection, labelling, and organisation practices. Feminist and women's archives are supposed to document a large, varied subsection of the populace with historically contested boundaries. Further, the words used to describe collective political struggle have historical trajectories, as activists and marginalized groups adjust to the rhetorical and political contexts in which they operate, identify new goals, and discard old ideas. Archival collection and description practices typically demand the imposition of hierarchies and static naming systems on materials, a process that can at best vastly simplify and at worst seriously distort the historical messiness that is so productive to social movements (Taves Sheffield 2020). These practices are not just potentially ahistorical but may also work against use of these archives as a basis for contemporary community cohesion and ongoing activism, a use emphasized by recent research on community archives (Bastian & Flinn 2020).

But how archives might best represent movements to demonstrate their historical complexity and contingency is still a live question. As research on early women's archives demonstrates, acknowledging a longer history can atomize and mainstream even those collections that started out as community archives, as the collections grow and the resources needed to maintain them metastasize (Mason & Zanish-Belcher 2007; Voss-Hubbard 1995). At the same time, as Caswell notes, many disempowered communities employ a strategic essentialism to find themselves in the past, linguistically fixing identity categories that are historically variable as a method of self-preservation (Caswell 2014).² Scholars of social justice archives need to extend their gaze backwards from the 1960s, in order to understand how groups represent and archive themselves over time. Without a longer historical view, scholarship may miss the historical and archival patterns that create "indexical absences" and "historiographical ghosts," in the words of historian Zeb Tortorici (2015). These absences obscure the activities and roles of historically disenfranchised communities.

Greater interest in the social justice possibilities of digitisation is warranted because metadata offers descriptive opportunities that align with queer theorizing about the need to embrace flexibility, multiple meanings, and outliers (Ruberg, Boyd, & Howe 2018). Researchers have repeatedly noted that the hierarchical, fixed structures of archival and library cataloguing do not provide the flexibility necessary to describe materials whose meaning is in flux, especially those documenting movement and identity politics (Thompson 2016). By removing individual materials from their archival *fonds*, by lifting them out of their physical contexts, cultural heritage institutions can facilitate access to multiple contexts via single documents. As van Dijk argues, "[t]he making of links, jumps and associations" provides a method of seeing interconnections across spans of time and space, within history and across cultural heritage institutions (2001: 193). Digital tools are well suited to represent the fusion of contextual messiness and order – the "ecology" of a boundary object, in Bowker and Star's (2000) terms – within which the ties between individuals and identity group categories are embedded.

Definitional multiplicity and fluidity are most important for the "ephemera" so important to archives created by and depicting historically disenfranchised communities. Like zines and other feminist cultural objects, digitized materials are easily reproducible, leading to their proliferation. As Michael Lesy observes, the description of photographs online is structured by the fact "not that there are too few images, but too many" (2007: 144). The same item may represent different phenomena in different communities and collections (Eichhorn 2013: 98). Perhaps due to a combination of illegibility and indexicality, visual materials are also uniquely important for individual and collective memory formation and identity group definition (Van Dijck 2004). How metadata works across collections housing similar materials or reproductions of the same materials defines the online archival ecology of movements and activists.

There is general consensus on the need for more exposure to and knowledge of materials integral to the construction and expression of racial, gendered, and sexed discrimination, and digital tools are frequently recognized as one of the most obvious ways of making these materials more widely accessible (Ruberg et al.

---

2   The term "strategic essentialism" was initially coined by the feminist theorist Gayatri Spivak, in the 1980s. She has since then attempted to fine-tune the term while disavowing some of its more nationalist and essentialist uses (Spivak 1990).

2018). However, scholars are very divided on how this should be done in practice. Some scholars recommend the retaining of harmful classification language as a teaching tool. Others recommend the adoption of new schemas that clearly identify materials as "trauma-causing" and constitutive of contemporary discrimination, recommending instead the application of metadata identifying racism, sexism, and other historic inequalities (for the former argument, see Drabinski 2013; for the latter argument, see Holterhoff 2017). The relationship between metadata and social justice is not simple.

These discussions underscore the inevitability of politically charged metadata, illustrating Bowker and Star's (2000) contention that classification is, at its heart, a profoundly political project. Choices in descriptive practice affect not just research avenues but also the wish of communities to be represented justly in archives and history, goals that as noted can seem at odds with one another. Movements and ideologies evolve, while the construction of metadata standards necessarily sets boundaries around and establishes relationships between concepts. Feminists, feminist organisations, feminist movements, and feminism are overlapping but conceptually distinct categories, covering the individual and historically specific to the broadly theoretical. Description of the relationships between specific individuals and broad, fuzzily defined movements is a kind of historiographical argument both about the meaning of an individual movement and the structure and boundaries of social movements themselves.

Rubenstein and Sluis argue that metadata functions "as a mediator between humans and computers" (2013: 152). Metadata has the potential to create a multiplicity of connections that form webs of context for individual documents. This multiplicity potentially facilitates a more expansive, contingent, and historically accurate definition of "the suffrage movement" than is possible with physical archival description. Yet there are also obstacles to overcome, including the individualisation not just of movements, but of the stuff of movements as well. Metadata best practices must acknowledge the individual and collective identities of historical figures who lived in different discursive and socio-political environments. These classification decisions have political consequences, shaping how the public understands key historical processes and peoples. Empirical examinations of metadata are necessary, in order to understand how intersectionality has be implemented in cultural heritage institutions. With this goal, this article investigates how two Swedish databases have used metadata to link individual documents and, through these links, define the Swedish suffrage movement.

Finding suffrage in the archive: Background and methods

The two institutions under analysis here have positioned themselves differently regarding the category "women". In the case of the National Resource Library for Gender Studies (KvinnSam), this is a recently visited conundrum – the institution was named the Women's History Collections until a series of name changes in 1997 and 2010.[3] Meanwhile, the Swedish Women's Biographical Lexicon (SKBL) is an attempt to institutionalize women's place in the historical record, assimilating women into mainstream Swedish history.[4] SKBL will eventually exist under the administrative purview of KvinnSam, but the projects have separate histories, created at different times and by different staffs. While SKBL does not provide access to their subject headings list, KvinnSam publishes their full list online.[5] As a result, the collections of KvinnSam and SKBL are interconnected but distinct, placing the concept of the suffrage movement in two discrete institutional contexts.

This article employs a qualitative content analysis of the array of the subject heading terms or keywords that hyperlink digitized documents tagged with the subject heading "Suffrage" (in Swedish, "Rösträtt"). The KvinnSam and SKBL data sets of keywords were assembled by going through each document tagged with "Suffrage" and recording the name and frequency of all subject headings attached to these items. The collection method is described below. Other searchable data attached to this material was excluded; only subject headings metadata functioned as hyperlinks on these sites, providing a structured and seemingly neutral process for understanding document meaning via a set of elaborated relationships between

3   KvinnSam was founded as a private archive in 1958, by librarians Asta Ekenvall, Rosa Malmström, and Eva Pineus, who was then the president of the Gothenburg branch of the Fredrika Bremer Association, a liberal women's rights association. In 1971, as a result of modern women's movement activism, this Women's Historical Archive was absorbed by Gothenburg University's library and archive system and renamed as the Women's Historical Collections. In 1997, the institution underwent its first name change under university auspices, to the National Library for Women's, Men's, and Gender Studies. The 2010 change simplified this name to the National Library for Gender Studies, removing the references to stable sex categories. The name changes indicate that KvinnSam follows research and theory developments in feminist scholarship.

4   Work on SKBL began after funding in 2015 from Riksbankens Jubileumsfond (RJ). The proposed database of 1,000 women's biographies written by academics was meant to counteract the emphasis on men in Swedish biographical volumes, where women made up between five and ten per cent of entries. Headed by historian Maria Sjöberg and literature scholar Lisbeth Larsson (both professors at Gothenburg University), the project received additional funding from RJ in 2018 to develop statistical frameworks that would support data visualization. The platform is partially supported KvinnSam but will also be maintained by the Danish Center for Research on Women and Gender (KVINFO).

5   KvinnSam's subject headings are available at http://www2.ub.gu.se/kvinn/kvinnsam/listor/amnesord.html (accessed 25 Jan 2021).

documents.[6] The keywords connected to the concept "suffrage" were then translated into English, thematically classified, and ranked from most to least used. This ordering provided a way of understanding the ontologies that define the boundary object "suffrage" within the KvinnSam and SKBL classification systems.

Figure 1: Screenshot of search results for the keyword "Suffrage", KvinnSam.[7]

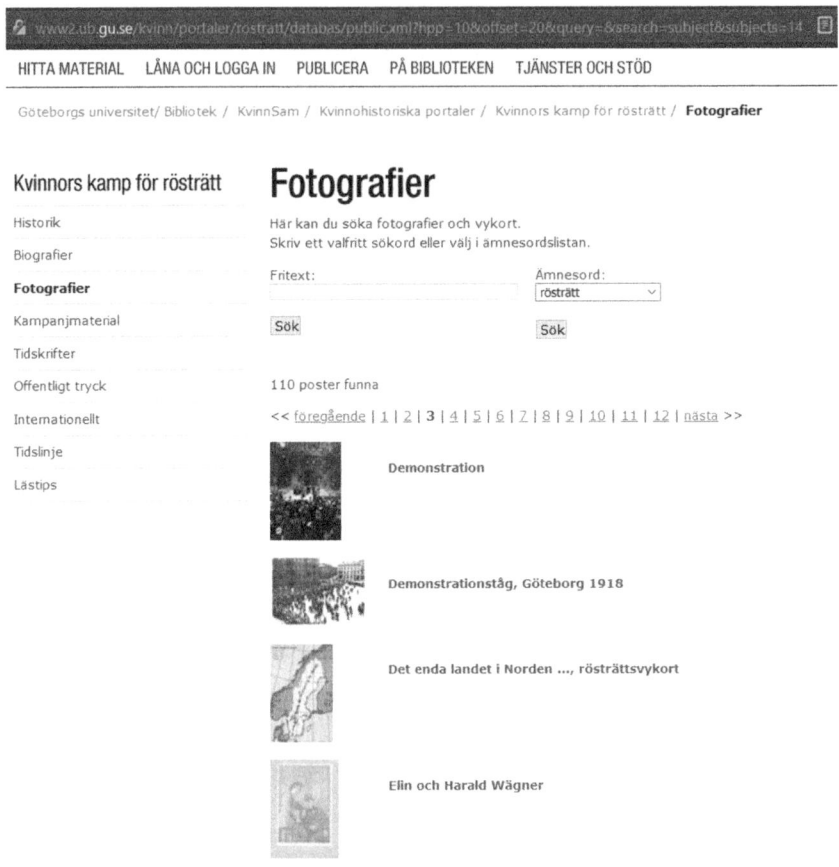

6   In the article, the terms "metadata", "subject headings", "tags", and "keywords" will be used interchangeably. All of these concepts refer to the terms that SKBL and KvinnSam use as hyperlinks between items.
7   The materials displayed here are, beginning at the top: "Suffrage shop, Uppsala, 1912"; "Suffrage Congress in Stockholm 12-17 June 1911"; "Suffrage Congress in Stockholm 12-17 June 1911 backside"; "Suffrage Congress in Budapest 1913, suffrage postcard"; "Suffrage Congress in Budapest 1913, suffrage postcard, backside". Available at (accessed 17 Dec 2020). Available at http://www2.ub.gu.se/kvinn/portaler/rostratt/databas/public.xml?hpp=10&offset=80&query=&search=subject&subjects=14 (accessed 17 Dec 2020).

The Swedish suffrage movement is defined organizationally on KvinnSam's site, which includes a series of pages dedicated to the movement within a "Women's history portal." The digitized image collection is a sub-category within this set of pages and is the only collection where subject headings – which are only in Swedish – have been applied and hyperlinked and materials have been made accessible via a search function. Searching can be done via free text or selection from a dropdown menu of metadata subject categories. Selecting the "Rösträtt" ("Suffrage") keyword within the portal's photography database returns all of the digitized images in the portal, a total of 110 objects (see Figure 1). Of these items. 62 are the front or backside of a suffrage-themed postcard (many featuring photographs), a popular way to both raise money for and advertise the movement. The other images are digitized photographic positives.[8]

Figure 2: Honorine Louise Hermelin entry, SKBL.[9]

---

[8] The results of a search for the metadata subject heading "Rösträtt" or "Suffrage" are available at http://www2.ub.gu.se/kvinn/portaler/rostratt/databas/public.xml?subjects=14&search=subject (accessed 25 Jan 2021). It is worth noting that the material with the applied subject heading of "Suffrage" is a substantial percentage of KvinnSam's digitized photography collection, which numbers 976 items in total.

[9] This image and set of keywords appears to the right of the biographical sketch. Available at https://www.skbl.se/en/article/HonorineHermelin (accessed 17 Dec 2020).

The SKBL site is lexical, privileging individual biographies linked through keywords. Digitized photographs of women are the only digitized archival material on SKBL. Each biographical page is composed of three parts. The first section is a textual biography authored by a scholar. To the right of each text is a second section with keywords, in most cases, located under a portrait of the women.[10] This structure is visible in Figure 2. The third section appears below the first two and lists family relationships, education, activities including professions, residencies, organizations with which the person was involved, prizes and awards received secondary sources of information, and a link to relevant material available in the Swedish national online catalogue Libris. Selecting the "Suffrage" keyword returns 97 biographical entries, a collection that is approximately the same size as KvinnSam's photographic suffrage archive.[11] These keywords are available in both English and Swedish, and a search in each language was performed to identify deviations between the two ontologies.

The assembled metadata from KvinnSam and SKBL was coded separately, using thematic categories make the patterns in each set of data visible. These results within each category were then organised by frequency of use, to facilitate the identification of central and peripheral keywords within the ontological ecology of the Swedish suffrage movement. The results of this analysis are available in Appendices A and B. The resulting keyword categorisation differs between the two data sets. KvinnSam keywords are coded using six categories: (1) Date, (2) Location, (3) Name, (4) Subject, (5) Organization, and (6) Profession/Role (see Appendix A). The SKBL collection falls into three of these categories: (1) Date, (2) Subject, and (3) Profession/Role (see Appendix B). The weighting across these categories varies quite a bit. The majority of KvinnSam keywords appear in the Name class (69 of 122 keywords, or 56.6 per cent), while SKBL's material is most findable via Subject keywords (47 of 76 keywords, or 61.8 per cent). The majority of these classes are highly traditional for archival collections, but both collections also include individual professions and public roles as hyperlinked keywords, which is a more unusual choice.

---

10   I have not investigated every SKBL entry to see what percentage of entries include an image, but not all entries include a photograph. See the "Contents" information at https://skbl.se/en/about-skbl (accessed 4 Mar 2020).

11   The results of a search for the metadata subject heading "Rösträtt" or "Suffrage" are available at https://skbl.se/sv/nyckelord/R%C3%B6str%C3%A4tt (accessed 25 Jan 2021). As with KvinnSam, the SKBL material with this applied subject heading is approximately 10 per cent of the collection, which numbers 1,000 entries in total.

Whose struggle for suffrage? Defining the movement in KvinnSam and SKBL

Collectively, these keywords wall off the boundaries of the suffrage movement in very different ways. Within the KvinnSam collection, the movement is restricted to the years between 1907 and 1921, a short timespan for a movement that some historians have argued spanned at least half a century (Sneider 2010). Both single year and decade keywords are in use, and collection materials are understandably most voluminous in the early 1910s (the tags for the years between 1910-1915 are used 28 times in total, while "1910s" is used 37 times) when collective suffrage activism was at its peak. In contrast, SKBL keywords encompass centuries. Because of the movement's spanning of the turn of the century, both "19th century" and "20th century" are used extensively, making for a far more temporally expansive definition that lacks the granularity of KvinnSam metadata, obscuring how this site actually defines the suffrage movement in time.

The collection keyword groupings also represent different movement geographies. While the movement is clearly centred in Sweden (a keyword for 86 images), there is an international reach to the KvinnSam materials, with "Hungary" (11 images), "United States" (6), "Denmark" (5 images), "Great Britain" (5 images), "Finland" (3 images), "France" (3 images) and "Germany" (2 images) represented alongside two regional tags ("Scandinavia", 5 images; "Europe", 1 image). This variation – often connected to postcards – makes clear how international inspiration, communication, and coordination shaped national and local fights for women's right to vote, a theme increasingly prominent in historical scholarship on the topic (Sneider 2010). In contrast to this range, the SKBL collection is fixed on Sweden, and other geographies are not made visible in the keywords. Instead, access to the SKBL collection is extended geographically by providing English and Swedish versions. Further, the variations between English and Swedish SKBL metadata underlines the centrality of language in expanding the flexibilities of description.

The name keywords of KvinnSam reinforce the collection's international scope while positioning the movement within a particular set of networks and influences. Individual names – 69 of them, in total – are uniformly employed as keywords in the KvinnSam materials. This different reliance on name keywords results in a wide gap between KvinnSam's and SKBL's coverage of suffrage movement participants, with only 16 names appearing in both collections. There are several ramifications of these two different choices. Internationally renowned women like Rosika Schwimmer (Hungary), Carrie Chapman Catt (USA), and Matilde Bajer (Denmark) appear, with women like Chapman Catt as icons used for marketing via photographic postcards, while Bajer and Schwimmer were women personally connected to Swedish suffragists. The suffrage movement depicted in KvinnSam's metadata includes men, all of whom are related to women involved in the movement. This is an interesting reversal of the gendered archival patterns that typically relegate women to the unseen periphery of collections, included because of their relationships to men (Bishop 2017).

Meanwhile, SKBL's keywords emphasize a different set of interconnections. With SKBL, the networks connecting the international and the local appear in the overlaps between "Suffrage", "Temperance movement" (16 tags), and "Peace movement" (11 tags), all three of which facilitated international cooperation through a variety of organisations with local chapters in Sweden. Making these movement overlaps visible is a key theme of women's history at the national level, emphasising the intergenerational political education necessary for movement sustainability (Sneider 2010). Interestingly, use of the "Women's movement" keyword parallels use of the "Suffrage" tag, appearing in an overwhelming majority of the SKBL entries (89 of 97 tags, or 91.8 per cent).

This focus on political topography – explicit, with the keyword "Politics," which appears 43 times (44.3 per cent of the collection) – is also reflected in keywords from all parts of the political spectrum, with "Liberalism" appearing most frequently (23 tags) alongside the less frequent "Conservatism" (9 tags), "Socialism" (1 tag), and "Communism" (1 tag). "Social democracy" is used nine times. Via keywords, the suffrage movement is also embedded in a broader Swedish political arena bridging activism and employment, including "Social work" (8 tags), "Union work" (7 tags), "Religious work" (1 tag), and "Sex education" (5 tags). Other areas of activism are mentioned as well, with the keywords "Environmental issues" (2 tags), "Public health issues" (2 tags), and "Public morality issues" (1 tag). These overlaps are evident in Figure 2. Subject keywords perform an entirely different kind of labour within the KvinnSam collection. There is a clear tendency towards clothing tags and kinds of events, including "Meetings" (14 tags) and "Hats" (9 tags). The keyword "Public awareness development" is by far the most common besides the "Suffrage" tag, appearing 61 times, covering 60 per cent of the collection.

Figure 3: A KvinnSam image "The Constellation" featuring the founders of the Women's Citizens School at Fogelstad.[12]

Both collections use profession/role keywords to define and connect materials and, in both cases, the suffrage movement is clearly made up of middle-class, well-educated individuals, mostly women, categorized as "Lawyers" (2 KvinnSam and 5 SKBL tags), "Politicians" (31 SKBL tags) or "Members of Parliament" (4 KvinnSam and 3 SKBL tags), "Doctors" (2 KvinnSam and 7 SKBL tags), "Librarians" (1 KvinnSam and 2 SKBL tags), "Teachers" (5 KvinnSam and 35 SKBL tags), and "Journalists" (2 KvinnSam and 10 SKBL tags). These keywords are used far less frequently in the KvinnSam collection, though Figure 3 provides one example of this use. While, these labels cover nearly 22 per cent of the KvinnSam materials, including in Figure 3, SKBL applies these keywords to every item. As a result, the professions represented are more numerous, although still dominated by the educated middle-class ("Seamstresses" is an exception, applied 4 times). Another major difference within this category is SKBL's use of the tags "Pioneer" and

---

12 The description of the image reads "The five founders of Women's Citizens School at Fogelstad. Standing from the left: Elisabeth Tamm, Ada Nilsson, Honorine Hermelin, Elin Wägner. Siting in a white rattan chair: Kerstin Hesselgren." The keywords featured to the left in blue are: "Suffrage"; "Wägner, Elin"; "Sweden"; "Nilsson, Ada"; "Doctors"; "1920s"; "Authors"; "Members of Parliament"; "Hesselgren, Kerstin"; "Knowledge"; "Women's Citizens School at Fogelstad". Available at http://www2.ub.gu.se/kvinn/portaler/rostratt/databas/public.xml?id=168&detail=1 (accessed 17 Dec 2020).

"First woman," both of which are used extensively. These keywords individualize women's and feminist history, as well as confirming Eichhorn's observation that "contemporary feminism may be structured by a longing, even nostalgia, for previous eras of feminism" (2013: 28). These keywords can also be read as an attempt to recover women in history, a goal of women's historians since the 1960s and a key goal of the SKBL project.

De-hierarchizing can only get you so far: Metadata politics and social movements as networks

As Denise Riley has asserted, "The individual subject can't quite either be or not be in the collective category, can't coincide with it or easily escape it" (Riley 2000: 85). The perils and opportunities of identity politics are reproduced and complicated in the documentation of historical movements, as generations of activists replicate, edit, and use that history to form their own individual and collective identities. This struggle is uniquely visible in digital projects designed to preserve that history and make it accessible; such projects require a distillation of content down to a few keywords that can be read as historiographical arguments. Description functions both as a classificatory and celebratory process. It is here, in collections like those of KvinnSam and SKBL, that Bowker and Star's observation about classification as a "site of political and ethical work" is most apparent (2000: 147).

These two digital archives demonstrate that historically situated categories and systems of classification can be built in a number of ways that overlap to create a fluid world with discernible boundaries. KvinnSam digital archival material confirms more closely to one camp, which relies on the avoidance of choices that could be considered ahistorical, instead emphasizing personal, professional, event, and organisational names ("Key, Ellen", "Demonstrations", or "Journalists") and specific years. The result is the definition of "suffrage movement" as a social project densely populated with women, built of networks between individuals and outreach to citizens, and tightly focused on a few key organisations and years. Meanwhile, SKBL's approach centres "pioneering" work, defined by individual professional advancement, political ideologies like "Socialism" and "Conservatism", and involvement in mainstream institutions, represented in keywords spanning political and professional activity like "First woman" and "Pioneers".

The much-criticized hierarchies of archival *fonds* are, as predicted by Yeo (2015), undermined by digital description, but there are choices here. Greater granularity – specific years, specific names – exists in the KvinnSam collection, while the SKBL archive employs flexible terms whose meaning is highly context-dependent and variable over time. The granularity of KvinnSam is useful in concretising movement work while also restricting the accessibility of materials – users may need to know names and dates to navigate the database, given that 69 names and 14 dates constitute 68 per cent of the keywords for the collection. Meanwhile, the SKBL collection uses terminology that is almost uniformly highly contested and historically variable, opening the materials up to definitional multiplicity and drift, as concepts like "Feminism" and "Conservatism" shift in response to new political contexts. The contestability is reflected in the occasional mismatch between English and Swedish metadata, which in one instance has translated the Swedish "Sedlighetsfrågan" or "Public morality issues" as the narrower and explicitly gendered "Female morality".

Political representation as evidenced in metadata is a flattened kind of politics; challenging movement history as hierarchical is connected to the deconstruction of hierarchical archival structure (Yeo 2015). This is the case in part because of the breadth of involvement; KvinnSam's keywords span 69 names, but the vast majority are mentioned only one or two times, with a small group of women at the centre (only five women appear in five or more images). Even with the SKBL group, the structure of the individual biographic lexicon and very broad keywords such as "Peace movement" and "Politics" create scope. With this kind of dispersion, the movement is characterised less by a geography of centre and margins than a web of keyworded personal and political connections that make visible various constellations of documents and people. This itemised classification results in the definition of individuals as within the suffrage movement if they corresponded with those in the movement, regardless of the extent of their investment or involvement in highly organised, national-level suffrage work.

This approach to hyperlinked metadata enhances the fragmentation of materials as individual documents existing outside the *fond* structure, which makes it harder to see the boundaries and structure of collections. Physical archives force an encounter with messiness and depth; this is their greatest charm for the historian (Farge 2013). They demand a wading through dozens of documents that seem irrelevant but provide checks on a researcher's preconceived notions about what the archive contains while through a finding aid presenting collections as discrete and finite. Digital archives do not eliminate these checks but instead reconfigure them, so that the messiness is in the metadata, what Rubenstein and Sluis call "the aggregations and topologies of data" (2013: 156). Users need to click through various keywords to understand how they are connected and form interwoven contexts for individual documents. The boundaries of individual collections are thus hard to see.

As a result, the invisibility of archival absences persists and indeed becomes more difficult to work against in the digital archive. Digitising historical materials reproduces patterns of historiography, where the proliferation of a particular paradigm runs the risk of naturalising past interpretation as historical fact and restricting the range of seen histories (Trouillot 2015). Multiple related digital archives produce productive disjunctures; the suffrage movement as defined by KvinnSam and SKBL focuses on contestation over geographic scope (the international coverage of KvinnSam versus the Swedish context depicted in SKBL) and periodization (suffrage as a 20-year project in KvinnSam versus SKBL's centuries-long depiction), which is central to current suffrage historiography (Blom 2012). At the same time, the collections create a few important boundaries around the movement as an historical object. They largely exclude men and a large subsection of women who did not or could not engage with a specific network of generally well-educated suffragists who worked on the national level with institutions like the "Association for Woman's Suffrage" or as "Members of Parliament". This infrastructure serves a purpose elaborated in Star: embodying and thus making invisible certain methodological standards in order to facilitate access to suffrage history (2010: 611). To study the Swedish suffrage movement, according to these digital archives, is to study a particular set of individuals and the relationships between them.

These webs of connection decentre the role of organizations without challenging a traditional focus on national activism and political citizenship. A traditional historiographical focus on pro-suffrage organisations has often obscured the involvement of individuals and undervalued the importance of friendships and communication patterns that upheld the movement (Sneider 2010). In these archives, social networks are clear, visible in both the visual and keyword information (see Figure 3). Yet this version of the movement is defined by a core of upper- and middle-class well-educated women from the centre of the political spectrum without naming them as such. In KvinnSam's case, keywords define a web of educated women in city centres via name keywords. In the case of SKBL, connections build on the professions at the heart of the suffrage movement as a national political force. SKBL cements this focus through its emphasis on "First woman" and "Pioneers" tagging, which privileges women who were in a position to obtain these largely professionally and politically defined "firsts." These metadata practices obscure the fact that the fight for suffrage was always also about economic citizenship and class, borrowing from and overlapping with labour and unionization movements (Kessler-Harris 2001; Blom 2012).

This tendency to collapse boundaries between (in this case movement-based) groups can work to reinforce the archive's top-down perspective. As Zeb Tortorici (2015) observes, erasures in the archive are often the result of interconnected government or organizational repression targeted at multiple groups seen to overlap in population and/or purpose: in his case, homosexuals, left-wing students, and political prisoners in Mexico. There are similar tendencies towards a top-down approach in SKBL. The prevalence of the "Women's movement" keyword within the suffrage collection indicates a synergy that might drown out other, more multicultural, international, and cross-class versions of both "Suffrage" and "Women's movement". Indeed, clicking on "Women's movement" leads to a larger collection that is dominated by white, middle-class Swedish women whose professional and political activities reached their height in the early 1900s.

This periodization supports a focus on a tight first "wave" of women's activism tightly tied to national suffrage work. Broader tags for movements and decades might serve to challenge feminist history's waves metaphor, which scholars increasingly criticize as linear and narrow, ignoring connections between turn of the 20th century national and international movements for minority rights, suffrage, women's labour rights, and educational opportunity, amongst other goals (Blom 2012; Sneider 2015). KvinnSam's keyword approach serves to support the waves interpretation of women's history, locating the suffrage movement between the years 1907-1929. And SKBL keyword use confirms as much as it challenges this historiographical argument. The century tags are clearly too broad to provide a useful critique, and collapsing movements obscures rather than challenges the overwhelming focus on turn-of-the-century activism.

By shifting description from the physical collection level to the level of the individual digitised document, the limits of the physical archive are aggregated and rendered less visible, even within primarily born-digital collections like SKBL, which are not directly tethered to archival collection practices that have historically favoured privileged groups. Yet the digital environment provides for multiple definitions of a concept, which overlap while also disagreeing about boundaries and definitions (Yeo 2015). The research here supports the argument that digital materials be viewed as processes rather than things, variable over time not just because of technical changes but because of a shifting contextual environment online (Hayles 2003). A deconstruction of hierarchy does not automatically produce a more historically accurate or feminist collection – metadata policies must actively deconstruct binaries and give space to outliers and silences. These concrete choices should be based in the understanding, as the explicitly, organisationally interconnected nature of these two digital archives illustrates, that a document's archival context online is connected to but fundamentally different from its physical context and infinitely more fluid.

Conclusion: Digital archivy and metadata as historical argument

Digital archiving projects must recognize that politics are implicated in metadata choices. The two most overtly political keywords evidenced in these two collections are "Feminism" and "Pioneers" – both SKBL tags. The use of "Feminism" as a SKBL keyword might be improved with a change to "Feminisms" in accordance with contemporary research on the multiplicity of feminisms that make up an intersectional feminist universe (Hemmings 2011). Meanwhile, the use of the keywords "Pioneers" and "First woman" in SKBL creates a linear and positivist historical narrative composed of "firsts," a celebratory approach that individualizes what might otherwise be seen as a complicated collective history rife with tensions within the group "women". Who gets to be classified as a pioneer is a question implicit in this category, and perhaps not a very productive one.

But the most glaring omission in these collections is a direct treatment of class, which could be seen both as a reflection of current feminist theorist disinterest in the category and an acceptance of middle-class positioning as normative, a set of decisions that support the LAM community's acceptance of the waves metaphor as a descriptive classificatory approach (Eichhorn 2013: 146-149). This failure to account for class re-entrenches the invisibility of the group least well-represented in the archive: poor and less educated women (Mason & Zanish-Belcher 2007). Beholden to the waves metaphor and restricted by archival collection and digitization practices that privilege groups with historical power, metadata for these two collections misses the fact that the suffrage movement was deeply entrenched in a politics of class throughout Scandinavia, and the gendered nature of Swedish party politics in the aftermath of suffrage cannot be explained without an understanding of the classed nature of the suffrage movement (Blom 2012).

Important too is the question of how to apply metadata to digitised ephemera, a kind of material more common in collections specific to movements by and for minorities and women and very popular online. Scholars such as Elizabeth Edwards (2012) have argued that photographs have a particular function, documenting the parts of life that are considered personal by their creators and grounded in physical context and collective use over time. Other visual materials like postcards, zines, and posters also have these relational histories that help social identities to cohere and persist. This analysis indicates that the reproduction of digitised ephemera documenting a movement multiplies and extends the definitions of these objects by linking materials across different ontological contexts. As the histories of feminism are written, more attention should be paid to how these histories are being shaped by the multiplication and increased accessibility of (some of) the stuff of history, extending networks as documents translated to dynamic digital environments or born in them, producing new collections where visual material is foregrounded.

The creators of digital projects devoted to political subjects do not necessarily understand that digital information is political too. The choice to structure a project around a historically disenfranchised community is not the end of the political decision-making process. These projects are equally vulnerable to fact that digital technologies, including hyperlinked metadata description, are embedded in a "cultural context" that "[determines] the opportunities it affords for making meaning from the world" (Ruberg et al. 2018: 119). Resistance to archival hierarchies does not necessarily translate to resistance to systematizing knowledge in digital environments. Further, undermining hierarchies built into the physical archive through digital description does not eliminate issues with the limits of collections and the silences created by constructing metadata within these limited contexts. Archivists of social movements must also think beyond "their" collections if they want to accurately represent the messiness of social movements and the archives that house the material residue of these movements. This metadata should not be perceived as stable either; the negotiation of identity and history occurring outside the archive will, inevitably, complicate any systematizing decisions made by archivists.

This negotiation also has to do with how individual materials are grouped, as metadata functions both as description and connection. As Geoffrey Yeo has asserted, "[t]he archives of the future will not be created as fixed aggregations, and the users of the future will not want materials presented to them as fixed aggregations" (Yeo 2015: 179). What these two suffrage collections demonstrate is that organising description around personal networks can open up and complicate the definitional boundaries of movements but does not necessarily challenge the general demographics or periodization of these boundaries. Indeed, this approach may even reify the individualization of materials and movements towards which item-level digitization already tends and that metadata is meant to rectify.

Finding ways to complicate what documents have in common is key to fully representing the archival messiness that is the "ecology" of boundary objects like the suffrage movement (Bowker & Star 2000). Digital archives are interconnected and overlapping processes, even within themselves through language differentiation. Their development must take this multiplicity and interdependency into account, and both archivists and researchers have an obligation to think more critically about the structure of and access points for digitized archival material. Collections online can be understood as new arguments about how to group the stuff of the archives. Without an understanding of this complexity, these digital archives run the risk of normalizing particular personal network boundaries as movement boundaries without making the archival ghosts at the centre of current historical archival practice visible.

Acknowledgements

The author would like to thank staff at the Swedish National Library for Gender Studies and the Swedish Women's Biographical Lexicon for approving the screenshots that appear in this text. Additionally, the author wishes to thank the two anonymous reviewers as well as the editors of this special issue for their comments, which have improved the article's clarity and argumentation. Thanks also, always, to Martin Öhman.

References

Allington, Daniel, Broullette, Sarah and Golumbia, David (2016): Neoliberal Tools (and Archives): A Political History of Digital Humanities. In: Los Angeles Review of Books, 1 May 2016 (https://lareviewofbooks.org/article/neoliberal-tools-archives-political-history-digital-humanities/).

Bastian, Jacqueline and Flinn, Andrew, eds. (2020): Community Archives, Community Spaces: Heritage, Memory and Identity, London: Facet Publishing.

Bishop, Catherine (2017). "The Serendipity of Connectivity: Piecing Together Women's Lives in the Digital Archive." In: Women's History Review 26/5, pp. 766-780.

Blom, Ida (2012): "Structures and Agency: A Transnational Comparison of the Struggle for Women's Suffrage in the Nordic Countries during the Long 19th Century." In: Scandinavian Journal of History 37/5, pp. 600-620.

Bowker, Geoffrey C. and Star, Susan Leigh (2000): "Invisible Mediators of Action: Classification and the Ubiquity of Standards." In: Mind, Culture, and Activity 7/1-2, pp. 147-163.

Caswell, Michelle (2014): "Inventing New Archival Imaginaries: Theoretical Foundations for Identity-based Archives." In: Dominique Daniel and Amalia Levi (eds.), Identity Palimpsest: Archiving Ethnicity in the U.S. and Canada, Sacramento: Litwin Books.

Cott, Nancy (1987): The Grounding of Modern Feminism, New Haven: Yale University Press.

D'Ignazio, Catherine and Klein, Lauren F. (2020): Data Feminism, Boston: MIT Press.

Drabinski, Emily (2013): "Queering the Catalog: Queer theory and the politics of correction." In: Library Quarterly: Information, Community, Policy 83/2, pp. 94-111.

Edwards, Elizabeth (2012): "Objects of Affect: Photography Beyond the Image." In: Annual Review of Anthropology 41, pp. 221-234.

Eichhorn, Kate (2013): The Archival Turn in Feminism: Culture in Order, Philadelphia: Temple University Press.

Farge, Arlene (2013): The Allure of the Archives, trans. T. Scott-Railton, New Haven: Yale University Press.

Hayles, Katherine (2003): "Translating Media: Why We Should Rethink Textuality." In: Yale Journal of Criticism 16/2, pp. 263-290.

Hemmings, Clare. (2011): Why Stories Matter: The Political Grammar of Feminist Theory, Durham: Duke University Press.

Holterhoff, Kate (2017): "From Disclaimer to Critique: Race and the Digital Image Archivist." In: Digital Humanities Quarterly 11/3.

Kessler-Harris, Alice (2001): In Pursuit of Equity: Women, Men and the Quest for Economic Citizenship in 20th Century America, Oxford: Oxford University Press.

Lesy, Michael (2007): "Visual Literacy." In: The Journal of American History 94/1, pp. 143-155.

Mason, Kären M. and Zanish-Belcher, Tanya (2007): Raising the Archival Consciousness: How Women's Archives Challenge Traditional Approaches to Collecting and Use, Or, What's in a Name? Library Trends 56/2, pp. 344-359.

McCann, Carole R. and Kim, Seung-kyung (2017): Feminist Theory Reader: Local and Global Perspectives, New York: Taylor & Francis.

Noble, Safiya Umoja (2018): Algorithms of Oppression: How Search Engines Reinforce Racism, New York: New York University Press.

Riley, Denise (2000): The Words of Selves: Identification, Solidarity, Irony, Stanford: Stanford University Press.

Rubenstein, Daniel and Sluis, Katrina. (2013): Notes on the Margins of Metadata: Concerning the Undecidability of the Digital Image. Photographies 6/1, pp. 151-158.

Ruberg, Bonnie, Boyd, Jason, and Howe, James (2018): "Toward a Queer Digital Humanities." In: Elizabeth Losh and Jacqueline Wernimonth (eds.), Bodies of Information: Intersectional Feminism and Digital Humanities, Minneapolis: University of Minnesota Press, pp. 108-127.

Sneider, Alison (2010): "The New Suffrage History: Voting Rights in International Perspective." In: History Compass 8/7, pp. 692-703.

Star, Susan Leigh (2010): "This is not a Boundary Object: Reflections of the Origin of a Concept." In: Science, Technology, & Human Values 35, pp. 601-617.

Spivak, Gayatri Chakravorty. (1990): The Post-colonial Critic: Interviews, Strategies, Dialogues, ed Sarah Harasym, New York: Routledge.

Strandgaard Jensen, Helle. (2020): Digital Archival Literacy for (All) Historians. In: Media History, DOI: 10.1080/13688804.2020.1779047.

Taves Sheffield, Roland (2020): "Archival Optimism, or, How to Sustain a Community Archives." In: Jeanette A. Bastian and Andrew Flinn (eds.), *Community Archives, Community Spaces: Heritage, Memory and Identity*, London: Facet Publishing.

Thompson, Kelly (2016): "More Than a Name: A Content Analysis of Name Authority Records for Authors Who Self-Identify as Trans." In: Library Resources & Technical Services 60:3, pp. 140-155.

Tortorici, Zeb Joseph (2015): "Archival Seduction: Indexical Absences and Historiographical Ghosts." In: special issue of Archive Journal, ed. Lisa Darms and Kate Eichhorn.

Trouillot, Michel-Rolph (2015): Silencing the Past: Power and the Production of History, Boston: Beacon Press.

van Dijck, José (2004): "Mediated Memories: Personal Cultural Memory as an Object of Cultural Analysis." In: Continuum: Journal of Media & Cultural Studies 18/2, pp. 261-277.

van Dijk, Jan (2001): The Network Society: Social Aspects of New Media, trans. Leontine Spoorenberg, London: Sage Publications.

Voss-Hubbard, Anke (1995): "'No Documents – No History': Mary Ritter Beard and the Early History of Women's Archives." In: American Archivist 58, pp. 16-30.

Yeo, Geoffrey (2015): "Contexts, Original Orders, and Item-Level Orientation: Responding Creatively to Users' Needs and Technological Change." In: Journal of Archival Organization 12/3-4, pp. 170-185.

Appendix A: KvinnSam keywords

Date	Location	Name	Organization	Subject	Profession/Role
1910s (37)	Sweden (86)	Wägner, Elin (19)	Association for Woman's Suffrage (40)	Suffrage (110)	Teachers (5)
1911 (11)	Gothenburg (12)	Petrini, Gulli (18)	Women's Citizens School at Fogelstad (5)	Public awareness development (61)	Authors (4)
1910 (9)	Uppsala (12)	Schwimmer, Rosika (9)		Meetings (14)	Members of Parliament (4)
1913 (8)	Hungary (11)	Holmgren, Ann Margret (5)		Hats (9)	Doctors (2)
1915 (6)	Stockholm (10)	Key, Ellen (5)		Knowledge (8)	Journalists (2)
1917 (5)	USA (6)	Andén, Eva (4)		Men (7)	Labour inspectors (2)
1920s (5)	Denmark (5)	Boheman, Ezaline (3)		Coats (6)	Lawyers (2)
1909 (3)	Great Britain (5)	Bugge Wicksell, Anna (3)		Suits (6)	Librarians[13] (1)
1907 (2)	Scandinavia (5)	Hagen, Ellen (3)		Demonstrations (5)	
1912 (2)	Finland (3)	Hesselgren, Kerstin (3)		General elections (3)	
1914 (2)	France (3)	Tamm, Märta (3)		Film (2)	
1918 (2)	Germany (2)	Whitlock, Anna (3)		Handbags (2)	
1916 (1)	Visingsö (2)	Bergman, Signe (2)		Agriculture (1)	
1921 (1)	Europe (1)	Brandell, Elin (2)		Reading (1)	
	Strängnäs (1)	Catt, Carrie Chapman (2)			

---

13 The entry does not include a digitised document.

Date	Location	Name	Organization	Subject	Profession/Role
		Cronquist, Maja (2)			
		Fischer, Ida (2)			
		Furuhjelm, Annie (2)			
		Helander, Emmy (2)			
		Helberg, Eira (2)			
		Hennings, Beth (2)			
		Lamm, Alfhild (2)			
		Landquist, Ellen (2)			
		Lindemann, Anna (2)			
		Lindhagen, Agnes (2)			
		Nilsson, Ada (2)			
		Odencrantz, Elin (2)			
		Peterson, Karin (2)			
		Pettersson, Anna (2)			
		Pettersson, Karin (2)			
		Rydelius, Ellen (2)			
		Schwimmer, Franciska (2)			
		Sheep-shanks, Mary (2)			
		Stéenhoff, Frida (2)			
		Svanström, Elin (2)			
		Wahlström, Lydia (2)			

Date	Location	Name	Organization	Subject	Profession/Role
		Wästberg, Barbro (2)			
		Öhrvall, Hjalmar (2)			
		Anthony, Susan Brownell (1)			
		Bajer, Fredrik (1)			
		Bajer, Matilde (1)			
		Billing, Ella (1)			
		Bremer, Fredrika (1)			
		Brisman, Ester (1)			
		Bromée, Emilia (1)			
		Carlberg, Frigga (1)			
		Condorcet, Jean Antoine Nicolas Caritat de (1)			
		Edén, Nils (1)			
		Ekberg, Ester (1)			
		Ekedahl, Lisa (1)			
		Ernander, Tyra (1)			
		Fjällbäck-Holmgren, Karin (1)			
		Fogelklou, Emilia (1)			
		Holmgren, Karin (1)			
		Huch, Ricarda (1)			
		Humla, Hildur (1)			

Date	Location	Name	Organization	Subject	Profession/Role
		Johansson, Gunhild (1)			
		Lindhagen, Carl (1)			
		Matson, Lydia (1)			
		Mattsson, Lydia (2)			
		Mill, John Stuart (1)			
		Munch-Petersen, Valfrid Palmgren[14] (1)			
		Palmstierna, Ebba (Ellen) (1)			
		Shaw, Anna Howard (1)			
		Starli, Katti (1)			
		Tonning, Augusta (1)			
		Widegren, Matilda (1)			
		Österhjelm, Hedvig (1)			
		Östlund, Agda[15] (1)			

14 The entry does not include a digitised document.
15 The entry does not include a digitised document.

Appendix B: SKBL keywords

Date	Subject	Profession/Role
20th century (96)	Suffrage (97)	Pioneers (54)
19th century (70)	Women's movement (89)	Teachers (35)
	Politics[16] (43)	Politicians (31)
	Liberalism (23)	Authors (13)
	Public education[17] (18)	Editors[18] (13)
	Peace movement (16)	School directors (13)
	Temperance movement (11)	First woman (11)
	Social democracy (9)	Journalists (10)
	Social work (8)	Doctors (7)
	Charity (7)	Entrepreneurs (7)
	Christianity (7)	Lawyers (5)
	Conservatism (7)	Photographers (4)
	Prostitution (7)	Seamstresses (4)
	Union work[19] (7)	Members of Parliament (3)
	Feminism (5)	Translators (3)
	Pedagogy[20] (5)	Building contractors[21] (2)
	Sex education (5)	Librarians (2)
	Social activities[22] (4)	Physiotherapists (2)
	Defence (3)	Publishers (2)
	Home[23] (3)	Actors (1)
	Cooperation (2)	Artists (1)
	Domestic handicraft (2)	County governors[24] (1)
	Domestic science (2)	Dentists (1)
	Environmental issues (2)	Economists (1)

16   In two instances, "Politics" appears amongst the English keywords but has no corollary in the Swedish keywords.

17   "Folkbildning" has been translated here as "Public education" but is translated as "Adult education" by SKBL.

18   SKBL does not offer the keyword "Redaktörer" in English.

19   "Facklig verksamhet" has been translated here as "Union work" but is translated as "Trade unionist" by SKBL.

20   SKBL does not offer the keyword "Pedagogik" in English.

21   SKBL does not offer the keyword "Byggherrar" in English

22   SKBL does not offer the keyword "Social verksamhet" in English.

23   "Hembygd" is not translated but is offered in the English-language SBKL as "Hembygd."

24   SKBL does not offer the keyword "Landshövdingskor" in English.

Date	Subject	Profession/Role
	Handicrafts (2)	Gardeners[25] (1)
	Public health issues (2)	Landowners[26] (1)
	Women's role (2)	Nurses (1)
	Advice columns (1)	Patrons (1)
	Agriculture (1)	Scholars[27] (1)
	Animal rights activism (1)	
	Children's and young adult literature[28] (1)	
	Children's rights[29] (1)	
	Communism (1)	
	Cookbooks (1)	
	Ethnology (1)	
	Fashion (1)	
	Gymnastics (1)	
	History (1)	
	Lesbianism (1)	
	Literary studies[30] (1)	
	Mental illness (1)	
	Public morality issues[31] (1)	
	Religious work[32] (1)	
	Sculpture (1)	
	Sex equality[33] (1)	
	Social politics (1)	
	Socialism (1)	

25 SKBL does not offer the keyword "Trädgårdsmästare" in English.
26 "Godsägare" has been translated here as "Landowner" but is translated as "Agriculture" by SKBL.
27 SKBL does not offer the keyword "Forskare" in English.
28 "Barn- och ungdomslitteratur" has been translated here as "Children's and young adult literature" but is translated as "Children's and youth literature" by SKBL.
29 SKBL does not offer the keyword "Barns rättigheter" in English.
30 SKBL does not offer the keyword "Litteraturvetenskap" in English.
31 "Sedlighetsfrågan" has been translated here as "Public morality issues" but is translated at "Female morality" by SKBL.
32 SKBL does not offer the keyword "Kyrkligt arbete" in English.
33 The keyword "Equality" is attached to one entry with no Swedish corollary, while "Jämställdhet" appears once with no English corollary.

Designing Digital Diagnostics
(Meta)data in Clinical Radiology

Kathrin Friedrich

Abstract

Since the 1990s Western clinical radiology has been confronted with a fundamental media-induced change – the so-called analogue-digital migration. Film-based diagnostics and archiving of radiological images are transformed into digital interfaces and infrastructures. Networked software applications, namely picture archiving and communication systems (PACS), provide a new basis for processing and displaying image data. The design and implementation of PACS and their (user) interfaces challenged, amongst others, the search for data standards for digital diagnostics. The data format DICOM (Digital Imaging and Communication) was developed to provide the technological basis for encoding image data. Simultaneously, DICOM determines how patients' bodies are rendered machine-readable and how radiologists are able to gain software-based insights. A main function of DICOM metadata is encoding and continuously actualising patient identification for technological and human actors. A misidentification of image data and specific patient could lead to fatal errors in the furthe+r treatment process. Accordingly, metadata themselves meander between being invisible to the human user and being essential and hence necessarily visible information for diagnostics. Shifting between normativity and fluidity, DICOM metadata enables new practices of radiological diagnostics, which literally bear vital consequences for patients and, on another level, for the profession of radiology. The paper analyses inherent politics and tensions of metadata from a media theoretical point of view by employing the case of the DICOM standard. Based on subject-specific discourses, data models as well as an in-depth examination of exemplary DICOM metadata it shows how (meta)data politics redefine diagnostic infrastructures and routines as well as gain impact on epistemic and aesthetic practices at the turn of the analogue-digital migration.

Keywords: digital imaging, data processing, clinical radiology, data model, DICOM, graphical user interface, analogue-digital migration, interoperability

The analogue-digital migration as a challenge for data politics

From business practices to everyday activities and scientific realms, many sociocultural domains have been and still are under significantly transformation due to processes of digitalisation. The alteration of established infrastructures and often material practices of information handling together with the introduction of networked digital services and their respective human-readable interfaces is overturning established modes of perceiving, thinking and acting. Such digitalisation processes pose a challenge to a multitude of actors to construct new modes and measures for technologically, operationally and aesthetically dealing with digital data.

Clinical radiology reveals a striking example of a domain in which digitalisation runs up against established practices of handling patient and image data with new technological opportunities. Only since around the year 2000 has such a media-induced change been taking place in Western clinical radiology, even though some medical imaging modalities, e.g. computed tomography (CT) or magnetic resonance imaging (MRI), were already digital in the 1980s. The term analogue-digital migration captures the changing infrastructures for processing and displaying imaging data and not primarily its digital acquisition. The analogue workflows and diagnostic modes, e.g. diagnosing with printed scans on a lightbox or managing the clinical processes on the basis of paper-based patient records, were successively transferred to digital environments and software systems. The relocation of once material things and processes challenged radiologists just as much as the designers of software applications and digital infrastructures. Radiologists now needed to diagnose soft copies, i.e. data sets of medical visualisations, within a graphical user interface by applying various digital tools, such as rulers or angle meters. As in other areas of digitalisation, professional expertise was confronted with "data avalanches", ramified network architectures and advanced modes of visualisation which cause far-reaching changes for the radiologists' workflows and diagnostic practices (Larsson et al. 2007: 235-240; Tellioğlu/Wagner 2001: 163-188). Many medical professionals and healthcare companies euphorically proclaimed the "digital revolution we are now living" (Bryan 2003: 299; Reiner et al. 2003: 299-304) would be just the thing for radiological diagnostics and care, thanks to the potential of a "fully digital radiology department", such as automatic data transfer and higher resolution visualisations.

How analogue-digital migrations unfold in a pragmatic sense and on a local level is rather complex, scattered and often the result of non-linear processes. Yet, in a more socio-cultural view, analogue-digital migrations in radiology demanded – and sometimes still demand – to negotiate data politics for a whole clinical discipline to ensure diagnostic standardisation, interoperability and validity. Such data politics take different media-based forms and scales as they address, amongst others, network protocols and visualisation modes within graphical user interfaces. Furthermore, actors from radiology, informatics and medical technology vendors participate in designing and establishing digital diagnostics.

Now, an established form of an encompassing and networked digital infrastructure in radiology are so-called picture archiving and communication systems (PACS), which provide a structural basis for processing and displaying image data. The design and implementation of PACS and their graphical user interfaces (GUI) challenged the search for common data standards. Such standards are both key to reliably process data from medical imaging modalities to the new fully digital workplaces of radiologist and to visualise imaging data with its corresponding metadata to identify patient-specific information. In clinical contexts this effort has resulted in the data format named Digital Imaging and Communication in Medicine (DICOM).

From a media studies point of view, PACS as a digital infrastructure and DICOM as a standard for processing and displaying image data provide an interesting case for tracing (meta)data politics in clinical radiology – both understood as a profession and a media practice. At the turn of the analogue-digital migration, it becomes possible to explore data politics in the making with regard to their conceptual, operational and aesthetic conditions. This basically implies questioning digital media – networks, software and data standards – with regard to their technicity rather than their technological ontology. "Technicity refers to the extent to which technologies mediate, supplement, and augment collective life; the extent to which technologies are fundamental to the constitution and grounding of human endeavor; and the unfolding or evolutive power of technologies to make things happen in conjunction with people." (Dodge/Kitchin 2011: 42) Technicity as a theoretical notion captures the interplays between technology, our conceptions of it and its contexts of application. The becoming and the transformation of technological (infra)structures becomes more interesting than questions of ontology.

What then is the "evolutive power" of digital imaging technology that "makes things happen" in clinical radiology at the turn of the analogue-digital migration? To critically explore this question, the following case study analyses the inherent politics and tensions of (meta)data (cf. Mackenzie 2003) at these three substantial points: first, it traces subject-specific discourses surrounding conceptual ideas for collectively establishing the software infrastructure PACS; second, this study examines data models of DICOM as onto-operational settings for processing image data; and third, it analyses an exemplary radiological visualisation and its GUI in-depth to demonstrate aesthetic and epistemic conditions of DICOM metadata.

Kathrin Friedrich

Collective negotiations of picture archiving and communication systems

One of the most obvious signs of the transformation from analogue practices to digitally encoded ones in radiology was the introduction of picture archiving and communication systems (PACS) throughout radiology departments and clinics. These software systems replaced once material and personnel intensive practices, such as delivering printed CT images to the lightbox of a certain radiologist for diagnosis (Saunders 2008: 159ff.). With the introduction of PACS into clinical contexts, the distribution and archiving of digital image data was fully transferred into automated software commands that replaced archive clerks and other administrative personnel, and – ideally – streamlined the flow of data from acquisition to visualisation to diagnosing and finally to archiving the patient-specific image data. This was also considered to boost the productivity of the "radiology assembly line" (Reiner/Siegel 2006: 75).[1]

Currently, several healthcare companies worldwide develop and sell PACS solutions and there are also open access versions available. The basic formal structure and the reliance on the DICOM standard of all these different versions of a PACS remain the same. From a medical data source, such as a CT scanner, image data is gathered and preliminary visualised by an imaging station. The data is distributed through a high-speed network to further workstations where radiologists conduct diagnosis. Within the network, there are archiving modalities as well as data interfaces to other digital infrastructures, such as the radiology information system or the hospital information system (Hanseth/Lundberg 2001: 355). Formally, the infrastructure of a PACS not only determines modes of exchange and distribution but already possibilities of visualisation, workflows and managing patient care. Picture archiving and communication systems are multi-

---

1 One of the potential gains and at the same time one of the biggest challenges for the work of radiologists is that more and more image studies by different digital imaging modalities, such CT or MRI, could be generated each day. For example, an informal study at the Department of Radiology at Mayo Clinic Jacksonville, Florida, evaluated "that roughly 1500 images were generated and stored in 1994. In that same practice in 2002, an average of 16000 images were acquired each day" (Andriole et al., 2004, 237). The potential of these "data avalanches" for medical research by employing methods of data mining were also addressed by several subject-specific publications: "Radiology has the opportunity to participate in the new era of big data and personalized medicine. [...] Every CT study, regardless of indication, such as 'evaluate for pulmonary emboli', has an enormous wealth of 'incidental' information, such as bone mineral density of the spine, coronary artery and other vascular calcifications, interstitial lung disease, and dozens of other potentially important information 'hidden' in its pixel data" (Siegel, 2013, 4).

layered and thus create conditions of data generation and exchange, and – literally – infrastructure certain contexts of application. "Study an information system and neglect its standards, wires, and settings, and you miss equally essential aspects of aesthetics, justice, and change. Perhaps if we stopped thinking of computers as information highways and began to think of them more modestly as symbolic sewers, this realm would open up a bit" (Star 1999: 379).[2] PACSs and in particular their data standard DICOM act as "symbolic sewers" as they open up the opportunity to capture the multifaceted relations of digital infrastructures and their impacts on aesthetic and epistemic practices. Looking at software systems and their different layers as "symbolic sewers" captures their technicity as both a technical and collective infrastructure.

The informatic idea to process imaging data by means of software applications dates back to the 1970s. In the subject-specific text *Applications of Picture Processing, Image Analysis and Computer Graphics Techniques to Cranial CT Scans* (1979) information scientists published their "vision of an all-digital department [that] includes, besides all-digital diagnostic devices, a complete new digital communication structure and standard" (Thomas et al. 2005: 332). The paper addresses all digital functions mentioned in its title and further the operational role of computer workstations as "possible working modes in such a system [distributed computing network, KF]" (Lemke et al. 1979: 341). The problem that the authors identify is basically media related: "In the process of medical diagnosis and therapy, information is usually presented by means of the written word, pictures, graphics and the spoken word. [...] In the interest of a patient oriented health care system there are a number of important if not vital requirements on how the information in the MR [medical record, KF] should be organzied and used" (Lemke et al. 1979: 341). As one of the "most desirable features of data representation and processing" they name "flexible conferencing and consulting mode facilities using MR's and all modes of communication (i.e. word, picture and voice communication)" (Lemke et al. 1979: 341). From the beginning, the informatic idea to develop an encompassing digital infrastructure for radiological diagnostics equally integrates technological as well as operational and human-centred considerations.

In the mid 1980s, more conceptual and organisational initiatives started to identify and negotiate needs of digital radiology (Friedrich 2016). While the consortium Transforming the Radiological Interpretation Process (TRIP) particularly addresses the challenges of digital diagnostics for radiological perception

---

2   Perspectives from the history of technology as well as from science and technology studies analyse different types of infrastructures and their impacts on material, epistemic and operational processes as well as their socio-technical effects (e.g. Akrich, 1992; Bowker et al., 2010; Star/Ruhleder, 1996). In reference to these studies also media theoretical approaches focus on the epistemic and performative status of code and software (e.g. Mackenzie, 2003; Mackenzie, 2005).

and training, the association Integrating the Healthcare Enterprise (IHE) stresses the necessity to establish common technological standards in PACS to grantee a "seamless data exchange"[3] between different imaging modalities and digital infrastructures. Starting in 1985, IHE developed "the *de facto* standard for representing and sharing medical imaging data, and now implemented as part of industry practice" (Bui/Morioka 2010: 98), which is the data format Digital Imaging and Communication in Medicine, DICOM for short. Members of the American College of Radiology (ACR) teamed up with actors from the National Electrical Manufacturers Association (NEMA) "with the purpose of developing a universal imaging standard that would be compatible with all future makes, modalities, and models of imaging devices" (Flanders/Carrino 2003: 272).[4] As a "universal imaging standard" DICOM (.dcm) defines "how individuals and communities meet infrastructure" (Bowker/Star 1999: 33), here in the PAC system. DICOM as both an image format like .jpeg as well as a network protocol standardises and encodes how radiologists can get hold of image data which are no longer printed out on film sheets but visualised within graphical user interfaces. If radiologists do not or cannot "comply" with these new modalities as part of the analogue-digital migration, they might not be part of digital diagnostics. Hence, it is not just an issue for medical technology companies to build their products, e.g. an MRI scanner, compatible to the collectively negotiated data standard, but it is also about whether an epistemic collective commits to being "standardised" by digital means (Bowker/Star 1999: 13).

"Compliance with this standard enables an open architecture for imaging systems, bridging hardware and software entities and allowing interoperability for the transfer of medical images and associated information between disparate systems" (Andriole 2006: 222). By referring to "compliance" and "interoperability" radiologist Katherine Andriole implicitly denotes the more-than-technological implications of data standards and their "symbolic sewing" with respect to politics of abstraction and coding. The search for a universal data standard for radiological imaging and diagnosing implies the idea to "seamlessly" integrate human and technological actors and render them interoperable within a digital infrastructure. Andriole's hinting at interoperability might exclusively draw on technological systems,[5] yet the ideal of seamlessness includes a strategic invis-

---

3   https://www.ihe-europe.net/ (last accessed 24.09.2020).
4   Today, the documentation of DICOM encompasses about 4200 printed pages and is being further developed for integration into more clinical specialities, such as neurosurgery. Besides, the DICOM standard for diagnostic radiology also needs to be adapted from time to time as new visualisation devices such as tablet computers and mobile phones enter the market (Kahn et al. 2011: 296).
5   According to the International Society for Standardization interoperability is defined as: "The capability to communicate, execute programs, or transfer data among various functional units in a manner that requires the user to have little or no knowledge

ibility for users: "Seamless data exchange is invisible to users who need the information, while intelligent for IT engineers who build the system."[6] Where and why there might be complications at the "seams" of the system does not seem relevant for users. Conceptually, for them only the semantic value of the data should count. This observation is similar to what Wendy Chun remarks for the introduction of graphical user interfaces: "GUIs have been celebrated as enabling user freedom through (perceived) visible and personal control on the screen. This freedom, however, depends on a profound screening: an erasure of the computer's machinations and of the history of interactive operating systems as supplementing – that is, supplanting – human intelligence" (Chun 2011: 59). In a different way, the introduction of ideally seamless digital infrastructures which draw on a profound division of labour between engineers and users, supplements and supplants formerly embodied and material practices of image distribution which now become uniform data practices. Nevertheless, the promise of seamlessness picks up on established analogue working routines of image production and transportation being almost invisible to radiologists as they have been carried out by technical staff ideally seamlessly as well. While this routine might appear not to have changed significantly with the introduction of digital infrastructures, the possibilities of individual intervention and iteration for medical personnel have. Ad-hoc coordination between radiologists and technical staff regarding the distribution and display of image data is now delegated to software-based tools which set their very own conditions of possibility for radiological diagnostics. These are collectively encoded and cannot be changed based on personal and *in situ* conversations. For technical staff being formerly responsible for handling film prints this development resulted in the socio-economic consequence: becoming redundant to newly establish digital routines. While the technological foundations of the analogue-digital migration were collectively negotiated, their role was sometimes only addressed in harsh statements such as: "Film room librarians were eliminated" (Reiner/Siegel 2006: 78).

DICOM as a network protocol for data processing

In analogue times, the typical workplace of a radiologist would have been a lightbox or light wall, probably yet accompanied by work at a computer for administrative reasons but the primary place of diagnostic viewing was in front of printed CT, x-ray or MRI images hung up at a lightbox (Saunders 2008: 13ff.). Nowadays, radiologists sit in front of computer screens of radiological workstations to review image data and mainly write diagnostic reports for attending physicians (Friedrich

---

of the unique characteristics of those units." (ISO/IEC 2382-01:1993, https://www.iso.org/obp/ui/#iso:std:iso-iec:2382:-1:ed-3:v1:en, last accessed 23.09.2020).

6 https://www.ihe-europe.net/ (last accessed 23.09.2020).

2018). Digital visualisations are no longer fixed on printed film but remain a steady stream of data within the PACS software. The GUI of the software now is not only the location where radiological diagnostics can be carried out but becomes a place where epistemic and aesthetic conditions of possibility are renegotiated between medical staff, healthcare vendors and ultimately patients. A radiologist remarks: "[...] CT exams with a thousand images are becoming common and simply cannot be managed effectively on film. PACS viewing software can be used to dissect, analyze, magnify, or reformat image data in an infinite number of ways" (Hirschorn 2006: 3-4). Therefore, software engineers need to determine beforehand how digital data is processed and made accessible at a workstation. For doing so, they need to translate diagnostic processes "into a mechanical process of action" (Trogemann 2010: 43). These diagnostic processes are abstracted to machine code, but they derive from and, on another level, retroact to a material, cultural and social world that is evidently affected (Trogemann 2010: 44). Therefore, designing the basic structure of data processing and visualisation in digital radiology also involves modelling the structure of digital work processes and entities.

The real-world and information models of the DICOM standard (Fig. 1 & 2) outline, for example, the conditions under which a person can be considered as a patient and how radiological workflows unfold. The flowcharts "show [...] the constraints on the system, its system boundaries and the general flow of information around the system. [They are] a common means of understanding complex data flows around a system within computer science and software engineering" (Berry 2011: 114).

Whereas the real-world model (Fig. 1) semantically specifies that an entity called "patient" "makes" a "visit" that "includes" a "study" and so on, it constructs a narrative about the sequence of an ideal-typical radiological exam. On the other hand, the information model based on this narrative is used to further abstract a "real-world" sequence to a schema that is finally transferable into machine code, i.e. into the algorithms and data structures of the DICOM standard and the PACS.

In the information model (Fig. 2), the patient is turned into an IOD, an information object, that is credited with specific attributes. The information object "patient" is defined as "a person receiving, or registered to receive, healthcare services, or is the subject of one or more [imaging, KF] studies for some other purpose, such as research" (NEMA 2014: 86). In this definition patients are primarily characterised as receivers of healthcare services or subjects of imaging studies, illness or sickness are not mentioned here. The information object patient is integrated into the information model of DICOM that further specifies relations to other information objects and ideal flows. But, whereas the patient in the real-world model (Fig. 1) is incorporated in human-comprehensible processes (e.g. patient – makes – visit – includes – study), the information model abstracts these processes into the semantically undefined category "references". The quality of referencing is not specified further, as solely the structural connections of different objects matter to the model and finally the programming of the data standard.

Fig. 1: Real-world model DICOM. NEMA – The Association of Electrical Equipment and Medical Imaging Manufactures (2014): DICOM PS3.3 2014c – Information Object Definitions, p. 91. (http://dicom.nema.org/medical/dicom/2014a/output/pdf/part03.pdf) (last accessed 27.09.2020)

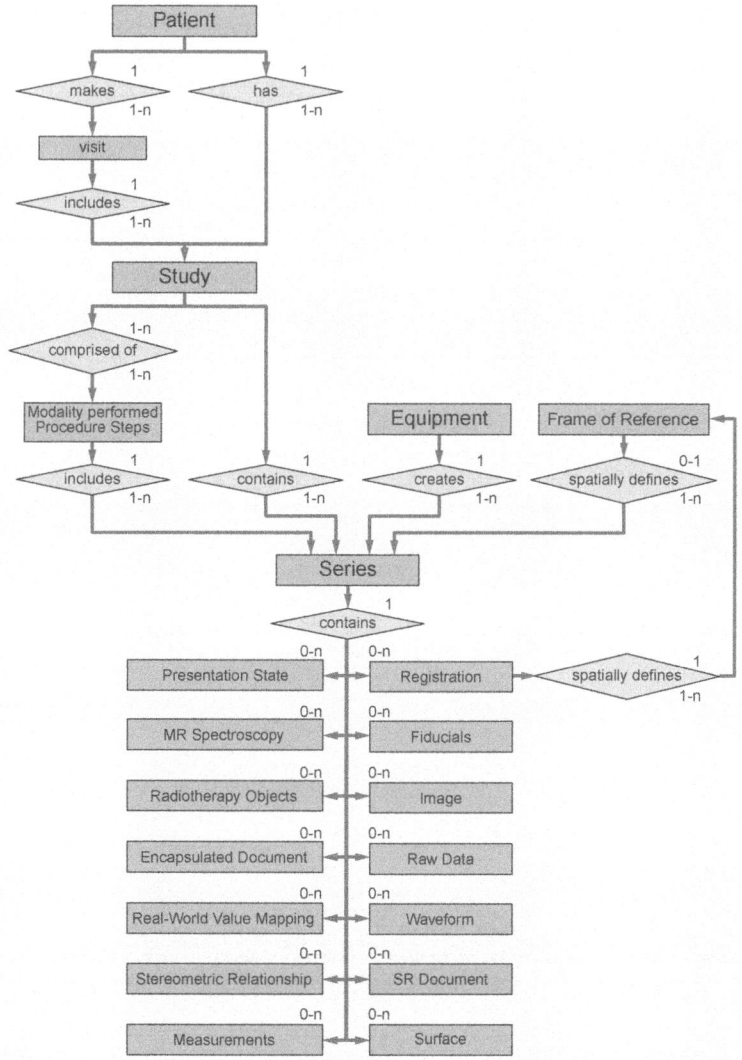

Fig. 2: Information model DICOM. NEMA – The Association of Electrical Equipment and Medical Imaging Manufactures (2014): DICOM PS3.3 2014c – Information Object Definitions, p. 89. (http://dicom.nema.org/medical/dicom/2014a/output/pdf/part03.pdf) (last accessed 27.09.2020)

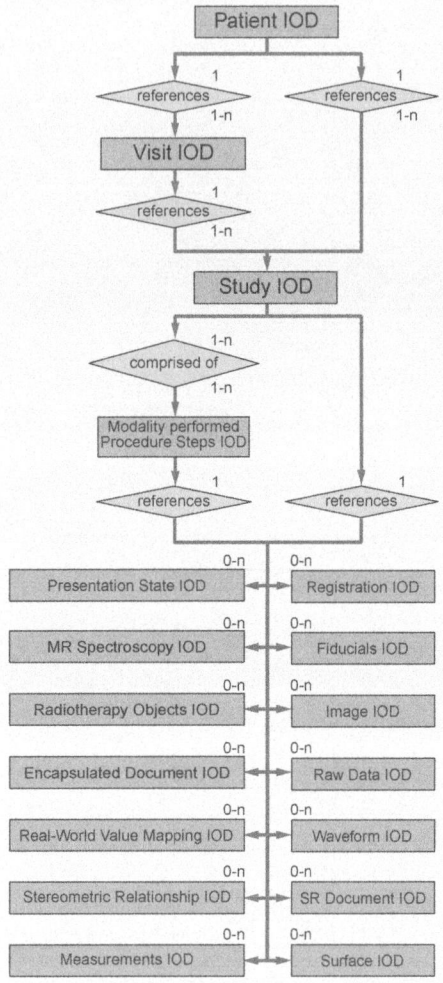

Not surprisingly, the DICOM information model addresses not just human beings as "patients" even though the definition mentions "a person". A short comment in the documentation remarks: "A patient may be a human or an animal" (NEMA 2014: 86). The comment addresses the "real-world fact" that imaging techniques are also applied for veterinarian diagnostics but also reveals that through computation everything is reduced to measurable and comparable entities, even unequal objects (Trogemann, 2014, 1). The formalisation of signals from living bodies – regardless whether they are human or animal – and their transformation into machine-readable data eliminates ontological qualities and thereby standardises the aspects that can be processed and further visualised by PAC systems. Or, as a subject-specific text from an information science paper puts it: "DICOM is not just an image or file format. It is an all-encompassing data transfer, storage, and display protocol built and designed to cover all functional aspects of digital medical imaging [...]. Without a doubt, DICOM truly governs practical digital medicine" (Pianykh 2008: 3).

Presumably without intending to do so, this quote points to the political dimension of data standards. The models and principles of software-based processing which were conceptualized in collaboration of radiological and engineering associations determine beforehand what can be executed diagnostically at a later stage and in situ at radiological clinics (Berry 2011: 124). Paradoxically, the process of digitalisation eliminates what seems to be the foundation of medical diagnostics: evaluating the vitality and liveliness of individual patients. Yet, the imaging process is designed to be highly standardised in order to guarantee reliable data acquisition and visualisation (de Rijcke /Beaulieu 2014: 137). A radiological image captures certain aspects and a certain state of an individual living body. Radiologists need to be aware of this basic paradox of radiological imaging and with their respective expertise about the human body create a more holistic image of the referring patient during diagnosis. Radiologists are challenged to supplement information derived by digital imaging by taking into account further information about a patient's individual condition (age, gender etc.), clinical symptoms and the diagnostic request of the attending physician.

Analysing DICOM metadata politics in the GUI

Picture archiving and communication systems, besides processing and communicating data, are also designed to archive patient data. As the A in PACS denotes, archiving is one of the main functions of the digital infrastructure. This function is reminiscent of former archival practices using paper folders, filing cabinets and archive rooms (Dommann 2003: 108-115). For a long time, archives were an inherent part of clinical architecture and radiological practice as spaces of orderly storage, and archive clerks were responsible for placing printed imaging studies and patient data in designated and retrievable locations (Hanseth/Lundberg 2001: 353ff.). But personnel were responsible not only for archiving printed data after diagnosis but also for distributing and delivering imaging studies within radiological departments and throughout the clinic for further diagnosis or consultation (Saunders 2008: 160-165). Hence, digital archiving not only implies developing modes for long-term storage of data on the basis of a digital infrastructure but also accounting for rather short-term "archiving practices" between data acquisition by imaging modalities, such as CT scanners, and their visualisation on computer screens for diagnostic purposes.

The main challenge of implementing PACS and using DICOM as an image format was to establish a new machine-readable, automated system for the reliable connection between patients, their image data and digital processes, e.g. archiving imaging studies in a database. Radiologist Steven Horii puts this problem quite pragmatically: "[...] how does a radiologist know what studies are to be read? With film, the answer was usually self-evident: studies to be read were put up by film library clerks on motorized film viewers together with prior studies if needed, or were placed into carts from which the radiologist would pick. With workstations and no film library clerks, what replaces the functions performed by those clerks?" (Horii 2006: 142).

A new system of data distribution was necessary to be both machine- and human-readable as files, and replace the printed imaging studies no longer distributed and archived by administrative staff and archive clerks. Data themselves needed to be identified and labelled in order to be clearly identifiably and diagnostically useful. As "data about data" (Manovich 2003:13), metadata should provide orientation in large data sets and ramified infrastructures. According to media theorist Lev Manovich, metadata can have several functions: "Metadata is what allows computers to 'see' and retrieve data, move it from place to place, compress it and expand it, connect data with other data, and so on" (Manovich 2003: 13). DICOM metadata are designed to guarantee that patient-specific data sets are both chronologically as well as spatially retrievable within a PACS network.

A DICOM file is composed of a body and a header which consists of metadata. The body stores image data acquired by a CT or MRI scanner. The header includes textual information like patient name, imaging modality and image size (Flanders/Carrino 2003: 275f.). Both body and header are integral parts for reliably connecting patient, data source and visualisations at a radiologist's workstation. Furthermore, both types of data – image data in the body and patient data in the header – are key to complement the visualised radiological images with further significant patient data to guide the diagnostic process.

The GUI of a PACS' workstation visualises not only image data as greyscale slices in various forms but also metadata "at the edges" of the visualisation. Figure 3 shows a screenshot of the GUI of a trial version of the PACS DICOM viewer *OsiriX Lite*. Visualised in the upper left corner of the central window, we can read information about the scanned body areas thorax and abdomen (Thorax-Abd) as well as the name of the data set (Brebix XsaDYa (-, -)). The image data visualised here is also a freely available and anonymised set of CT data named *Brebix*. In a clinical use case, the software would display important textual information in this area, i.e. the patient's name and birth date, for the radiologist to reliably identify the image data for a patient who is not physically present (Pianykh 2008: 15). It is mandatory and a main function of DICOM metadata to encode and continuously actualise patient identification data technological and human actors. A misidentification of image data and specific patient could lead to fatal errors in the further treatment process.

Fig 3: Screenshot of OsiriX Lite. Screenshot by the author. OsiriX Lite trail version (https://www.osirix-viewer.com/osirix/osirix-md/download-osirix-lite/) displaying data set Brebix (https://www.osirix-viewer.com/resources/dicom-image-library/) (last accessed 27.09.2020)

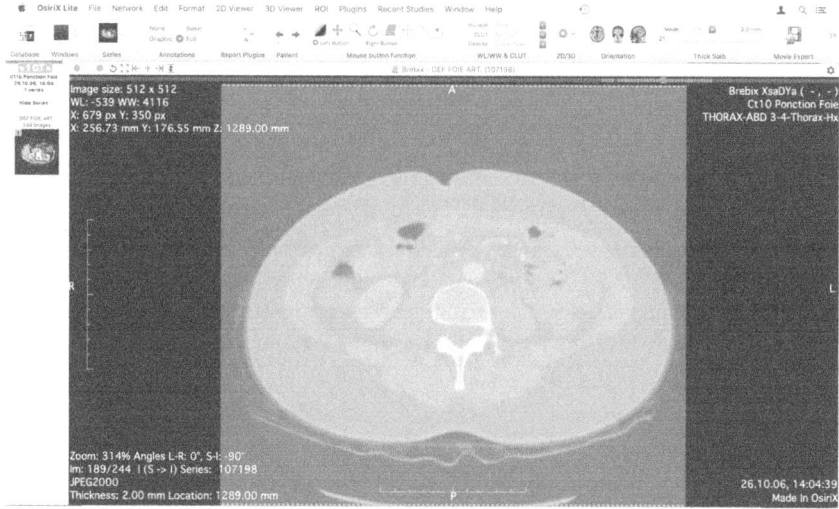

The other metadata displayed around the greyscale slice of the upper body also bear multiple orientation functions for radiologists. In a temporal respect, they provide information about the past scanning procedure, as in the lower right corner with date and time of data acquisition by a scanner. Further, as interactive annotations in the upper left corner, they provide a formal description of the displayed image data, e.g. by stating the image size (512x512) and position of the mouse cursor within the displayed slice (X: 679 px Y: 350 px). The latter metadata information changes according to the user's cursor operations within the image set. In this respect, metadata as digital annotations differ from annotations of analogue pictures because they are initially part of a data set and respond to changes made by the radiologist interactively in real-time.

In the case of diagnostic radiology, metadata from the header become an operational part of image data, even if they take a textual form. They provide information about radiological visualisation and thereby guide the diagnostic gaze and decision-making. As with film printing and distribution, technical staff are responsible for manually assigning patient data to its specific image series. Nevertheless, with digital diagnostics, technical and medical staff have to rely on PACS systems and their GUIs to automatically and continuously bridge the epistemic gaps between machine-readable information and images as aesthetic forms. As parts of an "invisible system of visibility" (Chun 2005: 27) digital metadata nowadays not only contain more detailed information about the imaging modality and modes of data processing. Metadata has become an essential visible and dynamic part of the radiological image as it operationally instructs radiologists' daily epistemic practice, e.g. by proving automated orientation within the image set. DICOM metadata encode formal data which otherwise cannot be known in digital infrastructures, such as the identification of image data and patient name. Even more – compared to analogue metadata practice – they operationally contribute to diagnostics by providing dynamic yet reliable information about the image itself.

Performing metadata

The analogue-digital migration in radiology significantly transformed diagnostic practices and workflows. Now software applications and their interfaces render the patient's body accessible for diagnostic operations (Friedrich 2018). The media-induced transformation challenged the design of data infrastructures and formal ontologies which, in practice, establish their very own data politics as they tie together technological and human-centred processes on multiple levels. From a media theoretical point of view, the question of how software programming and design establish epistemic conditions on a conceptual, operational and aesthetic level becomes important.

The conceptual negotiations between radiologists and engineers to establish the DICOM standard demonstrate that software design and programming not only implies formalisations and codifications but a certain programme of its own that retroacts on material, epistemic and social contexts (Trogemann, 2010, 44). As the example of PACS and the DICOM standard show, it is a fundamental requirement that programmers and designers conceptualise and therefore operationalise ideas of patients and radiologists as the primary users of such software systems. Within infrastructures and interfaces, both patients and radiologists – their habits and behaviours – are abstracted into patterns and models that can finally be incorporated into machine code and its different representations. Even though the abstractions are based on real-world models, they necessarily cannot fully bridge the gap between the qualitative aspects of certain processes and practices and the quantitative entities or models that can be transferred into machine code. Within this gap, digital media technologies and operations simultaneously need to incorporate the formal and normative ontologies of computation and the social and epistemic routines of human users, which often stem from analogue workflows.

Nevertheless, with mainly digital diagnostic processes, metadata and their representation within a GUI become a central point of investigation as they form a new place for radiological diagnostics. Analysing metadata – their formal and their dynamic and semantic aspects – offers a starting point to trace micropolitics within a GUI, which, at the same time, refer to broader professional politics (Mackenzie 2005: 76). In equal measure to image data, textually visualised metadata guides radiological diagnostics and provides peculiar "insights" into invisible digital processes. Not only do metadata, amongst others, connect the diagnostic situation to the dispositive of data acquisition, more importantly they should guarantee a reliable identification of physically absent patients and their image data. In this respect, metadata is not just an add-on or annotation. In radiology, the conception, operationalisation and visualisation of metadata fundamentally determines how digital diagnostics and subsequently therapy can be performed.

Acknowledgments

The author would like to thank Carmen Westermeier for text editing, Jacob Watson for proofreading and the Volkswagen Foundation for funding.

References

Andriole, Katherine and the SCAR TRIP Subcommittee (2004): "Addressing the Coming Radiology Crisis. The Society for Computer Applications in Radiology Transforming the Radiological Interpretation Process (TRIP) Initiative." In: Journal of Digital Imaging 17/4, pp. 235-243.

Andriole, Katherine (2006): "Image Acquisition". In: Keith J. Dreyer/David S. Hirschorn/James H. Thrall/Amit Mehta (eds.), PACS. A Guide to the Digital Revolution, New York: end edition, pp. 73-95.

Berry, David M. (2011): The Philosophy of Software. Code and Mediation in the Digital Age, London: Palgrave Macmillan.

Bowker, Geoffrey C./Baker, Karen/Millerand, Florence/Ribes, David (2010): "Toward Information Infrastructure Studies. Ways of Knowing in a Networked Environment". In: Jeremy Hunsinger/Lisbeth Klastrup/Matthew M. Allen (eds.), International Handbook of Internet Research, New York: Springer, pp. 97-117.

Bowker, Geoffrey C. /Star, Susan Leigh (1999): Sorting Things Out. Classification and Its Consequences, Cambridge, MA: MIT Press.

Bryan, Nick R. (2003): "The Digital rEvolution. The Millennial Change in Medical Imaging". In: Radiology 229/2, pp. 299-304.

Bui, Alex A. T./Morioka, Craig (2010): "Information Systems & Architectures". In: Alex A. T. / Ricky K. Taira (eds.): Medical Imaging Informatics, New York: Springer, pp. 15-91.

Chun, Wendy (2005): "On Software, or the Persistence of Visual Knowledge". In: Grey Room 18, pp. 26-51.

Chun, Wendy (2011): Programmed Visions. Software and Memory, Cambridge, Mass.: MIT Press.

De Rijcke, Sarah/Beaulieu, Anne (2014): "Networked Neuroscience. Brain scans and visual knowing at the intersection of atlases and databases". In: Catelijne

Coopmans/Janet Vertesi/Michael Lynch/Steve Woolgar (eds.): New Representation in Scientific Practice, Cambridge, Mass.: MIT Press, pp. 131-152.

Dodge, Martin/Kitchin, Robert (2011): Code/Space. Software and Everyday Life, Cambridge, Mass.: MIT Press..

Flanders Adam E./Carrino John A. (2003): "Understanding DICOM and IHE". In: Seminars in Roentgenology 38/3, pp. 270-281.

Friedrich, Kathrin (2016): "From Imaging 2.0 to Imaging 3.0. On the Crises of Radiology and Its 'Culture Shifts'". In: Bettina Krings/ Hannot Rodriguez/ Anna Schleisiek (eds.): Scientific Knowledge and the Transgression of Boundaries, Wiesbaden: Springer VS, pp. 35-58.

Friedrich, Kathrin (2018): "Screening Bodies. Radiological Screens and Diagnostic Operations". In: Luisa Feiersinger/Kathrin Friedrich/Moritz Queisner (eds.): Image Action Space. Situating the Screen in Visual Practice, Berlin/Boston: De Gruyter, pp. 93-101.

Hanseth, Ole/Lundberg, Nina (2001): "Designing Work Oriented Infrastructures". In: Computer Supported Cooperative Work 10, pp. 347-372.

Hirschorn, David S. (2006): "Introduction". In: Keith J. Dreyer/David S. Hirschorn/James H. Thrall/Amit Mehta (eds.): PACS. A Guide to the Digital Revolution, New York, 2nd edition, pp. 3-6.

Horii, Steven C. (2006): "Image Management Systems." In: Rostenberg, Bill (ed.): The Architecture of Medical Imaging. Designing Healthcare Facilities for Advanced Radiological Diagnostic and Therapeutic Techniques, New Jersey, NY: Wiley,pp. 133-150.

Kahn, Charles E./Langlotz, Curtis P./Channin, David S./Rubin, Daniel L. (2011): "An Information Model of the DICOM Standard". In: RadioGraphics 3/1, pp. 295-304.

Larsson, Wiveca/Aspelin, Peter/Bergquist, Marc et al. (2007): "The Effects of PACS on Radio rapher's Work Practice". In: Radiography 13, pp. 235-240.

Lemke, Heinz U./Stiehl Siegfried /Scharnweber, Horst /Jack.l Daniel (1979): "Applications of Picture Processing, Image Analysis and Computer Graphics Techniques to Cranial CT Scans, Proceedings of the Sixth Conference on Computer Applications in Radiology and Computer Aided Analysis of Radiological Images". In: Proceedings of the Sixth Conference on Computer Applications in Radiology and Computer Aided Analysis of Radiological Images, Newport Beach, CA: IEEE Computer Society Press, pp. 341-354.

Mackenzie, Adrian (2003): "These Things Called Systems. Collective Imaginings and Infrastructural Software". In: Social Studies of Science 33/3, pp. 365-387.

Mackenzie, Adrian (2005): "The Performativity of Code. Software and Cultures of Circulation". In: Theory Culture Society 22/1, pp. 71-92.

Manovich, Lev (2003): "Metadating the Image". In: Brouwer, Joke/Mulder, Arjen (eds.): Making Art of Databases, Rotterdam: V2 Publishers, pp. 12-27

NEMA - The Association of Electrical Equipment and Medical Imaging Manufactures (2014): "DICOM PS3.3 2014c - Information Object Definitions" (http://

medical.nema.org/medical/dicom/current/output/pdf/part03.pdf) (last accessed 27.09.2020).

Pianykh, Oleg S. (2008): Digital Imaging and Communications in Medicine (DICOM). A Practical Introduction and Survival Guide, Berlin/Heidelberg: Springer.

Reiner, Bruce I./Siegel, Eliot L. (2006): "Reengineering Workflow. A Focus on Personnel and Process". In: Keith J. Dreyer/David S. Hirschorn/James H. Thrall/Amit Mehta (eds.): PACS. A Guide to the Digital Revolution, New York, 2nd edition, pp. 73-95.

Reiner, Bruce/Siegel, Eliot S./Siddiqui, Khan (2003): "Evolution of the Digital Revolution. A Radiologist Perspective". In: Journal of Digital Imaging 16/4, pp. 324-330.

Saunders, Berry F. (2008): CT Suite. The Work of Diagnosis in the Age of Non-invasive Cutting, Durham, NC: Duke University Press.

Siegel, Eliot L. (2013): "PACS 2.0. Rebooting Pandora's Box for the Next 20 Years". In: Applied Radiology 1, pp. 3-4.

Star, Susan Leigh (1999): "The Ethnography of Infrastructure". In: American Behavioral Scientist 43, pp. 377-391.

Star, Susan Leigh/Ruhleder, Karen (1996): "Steps Toward an Ecology of Infrastructure". In: Design and Access for Large Information Spaces, Information Systems Research 7/1, pp. 111-134.

Tellioğlu, Hilda/Wagner Ina (2001): "Work Practices Surrounding PACS. The Politics of Space in Hospitals". In: Computer Supported Cooperative Work 10/2, pp. 163-188.

Thomas, Adrian M. K./Banerjee, Arpan K./Busch, Uwe (eds.) (2005): Classic Papers in Modern Diagnostic Radiology, Berlin/Heidelberg: Springer.

Trogemann, Georg (2010): "Code and Machine". In: Alexandra Gleiniger/Georg Vrachliotis (eds.): Code: Between Operation and Narration, Basel: Birkhäuser, pp. 41-54.

Trogemann, Georg (2014): Die Fülle des Konkreten am Skelett des Formalen. Über Abstraktion und Konkretisierung im algorithmischen Denken und Tun, (https://nbn-resolving.org/urn:nbn:de:hbz:kn185-opus4-501) (last accessed 27.09.2020)

Archiving the Leftovers of Science
Metadata and Histories of Scientific Institutions

Alina Volynskaya

Abstract

In this article, I focus on digital scientific archives which are made up of the leftovers of science, such as drafts, obsolete instruments, photographs, documentation, etc. The artifacts exhibited in such collections were neither meant to be representations, nor objects of gaze, but means used to achieve scientific results. As they lose functionality, they acquire aesthetic and historical value and emerge as clues, traces of past scientific practices and institutional histories. Therefore, the ways in which institutions situate these objects within the archive, the vocabularies and metadata they use, bear testimony on the manner they present and depict their past. How do the digital archives of the scientific institutions represent their histories? To address this question, I analyse the subject metadata of twenty-five institutional archives, turning them into objects of distant reading. Quantitative methods offer a way to discern the discursive frameworks that scientific institutions tend to adopt: Do they frame their collections as cultural heritage? represent them as corporate histories? emphasise technical specifications? scientific value? big names? A closer look at the metadata sets reveals that, in fact, these very different perspectives intermingle and clash with each other within the archive structures: the logic of heritage is juxtaposed with scientific classifications, institutional categories stand side by side with natural objects, and minority histories with celebrity narratives. Discussing this interplay of discourses, the article frames the digital archive of science as a specific mode of historical representation, which gives rise to a new (and still political) order of things.

Keywords: digital archives of science, subject metadata, archival discourses, digital historical representations, distant reading, history of scientific institutions.

Introduction

> A text always speaks to us; an archive doesn't.
>
> Franco Moretti

Figure 1: Ole Worm's cabinet of curiosities (1655).

Figure 2: The main interface of the Cavendish Laboratory digital archive.

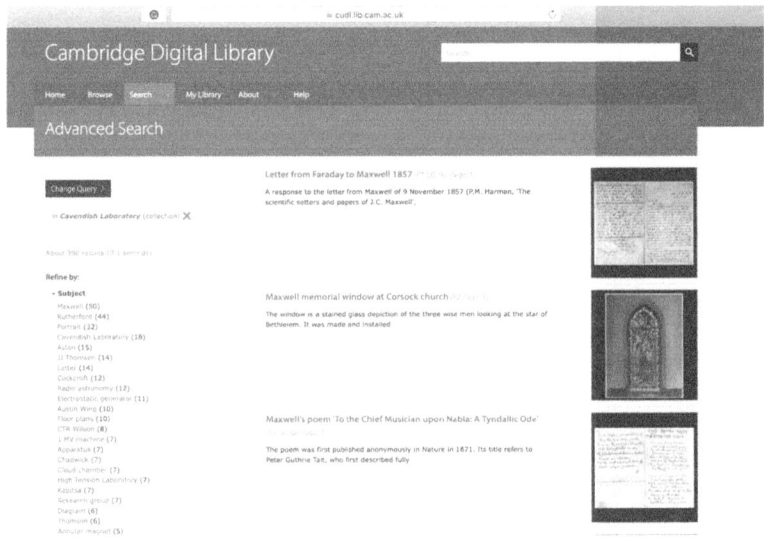

These two images represent two knowledge landscapes, separated by five centuries. The first is a *Wunderkammer*, cabinet of wonders – a theatre and laboratory of the mid-17th century, established by Ole Worm in Copenhagen. The second is a digital archive of the Cavendish laboratory, where the electron, the neutron, the DNA structure were discovered. The first one was set up towards the end of the Scientific Revolution, the second one stands in the midst of the era of Big Data, when science is being tirelessly memorialised and becomes interested in looking at itself.

Both constitute *theatrum scientiarum*, exhibiting carefully selected "scientific objects" – which are also objects of wonder and desire – for the general public. The very idea of scientificity and the public's curiosity have drastically altered over the last five centuries: from "crumbling shells, clumps of madrepores, coral branches, miniature busts, Chinese porcelain teapots, small medals, intaglio gems" (Stafford 1994: 238) to Maxwell's apparatus which detects the inertia of an electric current, the letter from J.J. Thompson to Rutherford dated 10 March 1919, a diagram of Aston's third mass spectrograph of 1937, and a vacuum pump gauge for the electrostatic generator.

In both cases, through certain practices of selection, classification and display these odd objects acquire meanings. The cabinet of curiosities arranges objects in such a way that together they reflect a unified world order, where all the things resonate and interact with each other. The Cavendish laboratory artifacts take on historical and scientific significance through classifications by authorship, by year, by type of instrument. These "orders of things" reveal and reflect different ideas of science, knowledge and the conditions of its production.

By placing these two interfaces next to each other, I seek to defamiliarize the image of digital collection we are used to, making the "invisible infrastructure" (Edwards 1996) apparent. Just like the *Wunderkammer*, the digital archive does not present things as they are, but rather constructs, follows and imagines a certain image of science. This article is to a large extent about this: the way in which scientific institutions represent and imagine their history in the digital archive and through it.

Scientific collections have recently gained a good deal of attention from historians of science, being treated as a form of scientific practice (Strasser 2012), as a form of relationship between science and its past (Daston 2012, 2017), as a locus of memory practices in science (Pestre 1999; Bowker 2005). These studies do not, however, consider those parts of scientific archive that are no longer of interest to science itself. Rather than structured, future-oriented scientific collections, those are the archives of institutions and laboratories, which cumulate administrative documents, personal collections handed over before one's retirement, various items retained by chance, etc. If the archives of science are addressed to "an imagined community of disciplinary descendants" (Daston 2012: 164), such a "para-scientific" archive is interpreted rather in terms of heritage, which serves to represent the history of scientific institutions.

In this article I will focus on this particular kind of scientific collections, which are made up of what I call the *leftovers* of science, such as drafts, obsolete instruments, outdated documentation, and other *inscriptions* and *inscription devices* (Latour 1987). Once in the archive, these very heterogeneous objects acquire a meta-value: experiment protocols, laboratory notebooks, technical drawings and other representations of nature no longer refer to nature, but to the very past practices of representation. They emerge as clues, traces by which a historian can retrace scientific practices of the past and the public can look behind the curtains of the scientific process. Take, for example, the photograph (fig. 3) of cloud chamber tracks observed by CTR Wilson in 1912. In the course of Wilson's research, this photograph served as a means to study the passage of particles. Within the archive context, it acquires another meaning: rather than being a representation of nature, it turns into a historical representation (as stated in the annotation, it "illustrates the remarkable quality of Wilson's cloud chamber images"), a documentary evidence of the "great discovery" ("one of the first cloud chamber photographs"). And even though it depicts the movement of particles, it already connotes not the laws of nature, but those of the history of science.

Figure 3: Clowd chamber tracks (1912) displayed by the Cavendish collection.

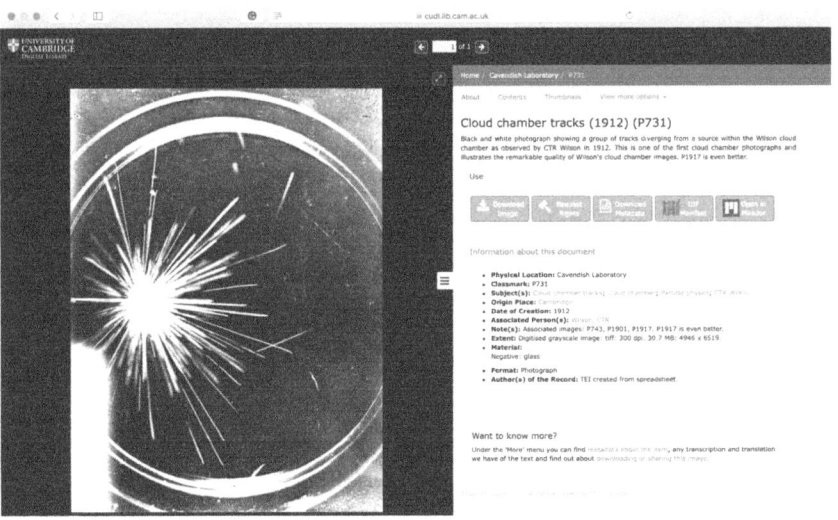

The digital archive of science displays objects of different pragmatics, which have been archived for various reasons: documentation routinely stored for administrative purposes; visualisations, experiment protocols, notebooks preserved for future research; objects associated with renowned scientists commonly referred to as heritage; photographs stored for the memory of the scientific communities. Through metadata, all these scattered and contingent pieces are linked together in the archive. In Latour's terms, the metadata may be interpreted as *meta-inscrip-*

tions meant to integrate objects into a common context of the archive and enhance combinability of representations.[1] This structural role of metadata – providing the integrity and continuity of the collection – entails a political dimension. Metadata emphasises and excludes categories, reveals and obscures connections, exposes and conceals. Therefore, the choice of vocabularies and metadata articulates the ways in which the institution presents, constructs and imagines its past.

While the politics of metadata and documentation for cultural heritage collections has already been addressed (Cameron/Robinson 2007; Navarrete/Mackenzie 2016), scientific collections have not yet received sufficient attention in this regard. So how do scientific institutions arrange and frame their collections? What discourses are involved in archival classifications and descriptions? Which aspects of scientific history do they render visible and which areas are left unmapped? To put it straight, how do the digital archives of scientific institutions represent their histories?

In my analysis, I draw on a corpus of twenty-five scientific collections (Annex A) chosen according to the following three criteria: 1) I deal neither with institutional repositories of publications nor with data collections, but with the archives of leftovers; 2) To narrow down the scope of the study, I focus on the collections of laboratories, research institutes and institutes of technologies, excluding more eclectic university repositories from consideration. In some cases, I have singled out one or more collections from large university archives (as in the case of the Cavendish laboratory); 3) Only collections organised through subject-based classifications are included in the corpus, since they are the main focus of my study. The resulting "collection of collections" encompasses archives from various countries, languages, formats and scientific disciplines.

This corpus is being subject to both close and distant reading (Moretti 2013). The quantitative research design is structured to examine classification discourses adopted in the collections. I manually gathered all the subject metadata of the collections into a single document, a sui generis vocabulary of the archive of science. To parse this vocabulary, I used Voyant Tools, an online platform which offers a variety of text-mining techniques. Firstly, I looked at the frequency with which words are used. These statistics give a general view of the archival discourses. Secondly, I applied manual topic modelling, classifying the individual words into thematic categories that I had established: natural objects, artificial objects, communal categories (Annex B). With such word lists, one can trace the frequencies of particular topics and discourses and their distribution across the archives.

---

1   For a broader perspective on metadata as well as an overview of metadata initiatives and controlled vocabularies cf. Pomerantz 2015, Gartner 2016. For the critical histories of information architecture and knowledge organization cf. Day 2001, Krajewski 2011, Blair 2011.

The quantitative analysis sheds light on the overall patterns of archival classification, but gives no insight into political implications of the metadata or its usage (e.g. the relationship between subject descriptors and item-level descriptions). The statistical data do not provide answers to the questions posed, but rather point the way forward, offering evidence for traditional interpretation which draws on classical concepts of critical theory, such as discourse, gender, canon. I discuss each of the quantitative findings through a series of examples, questioning not only the categories that the archives make visible, but also those that remain hidden (Geoffrey Bowker and Susan Leigh Star's (2000) analysis of the ICD structure furnishes a good example of such an approach).

In the next section, I discuss in more detail a number of theoretical points on how to read the digital collections (of science) through metadata. Building on this discussion, I then analyse the subject metadata of the twenty-five institutional archives, asking which discursive frameworks scientific institutions tend to adopt. In the following parts, I focus on three of those frameworks, tracing how the archives invoke institutional discourses, which vocabularies they use to represent scientific objects, and the ways in which they portray the actors of science.

Reading digital archives of science through metadata

1.1 Digital Humanities reading

In the field of Digital Humanities, digital archives have become an almost omnipresent *topos*, framed both as an object and a method of research. Lev Manovich seems to have been the first to declare database "a new symbolic form of a computer age" (Manovich 1999: 82). In his interpretation, database represents an alternative to the linearity of narrative. Manovich's opposition between database and narrative is by no means indisputable, yet his idea that database is a specific cultural form that needs to be analysed, has clearly provided a productive impetus for the Digital Humanities and New Media Studies. This approach has shown that databases and digital collections can be 'read' and interpreted: whether in terms of narratives (Anderson 2014), mediality (Ernst 2012), graphic interfaces (Drucker 2008), or reception practices (Rotman 2008; Vandendorpe 2009). Metadata in this perspective is presented as a technique that acts like paratexts (Genette 1997). Just as epigraphs, indexes, footnotes structure and contextualise our reading, so the metadata sets the context of data and determines a path of the user through the digital archive. The metadata links both pieces within a collection and the collection items with the discourse outside the archive. Take for example the subject arrangement of the American Institute of Physics. On the one hand, each category creates ties between objects that are unlikely to be close to each other in the physical archive (fig. 4, 5).

Archiving the Leftovers of Science   139

Figure 4: Heterogeneous items grouped together under the history category in the American Institute of Physics collections.

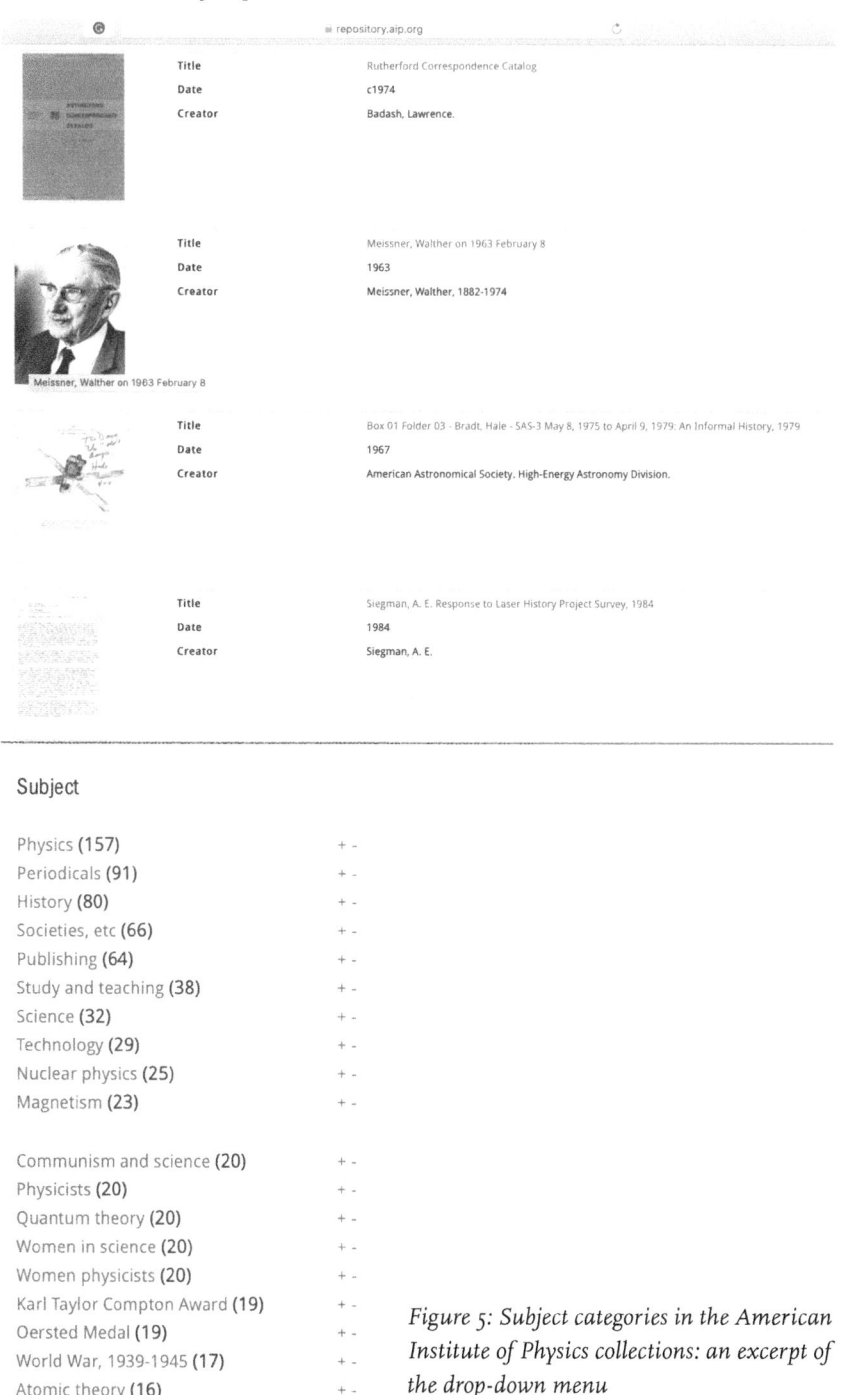

Figure 5: Subject categories in the American Institute of Physics collections: an excerpt of the drop-down menu

On the other hand, the metadata narrativises the collection by linking it to broader discourses. *Women in science* or *science and communism* categories are made as terse narrative formulas that participate in and respond to the debates beyond the archive. These tags make the objects speak by inscribing them into different discourses, be it historical discourse on the Cold War or gender criticism of science.

1.2 Archival science reading

While in the Digital Humanities the concept of archives has progressively expanded, archival science is in fact refusing to call many digital collections archives. The principal difference in the way archives are defined in the two domains was articulated by Kate Theimer (2012). Her main line of argument is that a great deal of digital collections does not adhere to the practices of contextualisation of objects that are in use in archival science, namely *respect des fonds*. Archivists preserve not only objects, but also their contexts, defined as the origins or provenance of a document, which are prioritised above the semantics of objects. This desire to put things in their place is reflected in the very multi-level archival structure divided by series and sub-series, fonds and sub-fonds.

Jacques Derrida treats this attachment to territory as a precondition for the archive's power: "Even in their guardianship or their hermeneutic tradition, the archives could do neither without substrate nor without residence. It is thus, in this *domiciliation* [original emphasis], in this house arrest, that archives take place" (1995: 2). The digitisation of the archive entails its democratisation: from the idea of the archive as a source of authority and power to the premise in the Digital Humanities that everyone may establish his/ her own archive.

Not that the digital archive is completely liberated from its territory, but it obviously works differently as regards to space. As an example of how the structure of an archive is transformed on the way from physical to digital, we can take a fragment of the Stevens Institute of Technology collection (fig. 6), which combines the logic of *respect des fonds* with thematic classification. In the category menu, between the *University of Illinois* and *Ray Stannard Baker*, one may find the *Alcoholism and employment* category, which seems puzzling for the university archive. The user intrigued by this conjunction will discover within this category the correspondence of Frederick Winslow Taylor, ideologist of scientific management, about the correlation between work efficiency and alcohol consumption.

In the traditional archive, there is a long way to go in finding these letters: one needs to follow the path from the *F.W. Taylor collection* to the *Biographical material* series, on to the *Miscellaneous* subseries, and further to a certain folder of a certain box. The search takes the form of an immersion into the archive, where each successive iteration further contextualises, narrows and specifies the search. The depth of the physical collection contrasts with the simultaneity of the digital archive, in which all elements are of one level and equal status. In the digital archive, the imperative of preserving the context is replaced (or at least supplemented) by semantic relationships provided by subject and descriptive metadata. The thematic categories shift the focus from the history of the collection to the history that objects represent (in our case, the history of scientific practices and institutions).

Figure 6: The Alcoholism and employment category within the subject list of the Stevens Institute of Technology collections.

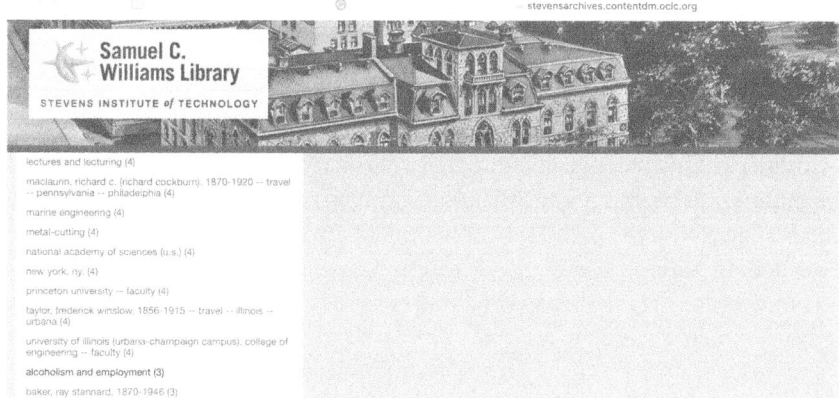

1.3 Digital Historiography and distant reading

Another range of issues has been raised by historians who question the epistemological implications of digital archives for historical research. This line of inquiry traces the way history is written through the agency of archives. To address the range of issues related to *digital* collections, Joshua Sternfeld introduced digital historiography – "a new interdisciplinary theory dedicated to the construction, use, and evaluation of digital historical representations" (2011: 547). This article echoes the key question of the new theory: how are historical representations constructed and contextualised? In responding to this question, Sternfeld identifies three types of contextualisation of digital representations: the selection of items in a collection, the search options that it offers and the metadata it applies – and asserts that each of them affects possible interpretations of the archives.

It is for a good reason that digital archives have raised so much enthusiasm in the Digital Humanities, so many doubts among archivists and so many questions among historians. Being neither a mere replication of tangible archive, nor a mere storage facility, the digital archive, in fact, participates in the production of knowledge, and as such needs to be problematised.

In my attempt to read archives (and not through archives), I look at how subject metadata – thematic categories that structure the collections – produce discourses on the history of scientific institutions. In the next section, I discuss the use of institutional categories before moving on to an analysis of how the archives represent the objects and actors of science.

Situating institutional history

One way to get an overview of archival categories is to calculate the list of the most frequent words in subject metadata (Annex C). What stands out in this list is the number of words referring to scientific organisations: *institute, university, observatory,* etc. In fact, more than a quarter of the fifty most frequent words points to institutional discourse. That is to say, institutions tend to use names of organisations as subject categories, mapping their histories through references to other institutions. This strategy is particularly characteristic for the archives of the Institute for Advanced Study, where organisations represent 59 per cent of the subject categories, the collections of the Cold Spring Harbor Laboratory (56 per cent) and the Yerkes Observatory (45 per cent).

By defining organisations as archival subjects, scientific institutions establish networks, map a (disciplinary, institutional, thematic) field and position themselves as an actor in this field. The context thus established varies from one institution to another. The Yerkes Observatory Archive, for example, only mentions observatories. The Institute for Advanced Study highlights both institutional diversity and broad international cooperation, referring to organisations ranging from the Soviet Commissariat for Education to the Brazilian Observatório Nacional. Conversely, the Florida Institute of Technology emphasises the cooperation with national American projects and agencies.

The history of an institution is thus construed as a history of relationships, cooperation and networks. It operates with links, references and relations rather than through scientific discoveries or inventions. Such a relational history puts internal, local institutional history behind the scenes, and does not shed any light on "science in action", but enables the study of influences, exchanges and inter-institutional interactions.

How influential is this discursive frame? To what extent does it conceal scientific activity itself? To address these questions, I compare two opposite cases of this institutional strategy: the archives of the Yerkes Observatory, which extensively refer to other organisations, and the Lick Observatory Archive, which is built without reference to other institutions.

Nearly 90 per cent of the Yerkes archive subjects is made up of people and organisations (fig. 7). The institutional part of the list is clearly structured: each institution is described in one category, regardless of the number of objects it refers to (e.g. *Pulkovo Observatory Buildings, Instruments, Equipment, Grounds* form a category). The remaining 10 per cent consists of astronomical bodies and objects (*comets, galaxies, meteoroids,* etc.) as well as several categories on solar eclipse expeditions.

Figure 7: A fragment of the subject list in the Yerkes Observatory Archive.

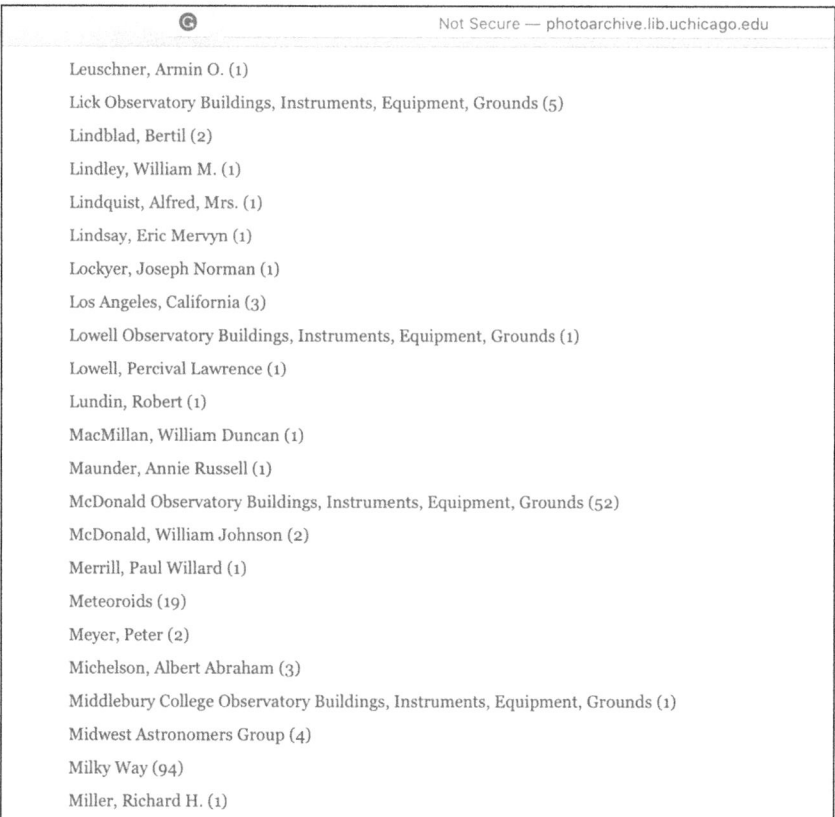

As far as the social and material history of the observatory is concerned, the institutional setting turns out to be the main reference point. No separate categories are defined at Yerkes for astronomers, domes, laboratories or telescopes – the only point of access to them is through a specific institution. The very act of naming institutions, singling out each of them into a separate category, is performative: it asserts the primacy of institutional affiliations over all other properties.

Interestingly, however, the institutional framework is being sidelined when it comes to astronomical phenomena. In this case, the main focus moves to the object itself: a photograph of the sun taken at the Mount Wilson Observatory comes under the category *sun* and not under the *Mount Wilson Observatory* (fig. 8,9). As far as the scientific process *per se* is concerned, categorisation is based on natural objects, rather than on institutions. The archive therefore maintains two separate and detached narratives governed by different logics: an institutional history and a "scientific" one.

Figure 8: Photographs grouped together under the Sun category in the Yerkes Observatory collection.

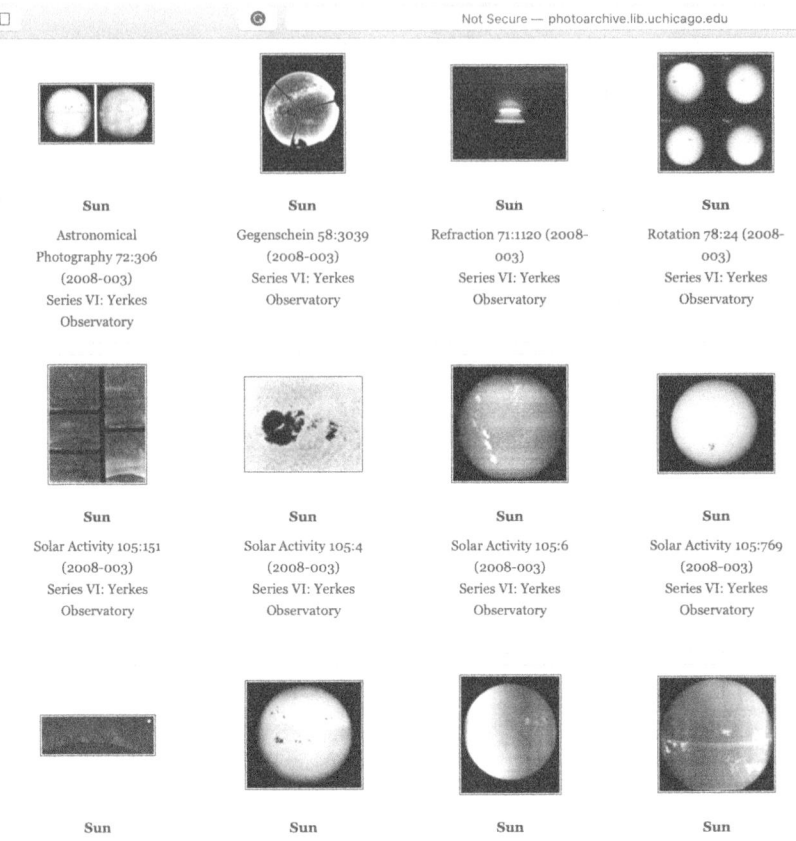

In terms of the institutional background, the structure of the Lick archive represents the exact opposite to the Yerkes collection: different observatories are brought together under the category *astronomical observatories*; separate categories are created for different types of instruments and techniques (*domes, refracting telescopes, seismometers*); social life is much more nuanced. In the absence of the generalised institutional categories, the archive represents a far more heterogeneous and multiple history of the institution, comprising the astronomical bodies and the instruments for studying them, representations of stargazing and social practices. In the diverse list of the Lick subjects, *picnicking* is placed between *observatories* and *galaxies*, and *children* stands between *solar eclipses* and *telescopes* (fig. 10, 11). As compared to the Yerkes archive, the structure of the Lick collection is much more chaotic and "tag-like", yet it provides far more opportunities for combination and recombination of archival items and meanings.

Archiving the Leftovers of Science   145

Figure 9: Photographs grouped together under the Mount Wilson Observatory category in the Yerkes Observatory collection.

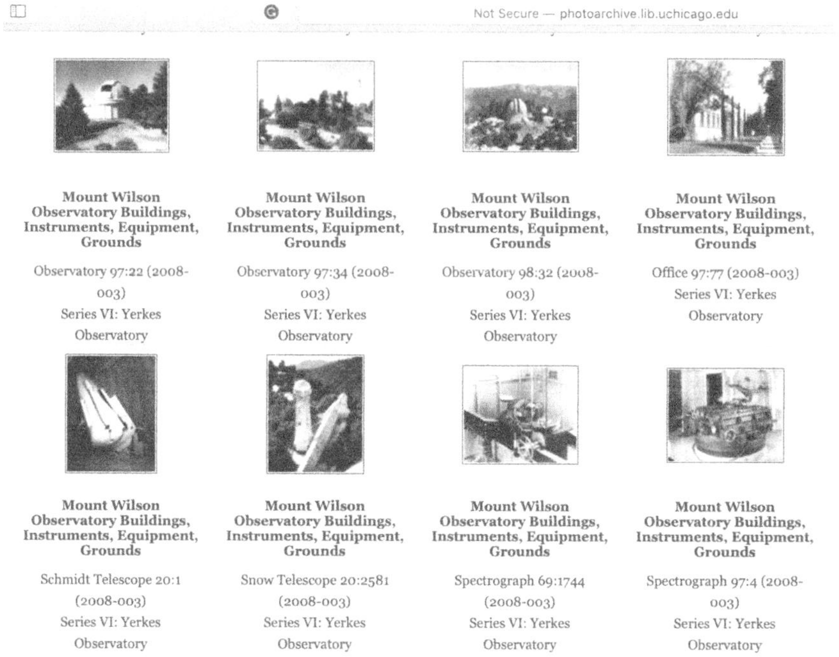

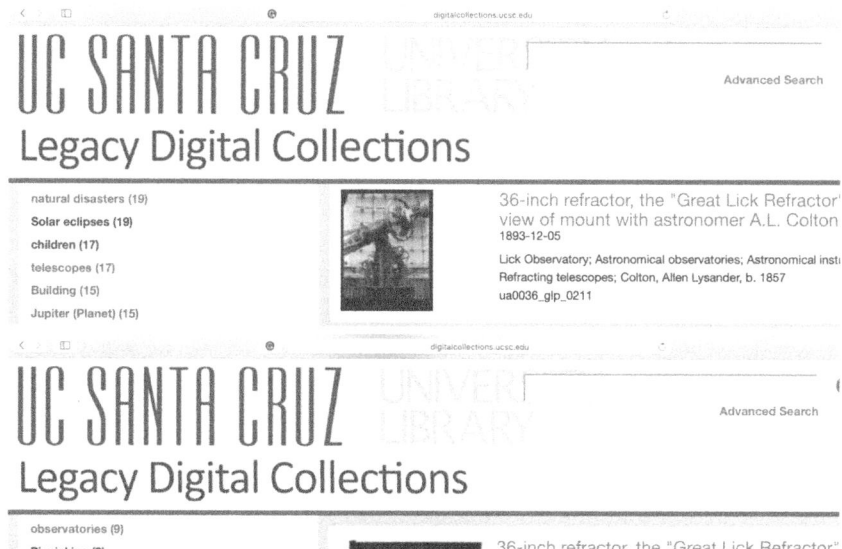

Figure 10 & 11: Excerpts of the drop-down lists of subjects in the Lick Observatory Archive

Another effect of the institutional mapping at Yerkes is that it highlights the resemblance of the observatories and obscures their differences. The digital archive establishes links, correspondences and similarities rather than differentiates or accentuates particularities. This becomes apparent when comparing the representations of the Yerkes Observatory in the archive and in an encyclopaedic article (e.g. in Wikipedia). Enumerating the Yerkes breakthroughs, discoveries, celebrities, and instruments, the Wikipedia article emphasises how the observatory stands out from other observatories. In the archive, everything that made up the identity of Yerkes, at least according to Wikipedia, is obscured. It does not give any familiar benchmarks or reference points: which people are great, which discoveries are important, which instruments are of particular interest. Instead, it equalises the various fragments and pieces of history, and ties them together through the unified set of descriptors.

So, if science in the digital archives is mainly defined in institutional terms, how does it differ from other domains? And how then are the specific objects of science represented?

Framing the objects of science

I have already pointed to how radically the value and pragmatics of scientific objects change once they are exhibited in the archive. Now the question is whether this transformation is captured in the archives. How are the scientific objects described and classified? To what extent do archival classifications include or reflect scientific ones? Do they borrow terms from the vocabularies of science, or perhaps adapt concepts from the history of science?

To address these questions, I singled out three classes of archive subjects: conceptual objects (concepts, theories, scientific terms), artificial objects (instruments and other scientific artifacts fabricated to study phenomena) and natural objects (phenomena). As for conceptual objects, my attempt to categorise them into a separate category failed. There is a good deal of formal reasons for that: often scientific concepts require context or consist of more than one word; many of them are mentioned only once, and after all archive deals with objects rather than theories. However, this very failure is quite significant. In my corpus, there are no less than ten institutes conducting physical research, but such basic notions of modern physics as *gravity* or *relativity* are not once mentioned among the subjects. At the very least, this reveals that the very vocabulary of science (scientific terms and concepts) is not engaged in the archival taxonomies. The leftovers of science displayed in the archives thus appear to be detached from their original (research) context – links to the theories, concepts and hypotheses that they embodied, described and maintained.

Eventually, I ended up with the classical division between natural and artificial objects (Annex B), *naturalia* and *artificialia*. This binary, to a certain extent, expresses the difference between the logic of a scientific library structured according to the research objects and that of an archive that accentuates and attributes the artifact's creation and preserves its provenance.

Generally, in the structure of archive subjects, both types of objects are present, yet some collections clearly gravitate towards this or that type of categorisation. For instance, the "scientific part" of the Yerkes collection is a good example of classification by *naturalia*. In it, classification by object clearly puts the logic of astronomers above that of historians. It stems from an interest in the object, not in the history of its representations, e.g. ways in which astronomical bodies have been captured and recorded since the late 19th century. The very fact of representation fades into the background, while the emphasis is placed on the properties of the natural object, be it *solar eclipse* or *galaxy clusters*. The archive adheres to the imperative of consistency and orderliness of scientific classifications, avoiding to bring together objects as different from an astronomical point of view as the sun and the moon. However, in keeping with the logic of scientific library, it readily draws together, for instance, photographs of different epochs.

Figure 12: Example of an item-level description in the Yerkes Observatory collection.

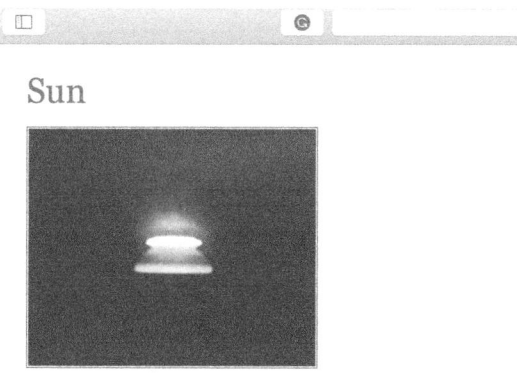

Whereas this classification is more suited for astronomical propaedeutics than for a study of scientific inscriptions, the item-level description follows an inverse logic. The metadata describing a particular image of the sun, after all, is silent on the properties of the depicted celestial body, instead emphasising the fact of representation and treating the photograph as a physical object (detailing its photographer, date, format (fig. 12)). It does not guide users' gaze, nor does it allow them to interpret these images in the way astronomers could do it. The metadata does not provide any context on the actual research: what was discovered, what was known at that moment, etc. So, the two grounds for description – on the one hand, the categorisation by type of celestial bodies, which promises user at least an astronomical exercise, and on the other hand, the logic of archival records, detailing the provenance and creation histories – confront and hinder each other.

In the case of classification by artificial objects, the juxtaposition of frames is even more intricate. A good example is the representations of scientific instruments in the ETH Zurich collection. The collection is structured around a classification by instrument type: *compasses, globes, horoscopes*, and so on. It is designed to enable user to draw a parallel between instruments of similar pragmatics: tools for measuring forces, mathematical models, optical instruments. Such categorisation emphasises the practical dimension, functionality of the instruments, or, so to speak, their *instrumentality* as opposed to aesthetic and formal properties.

At the item description level, however, what comes to the fore is not this practical dimension, but rather heritage value. The instruments are described by means of formulaic archival descriptors traditionally used for attribution of tangible cultural artifacts: *manufacturer, dimensions, material, physical measurements*. Detailing the formal properties of the instruments, such attributes seem self-evident and objective. Yet they often narrow down and replace the spectrum of meanings, the context relevant to an artifact, thus depriving it of its voice (Cameron/Robinson 2007). By focusing on the materiality, uniqueness and singularity of the instruments, such a description suppresses the pragmatic dimension: their uses, functions, applications. Instead, the instruments appear to be valuable in their own right, more as art objects than as part of an experimental set-up to be used for specific purposes.

Furthermore, these formal descriptions, intended to verify the authenticity of the objects, are complemented by technical descriptions such as the following one (fig. 13). Such "explanations" bring up the issue of elitism and accessibility of knowledge. Barely understandable to a non-specialist, they produce a distance between the object and the viewer. Whereas the instruments are made publicly available, becoming the object of gaze and desire, their annotations create an intellectual barrier, signalling that the knowledge they embody is still out of reach. Such attributions do not bring the user closer to the inner history of science, but, on the contrary, alienate him/ her from it by representing artifacts as static, isolated and closed for interpretation. The material history of science in the archives tends to be very formalised and not "reader-friendly". And what about personal histories of science?

Archiving the Leftovers of Science 149

Figure 13: Description of a mathematical model in the ETH Zürich collections. The caption reads: "Ennerper's minimum surface in the Weierstrass parameterisation ($u - u^3/3 + u v^2, v - v^3/3 + u^2 v, u^2 - v^2$) for u,v between -2 and 2".

Record Name: ETHZ-MATH-MOD-0006
Viewer: ZOOM

Title: Mathematisches Modell: Minimalfläche von Enneper
Creator:
Dating:
Caption: Ennerpersche Minimalfläche in der Weierstrass-Parametrisierung (u - u^3/3 + u v^2, v - v^3/3 + u^2 , u^2 - v, u^2 - v^2) für u,v zwischen -2 und 2.
Inscription: {-2,-3/2,-1,-1/2,0,1/2,1,3/2,2} sind angedeutet.
Begleitmaterial:
Footnote:

Portraying the actors of science: communities and personalities

Apart from institutional and "scientific-based" frames, the archives also represent the social dimension of science. In this section, I focus on one particular aspect, namely the identity of *scientific personae*. The digital archive is both extremely attentive to the individual names and surprisingly indifferent to them. The proper name, here, serves no more than a function for classifying archival objects. Converted into a thematic category, the name appears as a mere index sign structuring the collection.

Turning to the quantitative landscape, I have calculated what could be called a "personalisation index" of the collections, i.e. the proportion of proper names among the total number of subjects in each archive (fig. 14). In the graph, three groups of collections can be observed: the archives without proper names; those with less than 25 per cent of proper names and those with more than 50 per cent (up to 85 per cent at the MIT collections).

Figure 14: Personalisation Index of the collections showing the proportion of proper names among the archival subjects.

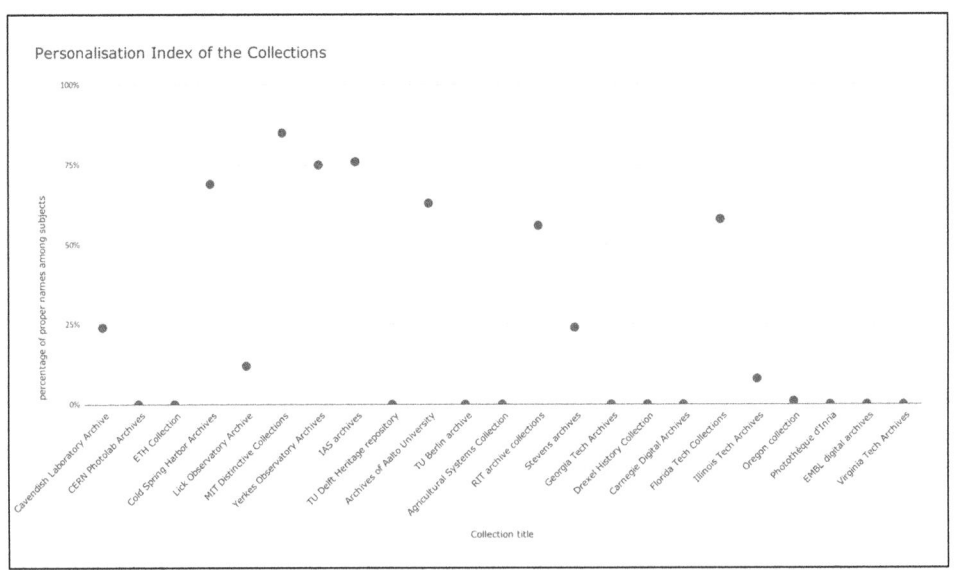

The two clusters of extreme values – both the highly personalised collections and the ones with no proper names – in fact represent roughly the same attitude towards personae. The classification structures they adopted put no emphasis on individuals. In the long lists of subjects sorted either alphabetically or by the number of items they point to, each individual name, no matter how renowned, occupies an equal position. At the structure level, the archive makes neither emphases nor distinctions: for instance, one of the big names of the Yerkes Observatory, Edwin Hubble, is as hidden in the long alphabetical list of the archival categories as much less well-known employees (fig. 15).

Figure 15: Edwin Hubble situated in the subject list of the Yerkes archive.

Hetzler, Charles (1)
Hill, George William (1)
Hiltner, William Albert (1)
Holden, Edward Singleton (1)
Horvath, Mr. (3)
Hoyle, Fred (1)
Hubble, Edwin Powell (5)
Huggins, Margaret Lindsay Murray (2)
Huggins, William (1)
Hughes, Stanley H. (2)
Hujer, Karel (1)
Hunter, Alan (1)
Hyakutake, Yuji (2)
International Astronomical Union (3)
International Astrophysical Conference on Novae and White Dwarf stars (1)
International Union for Co-operation in Solar Research (24)
Janssen, Pierre Jules César (1)
Jeans, James (2)
Jordrell Bank Observatory (1)
Joy, Alfred Harrison (1)
Justin, Edward M. (1)
Kamensky, M. (1)
Kapteyn, Jacobus Cornelius (1)
Keeler, James Edward (3)

The intermediate cluster, i.e. collections in which proper names do not exceed one quarter of the categories – are more of a special case. As a rule, the names in them have been specially selected, and this selection itself expresses distinctions, inequalities and hierarchies. In the archive of Cavendish laboratory, for example, only household names in physics get to become subjects. Within the archival subject structure, they appear almost as common names: *Maxwell, Rutherford, JJ Thompson*. In this case, the name carries a dual function. Firstly, it is used to recall a certain research field, to evoke a set of topics, experiments, tools and discoveries. For example, the *Aston* category includes only two Aston's portraits, the rest being apparatuses, charts and visualisations associated with him. Secondly, the name confers *aura* to the item: the magnetic detector from Rutherford's radio receiver is valuable and worthy of representation precisely because it belonged to Rutherford.

In this way, such an archive reflects and pursues a personalised history of science in which the names of prominent scientists serve as entry points into the scientific process.

An even more emblematic example of celebrity representations in the archives is the categorisation of Albert Einstein's photographs in the Caltech Archive. Einstein has been a visiting scholar at Caltech on several occasions since 1931, so the archive contains quite a few photographs of him. The following subcategories have been introduced for their arrangement: *Einstein in groups, Einstein with one other person, Einstein alone* (fig. 16). This set of categories reveals an overwhelming focus on the persona, particularly as it renders Einstein's entourage invisible. Nobody next to Einstein gets to be named (at the level of subjects): only his figure is worth being noted, the others are no more than his background, measured quantitatively. The category *Einstein with one other person*, for instance, in the majority of cases covers photographs of Einstein with his wife Elsa. Yet no separate category is set up for her; she appears to be merely "one person" next to him. That said, in and through such a representation, Einstein himself turns into a pure sign or tag. His very name does not require any additional details or categorisations: e.g., he is not presented as a visiting scientist, which would provide additional context and bring his figure into line with others.

Figure 16: Categorisation of Albert Einstein's photographs in the Caltech Image Collections: an excerpt of the drop-down list.

The opposite of the sharp focus on the famous personae is what I call communal categories (Annex B), i.e. various group denominations. One thing that stands out in this list is that there are virtually no categories assigned to scientific groups in public discourse. *Scholars* are never mentioned in any of the archives. Both *scientists* and *researchers* are listed only once (in the Aalto and Inria collections respectively). The same is true for the social categories emphasising the commonality: notably, there is virtually no mention of *community* or *team*. Instead, corporate identities are used quite extensively: notably, *employees* (Oregon, Florida Tech), *staff* (Aalto, Inria, Yerkes), *personnel* (Aalto), *people* (CERN, Inria). Institutional affiliations are once again prevailing over scientific practices: the tendency is rather to represent scholars as institutional employees than as a community of inquiry united by a common research interest. The only exception is the Inria collections, where the *project team (équipe-projet)* subject brings together portraits of researchers, their social interactions and fragments of the research. By bringing together both social and research dimensions, this category represents the very science in action.

Another set of collective identities I have captured are social and ethnic groups, namely *students, women, alumni, children, African Americans*. These subjects appear to map the social and role dimensions of the scientific process. One thing to note about this list is that no unified, general, and symmetrical grid of categories is established: having a *student's* category does not imply that there is a *teacher's* category, nor does having a *women* subject suggest the presence of *men* or *the third sex* categories.

In terms of the politics of equality, such asymmetries are quite controversial. Firstly, the recognition of only a few minorities stigmatises and makes even more invisible the other, unidentified ones. Not to mention the fact that the scientific milieu has specific marginalised groups, such as the 'invisible technicians' (Shapin 1989), which none of the archives explicitly identify. Secondly, such categories imply a certain image of the majority – essentially white and masculine. Separating *women* or *African Americans* as a category is meant to uncover the presence of the marginalised groups in the history of science, yet the effect can be quite the opposite. By singling out, for instance, women and not identifying men, the archives represent women's history as a peculiar marginal case in science, as a sideline of a "big mainstream history" of knowledge, constructed implicitly, out of categories.

The communal categories bring out very clearly the polyphony of perspectives and discourses in the digital archive of science. The two most numerous minor groups that often go together – women and children – fall under two almost contradictory logics. The widespread inclusion of female history in scientific archives is clearly a response to the recent gender criticism and a demand to acknowledge the presence of women in science. Identifying children as a category, on the other hand, seems to be driven by the desire to show life outside of science (and the fact that scientists may have one). The *African Americans* category highlights the diversity within science, while *staff* or *personnel*, in contrast, emphasise the unity of corporate identity. In this multi-faceted struggle for identity, each of the categories does not acquire meaning *within* the archive classifications, but instead appears as a performative response to certain discussions and discourses outside the archive. The fragments and remnants of these discourses are now forming part of the archival subject structures.

Conclusion

I started by asking how digital archives represent the histories of the scientific institutions. The succinct answer to this question does not sound very convincing: in diverse ways. The archives make use of institutional categories, scientific classifications, involve a variety of social groups, and differ greatly in their views on what constitutes history. In fact, very different and sometimes mutually exclusive categories and description modes may be found in the subject-based classification of the same collection. This multiplicity of narratives, discourses and meanings appears as one of the few constants of the digital archive of science.

If we define the digital archive through tensions and oppositions, it stands in contrast to the canon (rather than to the narrative, as Manovich believes). The canon, a definitive inventory of "the best which has been thought and said," to cite Matthew Arnold, clearly articulates values, giving preference to certain types of objects and discourses over other ones. The canon embodies the very essence of the archive concept that has been challenged by the famous critique of Michel Foucault (1972: 129):

> The archive is first the law of what can be said, the system that governs the appearance of statements as unique events [...] it is that which differentiates discourses in their multiple existence and specifies them in their own duration.

The canon is the ultimate expression of this very differentiation of discourses, the distinction between valuable and non-valuable, sublime and non-precious. It is based on the (political) operations of inclusion and exclusion, exaltation and suppression, which has caused waves of gender, post-colonial and other critiques.

The digital archive as a form of historical representation, in this sense, appears as a radical deconstruction of the canon. It gives the illusion that everything can be said – all it takes is to add a new subject! Essentially unfinished, fragmented, and willing to absorb everything, the digital archive brings together and gives equal rights to different logics, discourses and perspectives. Without giving preference to any point of view, it encompasses constellations of people and objects, fluctuations between institutional and scientific logics, aesthetics and pragmatics, scientific identities and external narratives about science.

Yet this deliberate disorder, as we have seen, also has political overtones. In the digital archives of science, the political manifests itself not in hierarchies, but at the intersection of discourses, at their borders and in their absence. We have seen how the clash between subject and descriptive metadata in the case of scientific instrument descriptions produces an elitist distance between the object and the viewer. The reverse example is when the boundaries and limits of the discourses are implicitly defined, as in the case of the institutional narrative in the Yerkes archive, which does not apply to the astronomical objects. In this case, it becomes clear that the scope and influence of certain discourses is limited to certain topics and objects.

As opposed to the physical collections, the digital archive brings semantic subject categories to the fore. The most explicit (and perhaps dangerous) political effect lies in their apparent neutrality. The poetics of alphabetical lists, number-based sorting, formalised descriptors convey the illusion that the archive simply presents things as they are. However, it is the structure of subjects and the choice of descriptors that constitute the most sensitive areas in terms of politics. Through them, the creators of the archive seek to impose order on the collection (the ethnography of how the institutions construct their archives is beyond the scope of this article, but definitely deserves a separate study). Through the metadata, fragments of various discourses penetrate into the archives and being deprived of context, take the form of a statement of fact. This is exactly what happens in the example of *alcoholism and employment* in the Taylor collection, or in the case of unbalanced gender categories that lead to the intervention of the same discourses of inequality against which they were directed.

Any category grid puts light on certain aspects and obscures the others. In this regard, the most significant absence in the categorisation of the digital archives that I have examined is the lack of concepts of the history and philosophy of science. This reveals that there is a great divide between the way sciences are interpreted in the humanities and the self-presentation of scientific institutions.

The digital archive apparently conveys some other history of science: one without *epistemic communities* or *memory practices*, but with *children*, *Einstein*, and *galaxy clusters* all at once. Treating the digital archive of science not just as an infrastructure for searching some pieces of historical data, but as a site of inquiry, allows one to read this history.

Bibliography

Anderson, Steve (2014): "Past Indiscretions: Digital Archives and Recombinant History." In: Marsha Kinder/Tara McPherson (eds.), Transmedia Frictions: The Digital, the Arts, and the Humanities, Berkley, CA: University of California Press, pp. 100-114.

Blair, Ann M. (2011): Too Much to Know: Managing Scholarly Information before the Modern Age, New Haven, London: Yale University Press.

Bowker, Geoffrey (2005): Memory Practices in the Sciences, Cambridge: MIT Press.

Bowker, Geoffrey/ Star, Susan Leigh (2000): Sorting Things Out: Classification and Its Consequences, Cambridge, London: MIT Press.

Cameron, Fiona/ Robinson, Helena (2007): "Digital Knowledgescapes: Cultural, Theoretical, Practical, and Usage Issues Facing Museum Collection Databases in a Digital Epoch". In Fiona Cameron/Sarah Kenderdine (eds.), Theorizing Digital Cultural Heritage: A Critical Discourse, Cambridge, Massachusetts: MIT Press, pp. 165-191.

Daston, Lorraine (2012): "The Sciences of the Archive." In: Osiris, 27/1, pp. 156-187.

Daston, Lorraine (2017): Science in the Archives: Pasts, Presents, Futures, Chicago: Chicago University Press.

Day, Ronald E. (2001): The Modern Invention of Information: Discourse, History, and Power, Carbondale, Ill.: Southern Illinois University Press.

Derrida, Jacques (1995): Archive Fever: A Freudian Impression, London: Chicago UP.

Drucker, Johanna (2008): "Graphic Devices: Narration and Navigation." In: Narrative, 16/2, pp. 121-139.
Edwards, Paul (1996): The Closed World: Computers and the Politics of Discourse in Cold War America, Cambridge: MIT Press.
Ernst, Wolfgang (2012): Digital Memory and the Archive, Minneapolis: University of Minnesota Press.
Foucault, Michel (1972): The Archaeology of Knowledge, New York: Pantheon Books.
Gartner, Richard (2016): Metadata: Shaping Knowledge from Antiquity to the Semantic Web, Cham: Springer.
Genette, Gerard (1997): Paratexts: Thresholds of Interpretation, New York: Cambridge University Press.
Krajewski, Markus (2011): Paper Machines: About Cards & Catalogs, 1548-1929, Cambridge, MA: MIT Press.
Latour, Bruno (1987): Science in Action: How to Follow Scientists and Engineers Through Society, Cambridge: Harvard University Press.
Manovich, Lev (1999): "Database as Symbolic Form." In: Convergence, 5/2, pp. 80–99.
Moretti, Franco (2013): Distant Reading, London: Verso.
Navarrete Trilce/ Mackenzie Owen J. (2016): "The Museum as Information Space: Metadata and Documentation". In Karol Jan Borowiecki/Neil Forbes/Antonella Fresa (eds.), Cultural Heritage in a Changing World, Cham: Springer, pp. 111-123.
Pestre, Dominique (1999): "Commemorative Practices at CERN: Between Physicists' Memories and Historians' Narratives," In: Osiris, 14, pp. 203–16.
Pomerantz, Jeffrey (2015) : Metadata, Cambridge, MA; London: MIT Press.
Rotman, Brian (2008): Becoming Beside Ourselves: The Alphabet, Ghosts, and Distributed Human Being, Durham, N.C./London: Duke University Press.
Shapin, Steven (1989): "The invisible technician." In: American Scientist, 77/6, pp. 554–563.
Stafford, Barbara (1994): Artful Science: Enlightenment Entertainment and the Eclipse of Visual Education, Cambridge, MA: MIT Press.
Sternfeld, Joshua (2011) "Archival Theory and Digital Historiography: Selection, Search, and Metadata as Archival Processes for Assessing Historical Contextualization," In: The American Archivist, 74/2, pp. 544-575.
Strasser, Bruno (2012): Collecting Nature: Practices, Styles and Narratives. In Osiris, 27/1, pp. 303-340.
Theimer, Kate (2012): "Archives in Context and as Context," In: Journal of Digital Humanities, 1/2 (http://journalofdigitalhumanities.org/1-2/archives-in-context-and-as-context-by-kate-theimer/).
Vandendorpe, Christian (2009): From Papyrus to Hypertext: Toward the Universal Digital Library, Urbana: University of Illinois Press.

Annex A. Corpus of the study: a list and overview of the digital collections examined.

Collection title	Institution, country	Total items	Items exhibited	Total subjects	Percentage of proper names in subjects	Metadata schema
Aalto University Archives	Aalto University, Finland	2623	photographs, physical objects, works of art, other	655	63%	LIDO
Agricultural Systems Engineering Collection	Technische Universität München, Germany	44402	photographs	561	0	
AIP Digital Collections	American Institute of Physics, US	95988	reports, correspondence, videos, oral histories, scrapbooks	55	listed separately	DCMI
Caltech Digital Image Archives	California Institute of Technology, US	9764	photographs, personal papers, scientific instruments, correspondence, manuscripts	27	listed separately	DCMI
Carnegie Digital Archives	Carnegie Mellon University, US	11549	correspondence, rapports, photographs, catalogues, brochures, yearbooks	100	0	
Cavendish Laboratory Archive	University of Cambridge, UK	390	photographs, correspondence, drafts, instruments	62	24%	DCMI
CERN Photolab Archives	CERN, Switzerland	21481	photographs, instruments, data visualizations	180	0	MARC

Collection title	Institution, country	Total items	Items exhibited	Total subjects	Percentage of proper names in subjects	Metadata schema
Cold Spring Harbor Laboratory Archives	Cold Spring Harbor Laboratory, US	22143	photographs, manuscripts, correspondence, notebooks	81	69%	
Drexel History Collection	Drexel University, US	523	photographs, yearbooks, correspondence, magazines, postcards, administrative records	62	0	DCMI
EMBL digital archives	European Molecular Biology Laboratory, Germany	606	photographs, interviews, documents, correspondence, brochures	7	0	DCMI, EAD
ETH Collection of Scientific Instruments	ETH Zürich, Switzerland	6373	instruments	57	0	
Florida Tech Digital Collections	Florida Institute of Technology, US	6320	photographs, manuals, correspondence, guides, personal notebooks, videos	2288	58%	
Georgia Tech Archives	Georgia Institute of Technology, US	12766	photographs, oral histories, reports, maps, sketches	50	0	

Archiving the Leftovers of Science

Collection title	Institution, country	Total items	Items exhibited	Total subjects	Percentage of proper names in subjects	Metadata schema
IAS archives	Institute for Advanced Study, US	4974	photographs, oral histories, reports, instruments, cultural artifacts, notes, correspondence	1387	76%	DCMI
Illinois Tech Archives	Illinois Institute of Technology, US	1387	photographs, magazines, reports, administrative documents, oral histories, plans	50	8%	DCMI, MODS
Lick Observatory Photographical Archive	UCSC, US	3279	photographs, data visualizations,	124	12%	
MIT Distinctive Collections	MIT, US	520	course catalogues, reports, oral histories, handbooks,	97	85%	DCMI
Oregon Campus History Collection	Oregon Institute of Technology, US	1938	photographs	100	1%	
Photothèque d'Inria	National Institute for Research in Digital Science and Technology, France	8273	photographs, data visualizations, web interfaces	1075	0	
RIT archive collections	Rochester Institute of Technology, US	3037	photographs, slides, correspondence, advertisement, posters	359	56%	

Collection title	Institution, country	Total items	Items exhibited	Total subjects	Percentage of proper names in subjects	Metadata schema
Stevens archives	Stevens Institute of Technology, US	1102	correspondence, bills, reports, photographs, student newspapers	100	24%	
TU Berlin Universitätsarchiv	TU Berlin, Germany	438	course catalogues, official gazettes, student leaflets	14	0	
TU Delft Cultural Heritage repository	Delft University of Technology, Netherlands	1381	technical drawings, reports, public lectures	13	0	DCMI
Virginia Tech Archives	Virginia Tech, US	7031	photographs, reports, correspondence, notebooks, postcards	60	0	DCMI
Yerkes Observatory Archives	University of Chicago, US	1300	photographs	328	75%	

Annex B. Categories of archival subjects.

The table represents the three thematic categories (term clusters) with words assigned to them and their frequency in percentages (rounded to two decimal places). The topic modelling was performed on the subject metadata of twenty-five archives, excluding proper names (a total of 12901 words and 3805 unique word forms). The list takes into account both the singular and plural forms of a word, with the table displaying the most frequently occurring form. Listed are only the words mentioned more than twice.

Natural objects		Artificial objects		Communal categories	
solar	0.23%	systems	0.54%	students	0.30%
energy	0.20%	equipment	0.45%	women	0.14%
air	0.17%	instruments	0.33%	alumni	0.09%
eclipse	0.14%	computer	0.26%	group	0.09%
satellites	0.13%	devices	0.16%	children	0.08%
animal	0.09%	machine	0.16%	employees	0.08%
planet	0.09%	vehicles	0.10%	nations	0.06%
natural	0.08%	spacecraft	0.10%	club	0.05%
stars	0.07%	detector	0.10%	engineers	0.05%
grain	0.06%	radio	0.09%	staff	0.04%
plant	0.06%	sensor	0.09%	musicians	0.03%
cells	0.06%	engines	0.09%	astronomers	0.02%
earth	0.06%	shuttle	0.09%	community	0.02%
saturn	0.05%	telescopes	0.09%	people	0.02%
water	0.05%	drawings	0.07%	vip	0.02%
light	0.05%	radar	0.06%	African Americans	0.02%
blood	0.04%	antennas	0.06%	architects	0.02%
corn	0.04%	atlas	0.05%	personalities	0.02%
lunar	0.04%	accelerators	0.05%	personnel	0.02%
beam	0.04%	calorimeter	0.05%		
comets	0.04%	charts	0.05%		
brain	0.03%	tools	0.05%		
moon	0.03%	magnet	0.05%		
muon	0.03%	aircraft	0.04%		
sea	0.03%	artificial	0.04%		
sun	0.03%	electronics	0.04%		
atmosphere	0.02%	interface	0.04%		
wind	0.02%	spectrometer	0.04%		
gases	0.02%	apparatus	0.04%		
particle	0.02%	diagrams	0.04%		
craters	0.02%	maps	0.04%		
jupiter	0.02%	hardware	0.03%		
lake	0.02%	lasers	0.03%		
ocean	0.02%	cathode	0.02%		
		cryomagnets	0.02%		
		algorithms	0.02%		
		boosters	0.02%		
		databases	0.02%		

Annex C. The fifty most frequent words among the subject metadata

The calculation is based on the subject metadata of twenty-five archives, excluding proper names (a total of 12901 words and 3805 unique word forms). Word frequencies are given as percentages, rounded to two decimal places. Words referring to the institutional discourse are highlighted in bold.

1	technology	0.87%	26	college	0.23%
2	institute	0.84%	27	n.j.	0.23%
3	united	0.74%	28	solar	0.23%
4	posters	0.73%	29	apollo	0.21%
5	states	0.72%	30	art	0.21%
6	systems	0.54%	31	new	0.21%
7	space	0.46%	32	computer	0.21%
8	equipment	0.45%	33	analysis	0.21%
9	research	0.44%	34	energy	0.20%
10	buildings	0.43%	35	advanced	0.19%
11	history	0.38%	36	congress	0.19%
12	university	0.38%	37	corporation	0.19%
13	study	0.37%	38	society	0.19%
14	international	0.36%	39	teaching	0.19%
15	u.s.	0.31%	40	association	0.19%
16	observatory	0.30%	41	service	0.19%
17	instruments	0.29%	42	center	0.19%
18	princeton	0.29%	43	foundation	0.18%
19	engineering	0.29%	44	air	0.17%
20	management	0.27%	45	industrial	0.16%
21	national	0.27%	46	office	0.16%
22	education	0.27%	47	program	0.16%
23	science	0.27%	48	studies	0.16%
24	department	0.26%	49	school	0.16%
25	american	0.25%	50	students	0.16%

Europeana, EDM, and the Europeanisation of Cultural Heritage Institutions

Carlotta Capurro, Gertjan Plets

Abstract

Over the past two decades, the European Commission has mobilised cultural heritage to bolster a European identity. One of the main flagship initiatives promoted to this end has been Europeana, the most extensive digital cultural project financed by the EU. At the core of the project stands europeana.eu, a digital cultural portal aggregating metadata provided by national and local heritage institutions.
Central in our analysis is the Europeana Data Model (EDM). Using standardised thesauri and vocabularies, EDM offers the possibility to create a semantic contextualisation for objects, allowing semantic operations on the metadata and their enrichment with Linked Open Data on the web. Due to its overarching nature, EDM cannot deliver the granularity that cultural heritage institutions need when documenting their resources. Nonetheless, heritage institutions accept to sacrifice accuracy to have their information represented in a Europe-wide collection.
We study how this digital heritage infrastructure was designed to enact a sense of Europeanness amongst national and local institutions. Policy documents, ethnographic research and a systematic survey amongst the European heritage institutions enabled us to trace how a standardised European metadata structure plays a role in governing local and national heritage institutions. The EDM might enable heritage stakeholders to benefit from Europeana's online exposure while enacting a European mindset. Ultimately, this study of the metadata model enriches the debate on the EU's cultural heritage politics, which has not fully explored the role of the digital. At the same time, it also taps into debates about infrastructure and digital governmentality.

Keywords: digital cultural policy, European cultural policy, digital cultural heritage, Europeana, Europeana Data Model (EDM), metadata, Digital Infrastructure

Introduction

Over the past two decades, the European Commission has actively invested in digitising the cultural sector, especially promoting cultural heritage's online accessibility. To this end, consistent financial support was allocated to projects designed to foster the cooperation between member states, supporting them in digitising their cultural resources and sharing them on the web or through new technological infrastructures. The political interest in the cultural sector's digital transformation became especially evident in 2005 when the Commission launched its i2010 strategy on digital libraries. The flagship of this strategy was Europeana, Europe's most extensive digital infrastructure centralising European cultural heritage. Over time Europeana has become one of Europe's largest and most costly initiatives in the field of culture, with a budget of about 62 million euros.[1] José Manuel Barroso (2005), president of the Commission, welcomed the digitisation and the online availability of cultural heritage preserved by European institutions as crucial for creating an economy and a society based on knowledge.

Thylstrup (2018) thoughtfully describes how, as a consequence of the substantial financial and political support to the European cultural sector's digitisation, an ever-growing amount of cultural data has been generated and aggregated in what she defines as the mass digitisation phenomenon. Cultural heritage institutions have produced digital resources with a variety of purposes: libraries, archives, and museums have embraced technology as an efficient tool to document, index, and disseminate their vast collections. Detailed metadata were increasingly used to describe these information resources. Allowing for more consistent retrieval, better management, and easy exchange of data records between software applications and institutions (Haynes 2018), metadata have become an essential requirement of information management for cultural heritage institutions (Baca 2016; Riley 2017).

At the same time, metadata allows cultural information to move out from institutions and serve other purposes on the web. Data provided by an institution are often aggregated with similar resources, joining local, national, or international databases (Presner 2010; Loukissas 2017). Thanks to this abundance of data, the research in the field of digital humanities has flourished, and extensive research infrastructures have been promoted to facilitate the reuse and the interpretation of cultural information in innovative ways, generating new scientific

---

1   This amount is calculated for the period 2006 - 2020, on the basis of the information available on the European repository CORDIS and on the Europeana Business Plans issued annually by the Europeana Foundation (available on pro.europeana.eu). It includes only the direct founds invested by the Commission for the development and the maintenance of the service, thus the projects financed to increase the collection are excluded from this amount.

knowledge (Gitelman 2013; Bunnik et al. 2016). However, not only academia has benefitted from the possibilities offered by these data. The European creative industry has also profited from the increasing amount of resources available on the web, reusing cultural information to produce books, games, touristic resources, or educational material (Howkins 2001; Schlesinger 2017). By enabling data interoperability, metadata allow the reuse of the cultural information in new settings and for different purposes.

Precisely due to the widespread uses of cultural heritage data, it is crucial to approach them critically, thoughtfully reflecting on their nature and inherent politics (Valtysson 2020). These are the cultural assumptions embedded in their creation, which produce wanted or unexpected consequences on the people using the data. Metadata about cultural heritage are "generated" (Manovich 2001, 224) from the interpretation of the records held by cultural heritage institutions, which are themselves subjected to cultural, social, and political biases (Hall 2001; Cameron and Robinson 2003; 2007; Smith 2006; Harrison 2013). Far from being neutral and objective descriptions (Gitelman 2013), metadata result from an array of conscious and unconscious decisions that underlie both the process of digitisation of cultural heritage and curation of digital objects (Thylstrup 2018). In this sense, they are authoritative and subjective *artefacts*, representing a set of cultural assumptions, and current and selective understandings of the past and the cultural heritage. Furthermore, in order to guarantee the interoperability and exchange of information, metadata rely on the use of certified thesauri and codes, resulting in a standardised and somehow simplified description of cultural heritage (Hodder 1999; Cameron and Robinson 2007). By imposing metadata schemas and selected vocabularies, cultural heritage institutions are de facto controlling the interpretation of objects in their collections (Bowker and Star 2000; Olson 2002).

Furthermore, the terminology and the structure of metadata determine how an object is retrieved from the database. In other words, metadata affect the context in which the digital item is on display. This context may or may not be relevant for the object, which has a history of its own and has been acquired by the institution as a result of specific selection criteria (Bennett et al. 2017). Ultimately, a digitally accessible heritage database should be conceived as a digital exhibition where the past is culturally assembled into heritage and objects are imbued with new meanings, generating unexpected connections (Fig. 1). Considering metadata as cultural products allows us to investigate their more profound impact on the society, so that we may understand how they determine the current interpretation of culture and heritage, contributing to the construction of narratives about identities and the past.

Metadata are at the core of the Europeana initiative. The digital portal *europeana.eu* (Europeana 2020), currently the largest aggregator of cultural heritage data in Europe, counts over 60 million digital objects,[2] provided by over

---

2   This data refers to the situation in September 2020.

4000 cultural heritage institutions, including libraries, archives, museums, and audio-visual collections.[3] As a metadata aggregator, Europeana developed the Europeana Data Model (EDM) as an infrastructure to deal with the variety of data provided by its partner institutions. However, Europeana's tasks are not limited to the aggregation of digital cultural heritage but include the support and promotion of the digital transformation of the European cultural heritage sector. To this end, Europeana has developed best practices and standards for cultural heritage institutions. To succeed in this task, Europeana has benefitted from extensive political and economic support, both of the European Commission and the member states. Therefore, this paper will consider Europeana not only as a digital service but as the result of a combination of political, cultural, economic, and technological forces.

This study argues that when cultural heritage institutions join Europeana, they actively contribute to the creation of *European heritage* by mapping their metadata into EDM and accepting to adhere to a procedure designed to bring them together despite their national, domain, or thematic differences. In this sense, EDM is more than a metadata model, representing an infrastructure for constructing the European identity of national and local cultural heritage institutions. In order to understand how Europeana has been conceived as a political and cultural product, the article first explores the evolution of European cultural and digital policy, focusing on how digital heritage tools have been used to meet the cultural goals set by the European Commission. The second section provides an overview of the Europeana project's role in the European policy. The rest of the article is dedicated to EDM and its specific impact on cultural heritage institutions. This analysis is based on policy documents and white papers,[4] interviews carried out at the Europeana Foundation headquarter in Den Haag,[5] and the data gathered through a survey distributed among cultural heritage institutions in Europe.[6]

---

3   A list of the data provider institutions is available at https://classic.europeana.eu/portal/en/explore/sources.html (Accessed on 20/08/2020).

4   These documents are issued both by the European Commission and the Europeana Foundation.

5   Interviews were carried out between May and August 2019 to ten employees of the Europeana Foundation (working in the R&D, Data Publishing, Aggregation Service, Collection Engagement and Management) in the frame of an institutional ethnography. Their answers informed the author's understanding of the internal procedures and the work of the Europeana initiative presented in this paper.

6   The survey, elaborated by the author, has been distributed to cultural heritage institutions in Europe with the support of Europeana Aggregators and domain associations, and through direct emails. The study primarily addresses those, within the institutions, with direct responsibility on digitization, to evaluate the impact of Europeana activity on the development of their internal digital policy. The information discussed in this article relies on the answers of 79 institutions from 16 European member states, collected between May and December 2020.

Europeana, EDM, and the Europeanisation of Cultural Heritage Institutions 167

Fig. 1: Print by M. Rapine in the different digital contexts of the Wellcome Collection and Europeana.

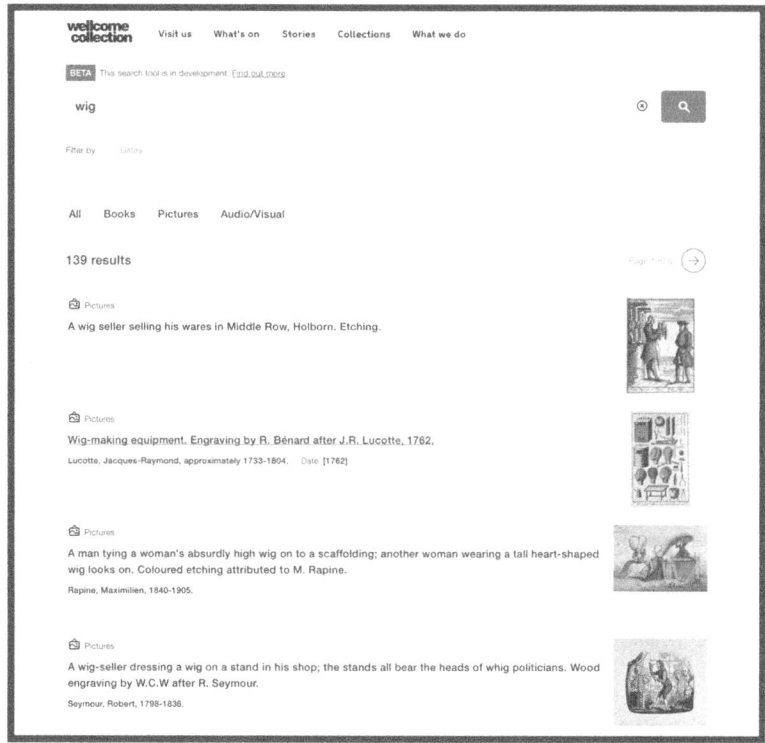

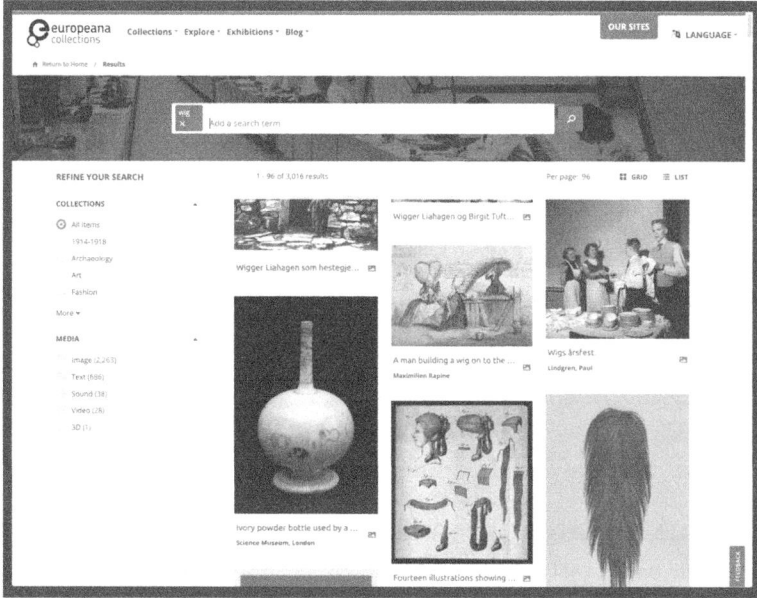

The European policies on culture and the digital

The introduction of culture to reinforce collective European belonging represented a turning point in the European Commission's political agenda. During the 1970s, the Commissioners realised that establishing a common economic and legislative framework for all the member states was not enough to create a union out of the heterogeneous European people (Haas 2004). Therefore, the Solemn Declaration on European Union promulgated in 1983 explicitly invited each member state to "promote a European awareness" (Council 1983, art. 3.3) and undertake joint action in various cultural areas.

Since the Solemn Declaration promulgation, the construction of collective European identity and memory has become an integral part of the Commission's cultural agenda (De Witte 1987; Shore 2000; Sassatelli 2006; Calligaro 2013). In 1992, article 128 of the Maastricht Treaty added culture to the list of areas under the sphere of European competence.[7] While offering a legal framework to the European actions in the cultural field, the Treaty opened the doors to the creation of funding schemes to finance cultural initiatives. By contributing "to the flowering of the cultures of the Member States, while respecting their national and regional diversity and at the same time bringing the common cultural heritage to the fore" (EC Council and Commission 1992, 128), the Treaty stressed the respect for national and local diversity, while emphasising the existence of a common cultural background. In this sense, then, article 128 embodied the cultural value of Europe's motto *Unity in Diversity*.

In line with this motto, the European concept of culture acknowledges and respects the variety of national and local expressions while accentuating the existence of a common background. This common trait is defined by the acceptance of a set of founding values promoted as European: the respect for human dignity and human rights, freedom, democracy, equality and the rule of law. Shore (2000) reveals how the Commission perceived European culture as more than a mosaic of each national cultural backgrounds: national diversity is celebrated with regard to how its specificity fits into the overall European design. In this sense, any local or national manifestation of culture represents a declination of a more comprehensive European history and identity. This process of cultural *Europeanisation* is a strategy of self-representation and a device of power wielded by the European institutions (Borneman and Fowler 1997). In the effort of creating a European cultural identity, Europe becomes itself a symbol (Swedberg 1994), in which the ambiguity among local, national, and European levels reinforces the possibility for citizens to identify with it (Sassatelli 2002).

---

7   Article 128 of the Maastricht Treaty was firstly amended in Article 151 of the Treaty of Amsterdam (1997), then in Article 167 of the Treaty on the Functioning of the European Union (2009).

However, Calligaro and Vlassis (2017) underline that culture is ambiguously addressed in the official documentation, noting that the Commission has dealt with it in the most disparate context, including policy about commerce, industry, communication, and development. These documents show that the European Commission values culture as a powerful economic driver for the continent (Littoz-Monnet 2012; Schlesinger 2017) and it is a field where institutional, political, and economic interests determine the composition of policy (Littoz-Monnet 2007). As Lähdesmäki (2012) notes, when financing cultural initiatives the European Commission is also pursuing its economic agenda since the cultural sector's support generates a direct spinoff in adjacent areas such as tourism, education, and the creative industries, and ultimately on the European economy as a whole. From a neoliberal perspective, culture is transformed into an exploitable resource (Yúdice 2003) and the cultural policy promoted by the Commission can be compared with the other economy-oriented policies designed to boost European competitiveness on the global market (Tretter 2011).

The economic and identitarian policies encoded in the European Commission's cultural actions have been addressed exhaustively in the academic literature. However, the digital policies of the EU have received less attention, although they are similar in scope and influence. As a matter of fact, from the early 1990s, the Commission identified the information society among the priorities for guiding the economic growth, boosting competitiveness, and increasing employment (EC 1994a). Besides the clear economic ambitions, digital policies were as well imbued with cultural goals. Reflecting on the social, societal, and cultural issues connected with the implementation of the information society (Kofler 1998), the 1994 Action Plan Europe's Way to the Information Society pointed out that "[it] provides the opportunity to facilitate the dissemination of European cultural values and the valorisation of a common heritage" (EC 1994b, 14). Therefore, the digital transformation was considered not only a driver of economic growth but also a central element in the development of a European culture.

From 2000 onwards, the European Commission has promoted two long-term development plans regulating all the European policy aspects, where the cultural and digital politics hold a central position. The Lisbon Strategy aimed at making Europe, by 2010, "the most competitive and dynamic knowledge-based economy in the world" (Council 2000, 1). At the heart of the plan were the development and use of the internet and internet-related technologies, and the improvement of European citizens' digital skills (Liikanen 2001). In this framework, the European Commission actively promoted cultural heritage digitisation, encouraging the member states to support digitisation initiatives (CDM 2001). In order to generate usable data for the information society, mass digitisation of cultural heritage became an imperative for member states and public heritage institutions, raising several political, legal and cultural issues (Thylstrup 2018).

With the launch of the Europe 2020 Strategy, the Lisbon Strategy's successor, 2010 represented a crucial year for the future development of European policy.

The new plan aimed at bolstering a "smart, sustainable and inclusive growth" (EC 2010a). One of the strategy's flagship initiatives was the Digital Agenda for Europe, which aimed at maximising the social and economic potential of ICT for the Digital Single Market. In particular, the development of widely accepted standards to reach the interoperability of IT products and services was the digital plan's central aim. In order to foster European identity by digital cooperation, standardisation was deemed essential. The plan presented digital heritage as one of the critical elements to address societal challenges in the digital era (EC 2010b). In the new Workplan for Culture, designed to align the cultural strategy of the Commission with the goals set by the Europe 2020 strategy (EU Council 2010), the standardisation of digital cultural and heritage data represented the optimal way to enforce their diffusion and their reusability on the web.

Europeana as a digital cultural policy instrument

The Europeana project exemplifies how the European cultural agenda is operationalised through instruments both from the digital and cultural policy frameworks. Ultimately, Europeana showcases that, when studying European cultural politics, both digital and cultural policy frameworks need to be studied in concert. Europeana is a cultural initiative financed by the European Commission with the support of the member states. Its activity is operated by the Europeana Foundation, who holds a service contract with the Commission. When, in 2005, the six heads of state called upon the Commission for the creation of a European digital library "to preserve and share Europe's cultural and linguistic identities and give them a more prominent place on the Internet" (Chirac et al. 2005), President Barroso gave to Viviane Reding and Ján Figel', the commissioners for Information Society and Media, and for Education, Training, Culture and Youth respectively, the task to plan its creation.

In accepting this duty, Reding emphatically declared that the internet was the most powerful medium at disposal to promote "our [European] collective memory" and make European libraries and archives accessible to all under a single unified portal. From his part, Figel' underlined the importance of institutional cooperation in ensuring the "preservation and access to our common cultural heritage for the future generations" (EC 2005). Europeana became the flagship initiative of the i2010 strategy, involving cultural heritage institutions from all over Europe. During the celebrations of the launch of the *europeana.eu* prototype in November 2008, Barroso described the portal as a "shop window" and a "digital doorway" to European culture "in all its glorious diversity" (Barroso 2008). Well aware of the portal's role in constructing a European identity, he stressed that "Europeana has the potential to change the way people see European culture. It will make it easier for our citizens to appreciate their own past, but also to become more aware of their common European identity" (ibid).

As Craith (2012) argues, despite its ubiquitous presence in policy documents, the notion of what constitutes the *common European heritage* is nowhere fully conceptualised, leaving room for multiple and ad-hoc interpretations. Lähdesmäki (2014a; 2014b; 2018) and others describe how Europe actively creates specific historical discourse by promoting those narratives that materialise the founding values of the EU through specific heritage sites and cultural icons (Sassatelli 2002; Patel 2014; Lähdesmäki et al. 2020). On the other hand, European heritage is also constructed through the appropriation of national cultural icons. Cultural heritage "is always both local and European" and "reveals what it has meant to be a European throughout time" (EC 2014, 3–5). Thus objects are reinterpreted in the frame of the European cultural narrative, becoming "an integral part of a common cultural heritage and [...] regarded as common property by the citizens of Europe" (Borchardt 1995, 73).

At the core of Europeana's action stands the online portal aggregating data about all the European digital heritage produced by the member states and their public heritage institutions. The loose definition of what, for Europeana, constitutes European heritage correlates with Craith's interpretation of an environment where multiple heritage discourses can operate. Since 2014, however, Europeana has more actively curated its repository producing virtual exhibitions around digital heritage objects embodying key European episodes and themes, such as the First World War, the fall of the Berlin Wall, or migration (Europeana 2014). These curated exhibitions have become prominent in the new website launched in spring 2020, and the financing of new European projects to enlarge Europeana collection increasingly relies on the thematics selected by the Foundation.

Although Europeana is indeed a digital portal enabling the European public to discover their shared European past, it is perhaps more oriented towards national and local heritage institutions. From the early phase of the initiative, and in order to optimise its business, the Foundation has worked towards the creation and implementation of an infrastructure for aggregating cultural data and stimulating the digital transformation of the European cultural sector. This infrastructure implied the design of EDM to document the resources and the creation of a network of people and institutions called to work together in line with the parameters created by Europeana. First, with the creation in 2011 of the Europeana Network Association (Europeana 2010), the Foundation involved representatives and practitioners from the cultural sector in a competence cluster, fostering institutional innovation through the adoption of the standards and best practices developed in collaboration with its members and promoted by Europeana, in line with the Commission's requirements.

Second, to facilitate the injection of new data into the portal, Europeana promoted the creation of the Aggregators' Forum (2020), a supranational network of content aggregators working locally, thematically, or by domain to aggregate cultural heritage data. Aggregators work as intermediaries between cultural heritage institutions and Europeana. They are expected to collect data from content providers, upload them into Europeana, and support institutions in solving their technical issues. At the same time, they promote best-practices and business models to standardise procedures among cultural institutions in the different member states. By positioning itself at the centre of these networks of professionals and institutions, Europeana reasserts its leading role in driving the cultural sector's digital transformation.

The robust political endorsement to Europeana's work granted by the Commission clearly emerges in the 2011 Recommendations on digitisation and online accessibility of cultural material. With that document, the Commission encouraged the standardisation of procedures and technologies for the cultural sector for the sake of the economy of scale, positioning Europeana at the heart of the sector's digital turn (EC 2011). Introducing a recommended target for minimum content contribution to Europeana, the Commission de-facto imposed upon the member states an acceleration in the digitisation investments. In this framework, Europeana is not a simple instrument in the hands of the European Commission to enforce its policy on digital cultural heritage, but a central actor in determining those policies' direction.

EDM: building European heritage by Europeanising cultural institutions

The conceptual model of EDM

The main operative obstacle posed by the creation of a digital repository aggregating the collections from many different European cultural heritage institutions has been the harmonisation of digital heritage objects. As a matter of fact, libraries, archives, museums, and audio-visual collections have very different standards to document their collections, which often are incompatible with each other. These differences are determined by the heterogeneous nature of the heritage preserved in each institution, the various authority vocabularies used to document resources (i.e. thesauri or controlled vocabularies that are discipline or domain-dependent), and the reference models for the metadata sets in use, such as LIDO for museums (McKenna, Rohde-Enslin, and Stein 2011), EAD for archives (Pitti 1999) and METS for digital libraries (McDonough 2006). To accommodate such a multitude of descriptions within the same digital collection, Europeana's developers had first of all to provide an architecture capable of bringing such a variety of data in relation with each other.

The first fundamental decision with a significative resonance on the Europeana service's architecture regarded the nature of the collected objects. From the early days, Europeana was not designed as a repository of digital heritage, but as an aggregator of *surrogates* of the digital resources owned by cultural heritage institutions (Purday 2009). Three mandatory components constitute these elements: a set of metadata describing the object, a thumbnail (a low-resolution image of the item for its preview on Europeana), and a URL linking the surrogate to the full resolution digital object preserved on the server of the owner institution (Gradmann, Dekkers, and Meghini 2009). This choice resulted in several advantages both for Europeana and the partner institutions. Europeana managed to overcome the issues posed by the diversity of digital resources' file formats, leaving the owner institutions responsible for the digital conservation and accessibility. On the other hand, partner institutions also benefitted from the surrogate model, keeping the control over their digital collections, especially concerning the copyright, and profiting from the increased internet traffic towards their website generated by Europeana. Thanks to the adoption of the surrogate model, Europeana could achieve a leading role in the governance of cultural heritage information on the web with a minimal investment in the management of digital resources.

The second constitutional decision that shaped Europeana's functionalities established how to accommodate the "information perspectives" of the different cultural domains within the same digital library (Aloia, Concordia, and Meghini 2011, 128). EDM thus was conceived as a standard for interoperability. Introduced in 2010, it was the follower of the Europeana Semantic Elements (ESE) used since the launch of the Europeana initiative (Doerr et al. 2010). Based on Dublin Core, ESE was conceived to extract from any digital resource the "lowest common denominator" (Isaac and Clayphan 2013, 2), meaning the minimum amount of information that each domain had in common when describing a resource. In its developers' intentions, the introduction of EDM had to overturn the limitation of such a model, accommodating the complexity of each domain's documentation requirements. In designing EDM, representative of libraries, archives, museums, and audio-visual collections worked in groups to identify their specific requirements for the novel metadata scheme. As a result, EDM is not based on any community standards in use, but "adopts an open, cross-domain Semantic Web-based framework" (ibid: 5) allowing each data provider to use its preferred metadata standard and vocabulary of reference. EDM thus represents a compromise between the needs of the different heritage domains. On the other hand, being such a generic layer, it can accommodate data from all the institutions, making sure that every domain can reuse each other's data (Charles and Olensky 2014). Thanks to its open model, then, EDM was designed to accommodate the variety of cultural heritage documentation in a univocal model, figuratively embodying the European motto *Unity in Diversity*.

On a conceptual level, EDM provides the structure to describe information about the who, what, when, and where of the heritage resource (Isaac and Clayphan 2013), and is defined by a set of specific design principles (Peroni, Tomasi, and Vitali 2013). First, it makes a clear distinction between the heritage item, either physical or born-digital, and its digital representation. They are represented respectively by the classes (edm:ProvidedCHO) and (edm:WebResource). In this way, EDM maintains the information about the object separated from those describing the digital item. They are brought together in the same entry by the class (ore:Aggregation). Second, EDM makes a distinction between the object and the metadata records describing the object. Thanks to this distinction, EDM allows the description of the information about the digital object's lifecycle. Third, EDM allows multiple records about the same object. This option allows more than one institution to provide different, potentially contrasting, information about the object. Fourth, EDM allows describing an object as composed by other items, facilitating the characterisation of compound heritage, such as each building in a monumental complex or each of the poems of which an anthology is comprised. Fifth, EDM makes data describing the resource with different levels of abstraction compatible with each other. In this way, it is up to the data provider to decide the degree of detail when describing the object. This characteristic makes EDM a ductile model capable of putting generic information from an institution in relation to the more detailed ones provided by another partner.

Lastly, EDM supports the use of contextual resources, which are a set of classes to describe contextual entities such as people, organisations, events, locations, time periods, and concepts (Isaac and Clayphan 2013), like controlled vocabularies and thesauri. These descriptions facilitate the automatic semantic enrichment of the data and support the research among multilingual resources (Gradmann 2010; Stiller, Isaac, and Petras 2014). The semantic enrichment of metadata consists of adding extra topical metadata so that machine can understand it and build connections with other resources (Clarke and Harley 2014). Whenever a contextual entity is detected, it is linked with all the related existing data already available in the Europeana database. By virtue of these compositional principles, from a data scientist perspective, EDM is an adaptable standard that can be extended to provide a higher degree of information specialisation when requested either by the data provider or specific projects (Isaac and Clayphan 2013).

In order to have an object included in Europeana, institutions must provide at least the metadata necessary to create a link between the *surrogate* and the digital resource on their websites. This information is described by the metadata fields (edm:object), which is a hyperlink to the object that is used to automatically generate a preview of the resource; (edm:isShownAt), which is a hyperlink to the website where the digital object is stored; and (edm:isShownBy), which is a direct hyperlink to the resource. In addition, Europeana asks institutions to provide information about the digital resource's copyright status using the field (edm:rights). The degree of completeness of the provided information determines the *tier* of the resource. Europeana has introduced a four-tier system to classify the quality of its contents, showing to data providers what are the benefits for them and the users when data are complete and accurate (Europeana 2015). Promoting the improvement of metadata quality using the catching motto "the more you give, the more you get" (ibid), Europeana sensitises heritage institutions of the importance of good-quality data to benefit from the data economy's advantages.

Cultural heritage institutions and EDM

In order to smooth the process of contributing new datasets, Europeana devised an operative supply chain working at the national, domain, or thematic levels, which is based on a network of data aggregators. They are cultural heritage institutions acting as intermediaries, with the duty to support data providers in mapping their data to EDM, gather the metadata, and verify the quality before injecting them into Europeana. These institutions have been identified by national governments, in the capacity of national aggregators, or have resulted from specific projects funded by the European Commission to increase the volume of Europeana collection (Purday 2009), such as Carare for archaeological heritage, OpenUp! for natural heritage, or Europeana Sound for audio heritage ('Aggregators Forum' 2020). Therefore, Europeana is positioned at the centre of a Europe-wide network of cultural institutions, which are strongly encouraged to digitise their collections and make them available on the portal. In constructing this operative infrastructure, Europeana is imposing its technical and operative requirements on institutional procedures.

Through the content aggregators, cultural heritage institutions are Europeana's data providers. They send to Europeana the datasets that have to be processed and validated before being published on the portal. Datasets are packages of information (IASA 2009) that can be about a particular topic, originate from a specific source or project, or aggregated by a certain custodian (Europeana 2016). Since the provided datasets have to comply with EDM requirements, cultural heritage institutions must define a mapping between their original data model and EDM (Charles and Olensky 2014). The process of mapping metadata consists of describing how to link the information provided by the institution with the corresponding element in the EDM scheme, defining the structural and semantic relationship between two metadata schemes (Haslhofer and Klas 2010). Ultimately, the responsibility for the data that are published on Europeana belongs to the cultural heritage institutions.

In order to assess the impact of Europeana's activities on cultural heritage institutions, a questionnaire was distributed online. Some of the questions targeted the experience with EDM, also investigating whether institutions have adopted it as their internal metadata model. Among the 79 respondents, only 19 declared to be data partners of Europeana, collaborating in the capacity of data providers or aggregators.[8] Among them, three declared to have adopted EDM for internal purposes, one to use an enriched metadata model based on EDM but customised to meet the institution's necessities, and one to plan to switch to EDM when improving the quality of its internal database. The remaining institutions expressed a series of concerns about the quality of the data available on Europeana.

---

8   These data refer to the answers collected up to December 2020.

Fig. 2: "Carl Larsson" query in Europeana. The results mix the work of two homonymous artists. There is no distinction between the two entities in the database.

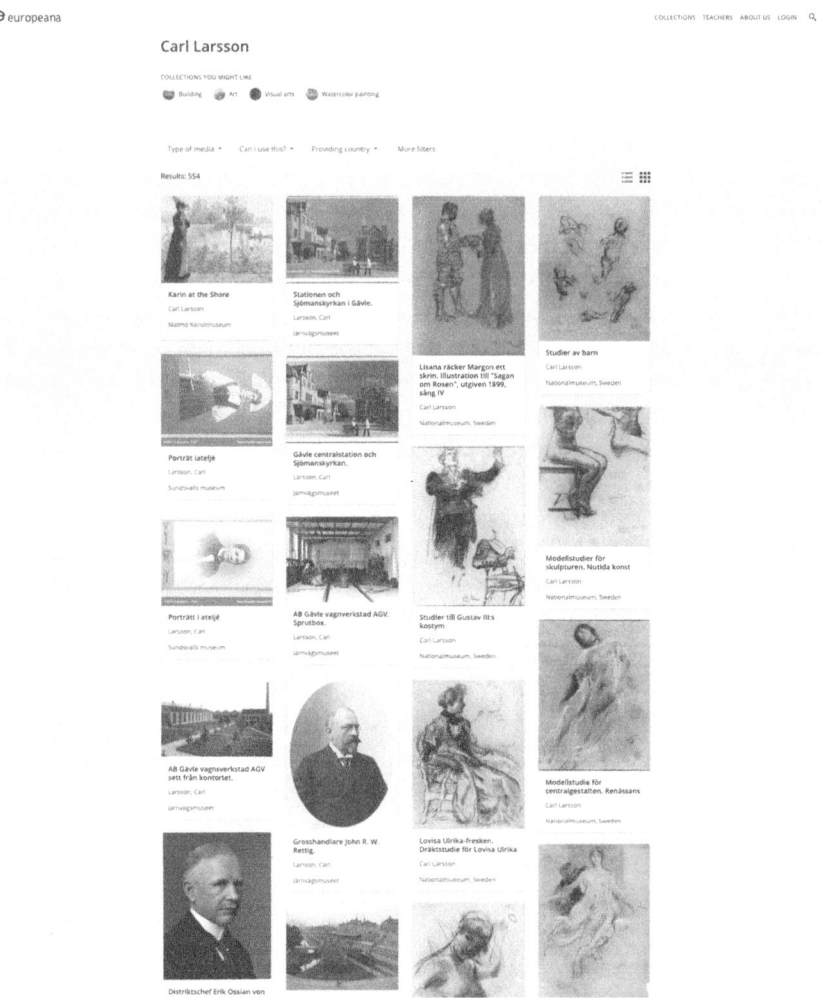

The most shared concern surfaced among the respondents regards the wrong information generated through automatic data enrichment. During the process of validation, datasets are enriched with pertinent data already available in the collection (EuropeanaTech 2015). In EDM, the data provided by the institutions are kept separate from those generated by the process of enrichment, preserving the authority control of the institution on the information. Despite this conceptual differentiation in the model's architecture, the two categories of data appear without any distinction on the user interface, that is the *europeana.eu* portal, making it impossible for a user to distinguish which data is automatically generated. This is especially problematic in the case of erroneous enrichment that may occur when two entities have the same name (such as homonymous authors or locations), which the algorithm is unable to distinguish. Despite recognising the benefits of placing their objects in relation with those in the collections of other institutions in cross-domain collections, cultural heritage institutions express concerns and annoyance over the misleadingly enriched data that, for Europeana's users, appears to be their responsibility.

Fig. 3: Ambiguity in the attribution of works to Egbert van Heemskerk I, II or III. Despite the different names attributed to the authors in the "Creator" field, the hyperlinks generate the same research results.

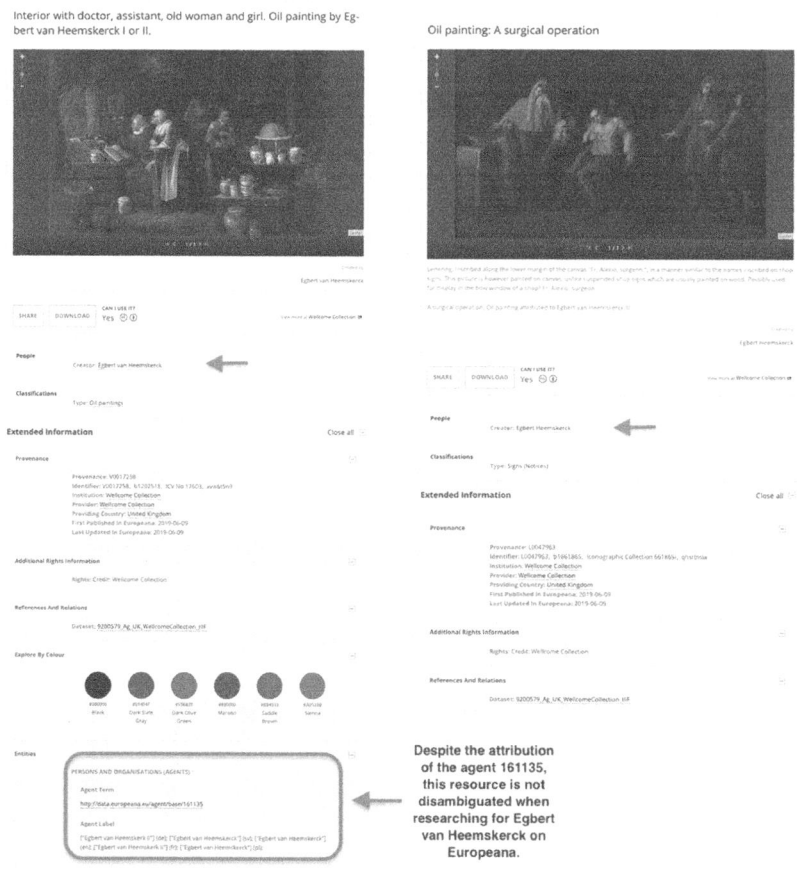

Europeana struggles especially in the case of homonymous authors when there is no possibility of automating the process of data enrichment with one specific entity. This is the case, for example, with Carl Larsson and Egbert van Heemskerk. First, the name Carl Larsson belongs both to a Swedish painter (Stockholm 1853 - Falun 1919) who is famous for his family scenes (Carl 2018), and a Swedish photographer (Stockholm 1866 – Uppsala parish 1947) active in the city of Gävle (SPA

1911). When browsing Europeana, the results mix the works of the two authors, without any possibility of disambiguation (Fig. 2). This suggests that there is only one generic entity about Carl Larson, to which the works of both artists are connected. Even more confusing is the research of works from Egbert van Heemskerk, a name which belongs to three different artists. In Europeana, there is no differentiation in the attribution of works to Egbert van Heemskerk I and II, father and son (Bredius 1925), or III, the nephew (Einberg and Egerton 1988, 237). Despite the owner institutions know who the author of their artworks is, the database does not provide any automatic differentiation in the authors' entities, failing to provide disambiguation for the users. An entity called "agent:161135" identifies Egbert van Heemskerk II. However, it is not systematically associated with all his works in the database, failing to be a useful element to disambiguate the collection (Fig. 3).

A second concern shared by many cultural heritage institutions regards the copyright of the metadata. Metadata provided to Europeana are CC0 licensed, this means that they can be reused by anyone, without any restriction (CC 2020). Europeana has promoted this requirement in line with the Open Culture campaign undertaken in 2011 with the support of Neelie Kroes, the European Commissioner for the Digital Agenda. If the European Commission already solicited cultural heritage institutions to preserve the public domain copyright status of their objects once digitised (EC 2008, 7), open culture was praised as a stimulus for boosting the European creative industry (Kroes 2012). This approach turned out to be problematic for many institutions, which consider part of their documentation the result of intellectual work, either by curation or research activity. Consequently, they publish their metadata using the CC-by licence, which requires the user to make a reference to the source.

In the survey, these institutions declared that, when sharing their data with Europeana, they had to decide what information to provide in CC0 and what to retain in their database, resulting in a minimal dataset available in EDM. Due to different approaches to the nature of cultural heritage information, as indisputably public domain or as the result of intellectual work, a consistent amount of data ultimately is not provided to Europeana, generating a disparity between the information available on the portal and that available on the website of the providing institutions.

This issue becomes evident when exploring the natural science collection on Europeana. The OpenUp! Project, which ran between 2011 and 2014 laying the foundation for the OpenUp! Natural History Aggregator, enriched Europeana's collection with natural heritage items ('OpenUp!' 2020). Among the project participants, the Royal Belgian Institute of Natural Science provided over 4000 images of insects from its entomology collection using the CC-by copyright license. This status, which also pertains to the digital collection available on its website, has significant consequences on the data available on Europeana. Exploring the *Diloboderus abderus* entry (Fig. 4), it is evident how the only information about the heritage item, an insect, in this case, is the title, which provides the scientific name of the species, and the (edm:hasType) property, which specifies the classification of the item as a *preserved specimen*.

Fig. 4 – Diloboderus abderus page on Europeana. When forcing institutions to adopt a different copyright status, the risk is a scarcity of information provided to Europeana.

The remaining information provided by the metadata is about the owner of the resource and the circumstances around the creation of the entry in the context of the OpenUp! Project. While the *Relations* field is used to provide a hyperlink towards the bibliography over the species (available on the Biodiversity Library), there is no information about the Diloboderus as an insect, such as the characteristics of the species, nor as an *heritagised* item, such as the moment it entered the collection or the place where it was captured. This scarcity contrasts with the detailed information provided in the Royal Belgian Institute of Natural Science database. There, each object also reports the name of the conservator responsible for the collection, recognising the status of the database as intellectual work. The discrepancy in the copyright license of these digital collections, thus, not only determines a discrepancy between the information owned by the institution and those available online but ultimately deprive the Europeana users of many essential data, making the resources unattractive to be reused in another context.

Another matter that generates some discontent among cultural heritage institutions is the generic nature of EDM. As previously described, EDM was conceived as "an integration medium for collecting, connecting and enriching the descriptions provided by Europeana content providers" (Europeana 2017). While making it possible to accommodate data from cultural heritage institutions in different domains, this overarching function reduces the granularity of the information provided. As a matter of fact, many institutions, and also some aggregators among them, lament that EDM is too generic to accommodate the complexity of their internal documentation. Therefore, cultural heritage institutions are providing data to Europeana that result in simplification when compared to the wealth of information in their databases.

Nevertheless, a consistent number of institutions have decided to share their data with Europeana, recognising the benefits of this European initiative. They accept to sacrifice part of the accuracy of their information and the total control over their online circulation for benefitting of better online exposure and an increment in the number of visits to their websites along with the reuse of their resources in external cultural projects (such as in user-generated pages on Wikipedia or in didactical material for schools). They acknowledge the value of having their objects connected with those of the other institutions and enriched by complementary heritage in a Europe-wide collection. By entering the Europeana catalogue, digital heritage ceased to express only a particular national or local identity but instead becomes part of European shared memory. Therefore, it can be said that Europeana actively engineers the creation of a European cultural heritage.

Governing through metadata: the politics of EDM

With the creation of EDM, Europeana not only introduced the new standard for documenting European cultural resources on the web but also established a new set of procedures around the documentation policy of European cultural heritage institutions. To benefit from the advantages of sharing their collection on Europeana, institutions now have to think through their metadata models to identify and map the correspondences with EDM. This also means that they have to reconsider the legal status of their data and decide which information they are willing to release in a complete open access. Then, they have to collaborate with their aggregators of reference to prepare the dataset for Europeana. Finally, they have to check the validation process results, assisting Europeana's team in case of mistakes. This iterative process, repeated at any new data ingestion, forces institutions to compromise with their internal policy to adhere to a Europe-wide collection requirements. When mapping their metadata in EDM, cultural heritage institutions are actively producing a European heritage collection.

In order to understand the politics enforced by mapping digital cultural heritage in EDM, it is useful to reflect on the three main cultural assumptions that it encodes. First, Europeana receives data exclusively from cultural heritage institutions, entrusted as the most accurate sources of cultural heritage information. Aiming at building a "comprehensive, trustworthy and authoritative source" (Europeana 2010, 12) of cultural heritage data, Europeana intends to become the primary "trusted source of Europe's collective memory" (ibid: 4). Europeana's approach openly contrasts with other digital cultural initiatives, such as Wikidata (2020), which relies on the collaboration between cultural heritage institutions and the wiki community to check and integrate data. Heritage institutions eagerly share their data and digital resources with the wiki initiatives to have them widely circulating on the web. Anyhow, a survey conducted in 2019 by the Swedish National Heritage Board revealed that they are reluctant to integrate the crowd-contributed information back in their database, also due to a lack of trust in those who operated the changes (Zeinstra 2019). In this sense, the Europeana approach seems to better respond to cultural heritage institutions' demand for retaining control over their cultural information. Consequently, the adjective "authoritative", used by Europeana to describe the quality of its data, also applies to the nature of its collection, in that it expresses a traditional, top-down, and authority-led relation with the past, exemplifying what Smith (2006) defines as *authorised heritage discourse*.

Second, Europeana supports and encourages the use of internationally recognised vocabularies and thesauri to facilitate information standardisation. This approach, which is essential for the optimal diffusion of interoperable and reusable data on the web (Wilkinson et al. 2016) is far from being neutral or culturally unbiassed. While promising a more open and accessible cultural heritage, the digitalisation of heritage collections raised the question which heritage is made open and accessible. Cultural heritage institutions are well aware of the biases hidden in the documentation of their collections (Hall 2001; Cameron and Robinson 2003; 2007) and have worked consistently towards a more inclusive (Simon 2010), decolonised (Senier 2014; Petrešin-Bachelez 2015), and diverse representation in their archives (Smith 2006; Harrison 2013; Wallace et al. 2020). Institutional digital collections and databases have been scrutinised, and efforts have been made to turn them more representative and inclusive (Geismar 2018; White 2018; Foka 2019; Risam 2019), also thanks to the adoption of new, user-generated, and specialised vocabularies (Cairns 2013). These words and descriptors are often not included in controlled vocabularies and standardised thesauri (Bergenmar and Golub 2020), making their use not recommended on aggregators such as Europeana. Therefore, by promoting the use of standardised concepts and vocabularies, Europeana risks jeopardising institutional efforts of enforcing diversity and inclusion in their archives, involuntary becoming the perpetrator of an authoritative and exclusive vision of cultural heritage.

Third, Europeana establishes a clear definition of digital cultural heritage. EDM makes a conceptual distinction between the physical object (edm:ProvidedCHO), its digital reproduction (edm:WebResource), and the metadata provided for each of these elements. In this sense, EDM remarks the contrast between the digital and the real, and the set of specific information belonging to each of these realms. On the other hand, the structure of the model brings together the data on the physical object and the digital reproduction in the same entry (ore:Aggregation), establishing a tight relationship between the two realms. In doing so, EDM allows for the conceptual representation of digital heritage as an assemblage of physical and digital properties. According to Cameron and Mengler (2015), such an entanglement is motivated by the shared components, relations, and effects between the physical and the digital objects, which are immersed in a network of connections with people, cultural meanings, and technical qualities (Forte 2003). Within this perspective, the contextual meanings attributed to an object in the digital world become an inextricable part of its cultural value. As a consequence, considering digital heritage as an assemblage allows transferring the value of Europeanness from the digital surrogate in the Europeana collection, to the item preserved by the cultural institution.

Conclusion

This article analysed the implication of the metadata scheme EDM on the construction of the European concepts of culture and heritage. With the introduction of EDM, a European model to represent cultural heritage information on the web, Europeana has established a new international standard that profoundly impacts the internal procedure of European cultural heritage institutions. When sharing their collection on the *europeana.eu* portal, institutions accept to adhere to a set of practice that forces them to adapt their internal policy to the European requirements. At the same time, they are actively producing a collection of *European heritage* which appropriate on a European level all the resources held by the member states as national heritage.

EDM is one of the instruments used by Europeana to govern the digital transformation of the cultural sector. Europeana has proactively engineered the Europeanisation of the sector by establishing an infrastructure of procedures and standards for heritage institutions. The portal promotes a European engagement with cultural heritage by operating on three levels: first, by aggregating local and national heritage into a European repository, *europeana.eu*, that makes visible commonalities and connections among the objects; second, by promoting the unlocking of heritage that was hidden behind the institutional walls of libraries, archives, and museums; and lastly, by creating EDM, a model that provides a uniform structure to describe the resources. Clearly, in a European perspective, Europeana has to be approached similarly to how national archives have been widely described in academic literature, as important nodes in assembling the nation and promoting nationalist framings of the past.

Europeana is a product of political determination, manifested by the member states and endorsed by the European Commission with conspicuous financial support. As a digital infrastructure, it is an instrument of the European cultural policy, showing that the European cultural agenda's objectives play a crucial role in understanding the ethics and politics embedded in the digital development of the sector. In this sense, the *europeana.eu* portal embodies a European design for culture, becoming a showcase of European know-how and a manifesto of the shared European history and identity.

Due to the creation of democratically approved procedures and in line with the European Commission's main guidelines, Europeana has become an intermediary body that leads the digital transformation of European cultural institutions. The digital turn had transformed their practices and methodologies and forced them to adhere to common standards and procedures. By enforcing the cooperation in a Europe-wide network and financing projects to align with the required parameters, Europe created a digital cultural policy that is shaping the digital identity of cultural institutions. In this way, Europeana is "transforming the world with culture"[9] thanks to its impact on the institutional network it has created.

The analysis of EDM presented in this article reveals how crucial it is to approach digital infrastructures critically. A thoughtful evaluation of their social significance from a political and ethical perspective is especially relevant for the field of heritage studies that still focuses on brick-and-mortar heritage institutions. This work, which relies on policy documents and the results collected by directly addressing cultural heritage institutions, may well be enriched when more institutions and other professionals will offer their perspective on Europeana. Understanding how and what politics are intrinsically imbued in the EDM metadata model is only the first step towards a comprehensive analysis of the dynamics of representation or exclusion that this model enforces towards cultural expressions in Europe.

---

9   Until the launch of the 2020-2025 strategy in Spring 2020, this sentence was part of Europeana's mission.

Acknowledgements

We would like to thank the interviewed at Europeana and the respondents to the survey, for the information provided. A special thanks to Jaap Verheul and Lorena De Vita for reading the first draft of this paper; to the reviewers and the editors of this journal for their precious feedbacks and support; and to the CHEurope group, for the valuable comments on a preliminary version of this work presented at the CHEurope final seminar. This work was supported by the European Union's Horizon 2020 Research and Innovation programme under the Marie Skłodowska-Curie Grant Agreement Nr–722416 (CHEurope).

List of References

'Aggregators Forum'. 2020. Europeana Pro. 2020. https://pro.europeana.eu/page/aggregators.

Aloia, Nicola, Cesare Concordia, and Carlo Meghini. 2011. 'Europeana v1.0'. In *Digital Libraries and Archives*, edited by Maristella Agosti, Floriana Esposito, Carlo Meghini, and Nicola Orio, 127–29. Communications in Computer and Information Science. Springer Berlin Heidelberg.

Baca, Murtha, ed. 2016. *Introduction to Metadata*. Third edition. Los Angeles: Getty Research Institute.

Barroso, José Manuel. 2005. 'Barroso Letter on the European Digital Library', 7 July 2005. European Commission.

———. 2008. 'Europeana: A Shop Window on Europe's Cultural Heritage'. SPEECH/08/632. European Commission - PRESS RELEASES.

Bennett, Tony, Fiona Cameron, Nélia Dias, Ben Dibley, Rodney Harrison, Ira Jacknis, and Conal McCarthy. 2017. *Collecting, Ordering, Governing: Anthropology, Museums, and Liberal Government*. Durham London: Duke University Press.

Bergenmar, Jenny, and Koraljka Golub. 2020. 'Subject Indexing: The Challenge of LGBTQI Literature'. *DHN*, 203–10.

Borchardt, Klaus-Dieter. 1995. *European Integration: The Origins and Growth of the European Union*. 4. ed. European Documentation, periodical 1995. Luxembourg: Office for Official Publications of the European Communities.

Borneman, John, and Nick Fowler. 1997. 'Europeanization'. *Annual Review of Anthropology* 26 (1): 487–514.

Bowker, Geoffrey C., and Susan Leigh Star. 2000. *Sorting Things Out: Classification and Its Consequences*. First paperback edition. Inside Technology. Cambridge, Massachusetts, London, England: The MIT Press.

Bredius, A. 1925. 'Bijdragen Tot de Biographie van Egbert van Heemskerck'. *Oud Holland - Quarterly for Dutch Art History* 42 (1): 111–14.

Bunnik, Anno, Anthony Cawley, Michael Mulqueen, and Andrej Zwitter, eds. 2016. *Big Data Challenges: Society, Security, Innovation and Ethics*. Palgrave Macmillan UK.

Cairns, Susan. 2013. 'Mutualizing Museum Knowledge: Folksonomies and the Changing Shape of Expertise'. *Curator: The Museum Journal* 56 (1): 107–19.

Calligaro, Oriane. 2013. *Negotiating Europe: EU Promotion of Europeanness since the 1950s*. Europe in Transition: The NYU European Studies Series. Palgrave Macmillan US.

Calligaro, Oriane, and Antonios Vlassis. 2017. 'The European Policy of Culture'. *Politique Européenne* No 56 (2): 8–28.

Cameron, Fiona, and Sarah Mengler. 2015. 'Transvisuality, Geopolitics and Cultural Heritage in Global Flows: The Israeli-Palestinian Conflict and the Death of the Virtual Terrorist'. In *Transvisuality: The Cultural Dimension of Visuality*, II:59–72. Liverpool University Press.

Cameron, Fiona, and Helena Robinson. 2003. 'Knowledge Objects: Multidisciplinary Approaches to Collections Documentation'.

———. 2007. 'Digital Knowledgescapes: Cultural, Theoretical, Practical, and Usage Issues Facing Museum Collection Databases in a Digital Epoch'. In *Theorizing Digital Cultural Heritage*, edited by Fiona Cameron and Sarah Kenderdine, 165–91. The MIT Press.

Carl, Klaus H. 2018. *Carl Larsson*. New York: Parkstone International.

Charles, Valentine, and Marlies Olensky. 2014. 'EDM Mapping Refinement Extension Report'. pro.europeana.

Chirac, Jacques, Schroeder, Berlusconi, Zapatero, Kwasniewski, and Gyurcsány. 2005. 'The letter to Barroso', 28 April 2005. European Commission.

Clarke, Michael, and Pam Harley. 2014. 'How Smart Is Your Content? Using Semantic Enrichment to Improve Your User Experience and Your Bottom Line'. *Science Editor* 37 (2): 5.

CDM. 2001 - Coordination of digitisation mechanisms. 2001. 'Lund Actions Plan. Implementation Framework for Digitisation Coordination Actions in Europe'.

EC Council and Commission. 1992 - Council of the European Communities, and Commission of the European Communities, eds. 1992. 'Treaty on European Union'. Office for Official Publications of the European Communities. ec.europa.eu.

EU Council. 2010 - Council of the European Union. 2010. 'Conclusions of the Council and of the Representatives of the Governments of the Member States, Meeting within the Council, on the Work Plan for Culture 2011-2014'. OJ C 325, 2.12.2010. EUR-Lex.

Craith, Máiréad Nic. 2012. 'Europe's (Un)Common Heritage(S)'. *Traditiones*, November, 11–28.

CC. 2020 - Creative Commons. 2020. 'About The Licenses'. 2020. https://creativecommons.org/licenses/.

De Witte, Bruno. 1987. 'Building Europe's Image and Identity'. In *Europe from a Cultural Perspective: Historiography and Perceptions*, edited by Albert Rijksbaron, W. H. Roobol, and M. Weisglas, 132–139. The Hague: Nijgh and Van Ditmar Universitair.

Doerr, Martin, Stefan Gradmann, Stefan Hennicke, Antoine Isaac, Carlo Meghini, and Herbert van de Sompel. 2010. 'The Europeana Data Model (EDM)'. In IFLA2010. Gothenburg.

Einberg, Elizabeth, and Judy Egerton. 1988. *The Age of Hogarth: British Painters Born 1675-1709*. London: Tate Gallery.

EC. 1994a - European Commission, ed. 1994a. *Growth, competitiveness, employment. The challenges and ways forward into the 21st century. White paper (Parts A + B)*. Luxembourg: Office for Official Publ. of the EC.

———. 1994b. 'Europe's Way to the Information Society. An Action Plan'. COM(1994)0347 final. EU publications.

———. 2005. 'New Strategy on European Digital Libraries Unveiled'. News. CORDIS.

———. 2008. 'Europe's Cultural Heritage at the Click of a Mouse: Progress on the Digitisation and Online Accessibility of Cultural Material and Digital Preservation across the EU'. COM(2008)513 final. EUR-Lex.

———. 2010a. 'EUROPE 2020 - A Strategy for Smart, Sustainable and Inclusive Growth'. COM(2010)2020. EUR-Lex.

———. 2010b. 'A Digital Agenda for Europe'. COM(2010)245 final. EUR-Lex.

———. 2011. 'Commission Recommendation of 27 October 2011 on the Digitisation and Online Accessibility of Cultural Material and Digital Preservation'. OJ L 283/39. EUR-Lex.

———. 2014. 'Towards an Integrated Approach to Cultural Heritage for Europe'. COM(2014)0477 final. EUR-Lex.

Council. 1983 - European Council. 1983. 'Solemn Declaration on the European Union'. Bull. EC 6-1983.

———. 2000. 'Presidency Conclusions on the Lisbon European Council'. European Council.

Europeana. 2010. 'Strategic Plan 2011-2015'. pro.europeana.

———. 2014. '2014 Business Plan'. Den Haag: Europeana Foundation.

———. 2015. 'The More You Give, the More You Get. Europeana Publishing Framework'. pro.europeana.

———. 2016. 'Europeana Dataset Profile'. pro.europeana.

———. 2017. 'Definition of the Europeana Data Model v.5.2.8'. pro.europeana.

———. 2020. 'Welcome to Europeana'. 2020. https://www.europeana.eu/en.

EuropeanaTech. 2015 - EuropeanaTech Task Force. 2015. 'Enriching Europeana: New EuropeanaTech Task Force Report'. pro.europeana. 30 October 2015.

Foka, Anna. 2019. 'Women's (in) Visibility: In the Carl Sahlin Archive'. In *Digitala Modeller: Teknikhistoria Och Digitaliseringens Specificitet*, 95–106. Lund: Lund University Tekniska Museet.

Forte, Maurizio. 2003. 'Mindscape: Ecological Thinking, Cyber-Anthropology and Virtual Archaeological Landscapes'. *BAR International Series*, no. 1151: 95–108.

Geismar, Haidy. 2018. *Museum Object Lessons in the Digital Age.* London: UCL Press.

Gitelman, Lisa, ed. 2013. *'Raw Data' Is an Oxymoron.* Infrastructures Series. Cambridge, Massachusetts; London, England: The MIT Press.

Gradmann, Stefan. 2010. 'Knowledge = Information in Context'. White paper.

Gradmann, Stefan, Makx Dekkers, and Carlo Meghini. 2009. 'Europeana Outline Functional Specification For Development of an Operational European Digital Library'. Report.

Haas, Ernst B. 2004. *The Uniting of Europe: Political, Social, and Economic Forces, 1950-1957.* 3rd ed. Contemporary European Politics and Society. Notre Dame, Ind: University of Notre Dame Press.

Hall, Stuart. 2001. 'Constituting an Archive'. *Third Text* 15 (54): 89–92.

Harrison, Rodney. 2013. *Heritage: Critical Approaches.* 1. publ. London: Routledge.

Haslhofer, Bernhard, and Wolfgang Klas. 2010. 'A Survey of Techniques for Achieving Metadata Interoperability'. *ACM Computing Surveys* 42 (2): 7:1–7:37.

Haynes, David. 2018. *Metadata for Information Management and Retrieval: Understanding Metadata and Its Use.* Second edition. London: Facet Publishing.

Hodder, Ian. 1999. *The Archaeological Process: An Introduction.* Oxford: Blackwell.

Howkins, John. 2001. *The Creative Economy: How People Make Money from Ideas.*

IASA. 2009 - IASA Technical Committee. 2009. *Guidelines on the Production and Preservation of Digital Audio Objects.* Edited by Kevin Bradley.

Isaac, Antoine, and Robina Clayphan. 2013. 'Europeana Data Model Primer'. pro.europeana.

Kofler, Angelika. 1998. 'Digital Europe 1998: Policies, Technological Development and Implementation of the Emerging Information Society'. *Innovation: The European Journal of Social Science Research* 11 (1): 53–71.

Kroes, Neelie. 2012. 'Learning through Technology; Learning about Technology'. SPEECH/12/70. EC - Press Releases.

Lähdesmäki, Tuuli. 2012. 'Rhetoric of Unity and Cultural Diversity in the Making of European Cultural Identity'. *International Journal of Cultural Policy* 18 (1): 59–75.

———. 2014a. 'Transnational Heritage in the Making: Strategies for Narrating Cultural Heritage as European in the Intergovernmental Initiative of the European Heritage Label'. *Journal of European Ethnology* 44: 75–83.

———. 2014b. 'The EU'S Explicit and Implicit Heritage Politics'. *European Societies* 16 (3): 401–21.

———. 2018. 'Founding Myths of European Union Europe and the Workings of Power in the European Union Heritage and History Initiatives'. *European Journal of Cultural Studies* 22 (5-6): 781-798.

Lähdesmäki, Tuuli, Viktorija L. A. Čeginskas, Sigrid Kaasik-Krogerus, Katja Mäkinen, and Johanna Turunen. 2020. *Creating and Governing Cultural Heritage in the European Union: The European Heritage Label*. Routledge.

Liikanen, Erkki. 2001. 'EEurope - An Information Society for All'. SPEECH/01/180. European Commission - PRESS RELEASES.

Littoz-Monnet, Annabelle. 2007. *The European Union and Culture: Between Economic Regulation and European Cultural Policy*. Manchester University Press.

———. 2012. 'Agenda-Setting Dynamics at the EU Level: The Case of the EU Cultural Policy'. *Journal of European Integration* 34 (5): 505–22.

Loukissas, Yanni Alexander. 2017. 'Taking Big Data Apart: Local Readings of Composite Media Collections'. *Information, Communication & Society* 20 (5): 651–64.

Manovich, Lev. 2001. *The Language of New Media*. Cambridge, Mass: MIT Press.

McDonough, Jerome P. 2006. 'METS: Standardized Encoding for Digital Library Objects'. *International Journal on Digital Libraries* 6 (2): 148–58.

McKenna, Gordon, Stefan Rohde-Enslin, and Regine Stein. 2011. *Lightweight Information Describing Objects (Lido): The International Harvesting Standard for Museums*. Rome.

Olson, H. A. 2002. *The Power to Name: Locating the Limits of Subject Representation in Libraries*. Springer Netherlands.

'OpenUp!' 2020. Opening up the Natural History Heritage for Europeana. 2020. http://open-up.eu/en.

Patel, Kiran Klaus, ed. 2014. *The Cultural Politics of Europe: European Capitals of Culture and European Union since 1980s*. Routledge/UACES Contemporary European Studies 24. London: Routledge.

Peroni, Silvio, Francesca Tomasi, and Fabio Vitali. 2013. 'Reflecting on the Europeana Data Model'. In *Digital Libraries and Archives*, edited by Maristella Agosti, Floriana Esposito, Stefano Ferilli, and Nicola Ferro, 228–40. Communications in Computer and Information Science. Berlin, Heidelberg: Springer.

Petrešin-Bachelez, Nataša, ed. 2015. *Decolonising Museums*. L'internationale.

Pitti, Daniel V. 1999. 'Encoded Archival Description: An Introduction and Overview'. *New Review of Information Networking* 5 (1): 61–69.

Presner, Todd. 2010. 'Digital Humanities 2.0: A Report on Knowledge'. In *Emerging Disciplines: Shaping New Fields of Scholarly Inquiry in and Beyond the Humanities*. Rice University Press.

Purday, Jon. 2009. 'Think Culture: Europeana.eu from Concept to Construction'. *The Electronic Library*, November.

Riley, Jenn. 2017. *Understanding Metadata: What Is Metadata, and What Is It For?*

Risam, Roopika. 2019. *New Digital Worlds: Postcolonial Digital Humanities in Theory, Praxis, and Pedagogy*. Evanston, Illinois: Northwestern University Press.

Sassatelli, Monica. 2002. 'Imagined Europe: The Shaping of a European Cultural Identity Through EU Cultural Policy'. *European Journal of Social Theory* 5 (4): 435–51.

———. 2006. 'The Logic of Europeanizing Cultural Policy'. In *Transcultural Europe: Cultural Policy in a Changing Europe*, edited by Ulrike Hanna Meinhof and Anna Triandafyllidou, 24–42. London: Palgrave Macmillan UK.

Schlesinger, Philip. 2017. 'The Creative Economy: Invention of a Global Orthodoxy'. *Innovation: The European Journal of Social Science Research* 30 (1): 73–90.

Senier, Siobhan. 2014. 'Decolonizing the Archive: Digitizing Native Literature with Students and Tribal Communities'. *Resilience: A Journal of the Environmental Humanities* 1 (3).

Shore, Cris. 2000. *Building Europe: The Cultural Politics of European Integration*. London ; New York: Routledge.

Simon, Nina. 2010. *The Participatory Museum*. Santa Cruz, California: Museum 2.0.

Smith, Laurajane. 2006. *Uses of Heritage*. 1 ed. London: Routledge.

Stiller, Juliane, Antoine Isaac, and Vivien Petras. 2014. 'EuropeanaTech Task Force on a Multilingual and Semantic Enrichment Strategy: Final Report'. Europeana. pro.europeana.

Swedberg, Richard. 1994. 'The Idea of "Europe" and the Origin of the European Union – A Sociological Approach'. *Zeitschrift Für Soziologie* 23 (5): 378–387.

SPA. 1911 - Swedish Photographers' Association. 1911. *Förteckning Öfver Sveriges Fotografer 1911*. Stockholm: Svenska fotografernas förbund.

Thylstrup, Nanna Bonde. 2018. *The Politics of Mass Digitization*. Cambridge, MA: The MIT Press.

Tretter, Eliot. 2011. 'The "Value" of Europe: The Political Economy of Culture in the European Community'. *Geopolitics* 16 (4): 926–48.

Valtysson, Bjarki. 2020. *Digital Cultural Politics: From Policy to Practice*. New Directions in Cultural Policy Research. Palgrave Macmillan.

Wallace, David A., Wendy M. Duff, Renée Saucier, and Andrew Flinn, eds. 2020. *Archives, Record-Keeping and Social Justice*. New York: Routledge.

White, Hollie C. 2018. 'Decolonizing the Way Libraries Organize'. In IFLA-WILK2018, 13.

'Wikidata'. 2020. https://www.wikidata.org/wiki/Wikidata:Main_Page.

Wilkinson, Mark D., Michel Dumontier, IJsbrand Jan Aalbersberg, Gabrielle Appleton, Myles Axton, Arie Baak, Niklas Blomberg, et al. 2016. 'The FAIR Guiding Principles for Scientific Data Management and Stewardship'. *Scientific Data* 3 (1): 160018.

Yúdice, George. 2003. *The Expediency of Culture: Uses of Culture in the Global Era*. Post-Contemporary Interventions. Durham, NC: Duke Univ. Press.

Zeinstra, Maarten. 2019. 'Research Report – Returning Commons Community Metadata Additions and Corrections to Source''. Stockholm: Swedish National Heritage Board.

Paradata in Documentation Standards and Recommendations for Digital Archaeological Visualisations

Lisa Börjesson, Olle Sköld, Isto Huvila

Abstract

Digitalisation of research data and massive efforts to make it findable, accessible, interoperable, and reusable has revealed that in addition to an eventual lack of description of the data itself (metadata), data reuse is often obstructed by the lack of information about the data-making and interpretation (i.e. paradata). In search of the extent and composition of categories for describing processes, this article reviews a selection of standards and recommendations frequently referred to as useful for documenting archaeological visualisations. It provides insight into 1) how current standards can be employed to document provenance and processing history (i.e. paradata), and 2) what aspects of the processing history can be made transparent using current standards and which aspects are pushed back or hidden. The findings show that processes are often either completely absent or only partially addressed in the standards. However, instead of criticising standards for bias and omissions as if a perfect description of everything would be attainable, the findings point to the need for a comprehensive consideration of the space a standard is operating in (e.g. national heritage administration or international harmonisation of data). When a standard is used in a specific space it makes particular processes, methods, or tools transparent. Given these premises, if the standard helps to document what needs to be documented (e.g. paradata), and if it provides a type of transparency required in a certain space, it is reasonable to deem the standard good enough for that purpose.

Keywords: Archaeology, FAIR, Heritage Data, Metadata, Paradata, Provenance, Standards, Transparency, Visualisations

Introduction

Archaeology and cultural heritage preservation are heterogeneous disciplines. Global, local, formal and informal metadata standards and efforts to establish new standards hold them together and regulate activities from fieldwork documentation (e.g. Archaeology Data Service and Digital Antiquity, 2009-), to architectural reconstructions and visualisations (e.g. López et al., 2018), and virtualisation of heritage environments and intangible history (Papadopoulos and Schreibman, 2019). While many standardisation initiatives have focused on description of archaeological information objects like geographic datasets or visualisations, both archaeological (Bentkowska-Kafel and Denard, 2012; Richards-Rissetto and von Schwerin, 2017) and transdisciplinary (Pasquetto et al., 2019) research emphasise the parallel importance of documenting how these information objects were created. As a complement and in parallel to 'metadata', archaeologists dealing with visual data are increasingly using the term paradata to denote the provenance and processing history of visual objects. The term paradata is commonly used of data that aims to provide transparency of the operational and intellectual processes preceding image creation (Sköld et al., work in progress; Bentkowska-Kafel and Denard, 2012). "Naive" use of the term paradata has been criticised (Havemann, 2012), i.e. an assumption that paradata can give an exhaustive account of provenance and processing imparting a digital representation as neutral "redo property". In parallel, the absence and need of standards and comprehensive guidelines for documenting paradata has been recognised as a problem (Niccolucci, 2012; Borrero and Stroth, 2020). Even if no data description can recount all details, well-structured process descriptions are vital to maintaining insight into the production of visualisations. However, considering that several existing heritage visualisation-related standards and recommendations stipulate documentation of paradata-like information to a varying degree and extent, a question arises of what they do as they are clearly not deemed good or comprehensive enough.

To increase the understanding of how contemporary documentation schemes represent paradata, this article reviews a selection of major standards and recommendations frequently referred to as useful for documenting archaeological visualisations in search of how they document processes i.e. make explicit and implicit stipulations relating to paradata. The article inquires into what process descriptions the standards support, how processes are represented, and what space i.e. context the standards are encompassing. Building on the long tradition of critical and practical knowledge organisation research in information science, a critical close reading (DuBois, 2003) of a selection of documentation schemes in this article has two aims. First, it aims to provide insight into (1) how current standards can be employed to document provenance and processing history (i.e. paradata) to inform (as urged by Hansson et al., 2020) the development of existing and new metadata and paradata standards, and second, to attain a (2) critical understanding of what aspects of the processing history can be made transparent using the reviewed standards, and which aspects are pushed back or hidden.

Politics of metadata and paradata

A long line of earlier research has investigated the political nature of organising and describing knowledge (Leazer and Montoya, 2020). This subsumes also the creation of metadata and paradata, and the development and use of related standards. In contrast to the currently unpopular epistemic aspirations to neutral and universal description of knowledge, contemporary research, especially from the 1990s onwards, has disclosed the implicit and explicit subjectivity of any attempts to describe and organise knowledge (Smiraglia, 2014). Especially Olson's (e.g. 1994; 2002) groundbreaking work played a key role in uncovering bias and marginalising effects of knowledge organisation systems exposed the politics of organising knowledge and paved the way to study intersectionality in information and knowledge organisation and description (Fox, 2016). As the studies of folksonomies show (Adler, 2009; Gartner, 2016), even seemingly factual or neutral, open and 'democratic' schemes of organising knowledge are political (Hjørland, 2020), and follow the logic of the politics of formalism outlined by Star (1995): they are abstractions, simplifications, and incorporate choices of what is important and what can be discarded. Such formal arrangements can support existing practices but they have also capability to upgrade and redefine the socio-technical infrastructure of activities (Millerand and Bowker, 2008) with very real consequences (Moncrieffe and Eyben, 2007).

Beyond the generic factors outlined by Star (1995), there are several practical reasons why knowledge organisation systems, including metadata and paradata schemes, exercise their politics as they do. One is that language (in a broad sense cf. e.g.Manovich, 2001) is political. Even if concrete aspects of things tend to be less controversial to describe than abstract ones, it is difficult to find words that are and would remain neutral and reasonably resilient to change (Radio, 2018). The contemporary tendencies to mix different descriptive facets in metadata schemes (Gnoli, 2012; Radio, 2018) complicates the matter even further by obscuring what aspects of things are described.

Another parallel factor is the contextuality of all metadata and paradata. Contextuality pertains both to how knowledge organisation schemes often describe domain-specific matters and discourses (Szostak et al., 2016), and how different types of data (Jansson, 2018) and descriptive schemes themselves are contextual and incommensurate with each other (Jansson and Huvila, 2019). Further, the intended and potential scope of metadata or paradata is not necessarily understood well enough. For instance, personal descriptions of things are not necessarily meant to inform others (Feinberg, 2011). Moreover, descriptions are produced with different objectives in mind. Textbooks (e.g. Foulonneau and

Riley, 2008; Haynes, 2018; Gartner, 2016; Smiraglia, 2014) enumerate typically a fairly standard set of purposes for metadata, including resource identification and description, information retrieval, information resource management, management of information rights, supporting learning, research and working with information. Haynes (2018) introduces information governance as an additional category. The comparisons of folksonomies, and formal classification and indexing systems have made it more apparent than ever (e.g. Jansson, 2018; Adler, 2009) that similarly to how individuals and groups of users have different metadata (and paradata) needs (Hu et al., 2019), the explicit and implicit purposes of producing and using particular descriptors and descriptive schemes have repercussions on what is described and how.

As the unfolding of the 'hows' of how knowledge organisation systems exercise their politics inevitably indicates, the politics of paradata has repercussions beyond the technical viability of standards and descriptors. It also ties into the ethics, power and ownership of resources. Considering the intricacy and complexity of influences different actors, including institutions and individuals, have on practices of description and documentation (e.g. Mayernik, 2015; Bates, 2018), the key questions are who gets to organise and describe, who pays for the work, who gets access to the descriptions and who benefits from them. Moreover, an additional, equally relevant question is who owns the space that the paradata is meant to describe and who gets to decide how the descriptive standards are developed and put to use (Haynes, 2018).

Documentation of archaeological visualisations

Before engaging with standards and recommendations relevant to archaeological visualisations, we give a brief overview of archaeological visualisations, their documentation and role in archaeological work.

Different types of visualisations – site drawings, maps, plans, photographs, object illustrations, physical and digital models – have always been central to archaeological documentation and dissemination of knowledge (Moser, 2012; Watterson, 2015). Similarly, the acts of producing images and visualising from map making, drawing and photography to modelling have been at the heart of archaeological knowledge making (Morgan and Wright, 2018). Images and visualisations have a major impact on the knowledge about (pre-)history. Since it is not always possible to see or feel archaeological remains in person, an image can become, in a sense, more real than what it represents (Moser, 2012).

Many archaeological visualisations, whether they are 3D models (Champion, 2018) or other visual artefacts, lack both descriptive metadata and process information (Piccoli, 2017). The attention to different types of visual information has also been somewhat unevenly distributed in the literature. Spatial information and 3D has been discussed more than many other forms of visualisations such as drawings or photographs (Huvila, 2019; Morgan and Wright, 2018). The general intricacy of describing visual material (Lim and Liew, 2011; Huvila, 2019) and the difficulty to align different metadata schemes and descriptive needs to each other (von Schwerin et al., 2016) pertains also to archaeological visualisations. Another problem is the uneven availability and slow emergence of guidelines and metadata schemes for describing visual artefacts (Huvila, 2017).

The particular relevance of paradata for archaeological visualisation stems from that the insights developed during the process of creating visualisations can be more important than the final product (Morgan, 2009). The rapid development and proliferation of new, especially digital methods adds to the importance of documenting not only what but also why and how (Edmond and Morselli, 2020). Paradata can help to understand what was done and how (Richards-Rissetto and von Schwerin, 2017; Edmond and Morselli, 2020), make projects and their outcomes sustainable (Edmond and Morselli, 2020), and verify hypotheses and the authenticity of models (Kastanis, 2019), and contribute to "informed, critical and qualified interpretation" (Ogleby, 2007). A parallel question to the need of paradata, is how and in which form it should be preserved. As a form of processual information, (Agrifoglio, 2015) paradata can be difficult to capture and document. Proposed approaches range from writing free text narratives, producing annotations, developing virtual research environments and using information visualisation (Richards-Rissetto and von Schwerin, 2017), to 3D scholarly editions (Papadopoulos and Schreibman, 2019), video diaries (Hodder, 2000), written reports (de Kleijn et al., 2016) and formal modelling of intellectual and argumentative processes (Doerr and LeBoeuf, 2007; Marlet et al., 2019). At the same time, the digitalisation of archaeological practices has invigorated the earlier interest in standardisation and formal description of archaeological reasoning and workflows (e.g. Ogleby, 2007; Giovannini, 2018; Kastanis, 2019 cf. e.g. Gardin, 1980).

Besides the formats of descriptions, opinions diverge also on whether the best approach to improve the quality of documentation is to provide guidance or to increase standardisation. Studies of archaeological metadata confirm that the level of standardisation of descriptions and vocabulary is low especially between, but to a certain extent also within, investigation projects (e.g. Pavel, 2010; Oikarinen and Kortelainen, 2013; Henninger, 2018). There have been recurrent calls for increased standardisation (e.g. Quintero and Eppich, 2016; Gunnarsson, 2020) and specific new standards (e.g. Ogleby, 2007; Bendicho, 2013). In parallel, however, others argue that the complexity of the heritage field, its interdisciplinary and rapid development means that standards become too rapidly obsolete (Addison, 2007).

A parallel problem to obsolescence and finding a balance between too much and too little standardisation (e.g. Huvila, 2012) is that standards are not always implemented and used consequently (e.g. Molenda, 2020; Maron and Feinberg, 2018) and according to directives. Moreover, creating metadata takes is also often more time-consuming than anticipated and it requires skills both in the subject matter (Rejdovianova et al., 2018) and subject description (Llebot and Tuyl, 2019).

Standards for documenting archaeological visualisations

As noted earlier in this article, the existing standards and recommendations pertaining to archaeological visualisations make occasional, albeit as a whole, somewhat unsystematic references to the documentation of paradata. After reviewing current major standards and recommendations, we identified three broad categories of such references: 1) charters and recommendations, 2) metadata schemes and standards, and 3) conceptual models, exemplified here by CIDOC Conceptual Reference Model (CIDOC-CRM) and its extensions. The following three sections describe these categories before the text proceeds to explicate what and how the standards aim to standardise and how they represent processes.

Charters and recommendations

Much of the standardisation of archaeological visualisations conducted outside of individual organisations and information management systems has happened through charters and recommendations. *The Venice Charter on the Conservation and Restoration of Monuments and Sites* from 1964 notes that "all works of preservation, restoration or excavation" need to be documented in "analytical and critical reports, illustrated with drawings and photographs" including a documentation of "[e]very stage of the work of clearing, consolidation, rearrangement and integration, as well as technical and formal features identified during the course of the work" (Gazzola et al., 1964). Even if the text does not instruct how drawings and photographs should be produced or documented, it suggests that some types of drawings and photographs are a part of the apparatus of "analytical and critical" documentation of sites and monuments. Comparable general formulations on the role of illustrations can be found in several of the charters issued by the International Council on Monuments and Sites (ICOMOS) relating to conservation and restoration of sites and monuments (Petzet and Ziesemer, 2004).

Two recent documents originating from two international working groups, *the London Charter* (Denard, 2013) and *Seville Principles* (or the International Guidelines for Virtual Archaeology, International Forum of Virtual Archaeology, 2011; Bendicho, 2013) have focused specifically on computer-based archaeological and heritage documentation and visualisations. The objectives of the London Charter include an aim to "[e]nsure that computer-based visualisation processes and outcomes can be properly understood and evaluated by users" (The London Charter Organisation, 2009). The Seville Principles underlines similarly the importance of "scientific transparency" i.e. how visualisations need to be testable and confirmable or falsifiable by others. The document adds that "the incorporation of metadata and paradata is crucial to ensure scientific transparency of any virtual archaeology project. Paradata and metadata should be clear, concise and easily available. Besides, it should provide as much information as possible. The scientific community should contribute with international standardization of metadata and paradata" (International Forum of Virtual Archaeology, 2011).

A fourth document, *ICOMOS Charter for the Interpretation and Presentation of Cultural Heritage Sites* (Silberman, 2008) notes that "the information sources on which [..] visual renderings are based should be clearly documented and alternative reconstructions based on the same evidence, when available, should be provided for comparison" and that "[i]nterpretation and presentation programmes and activities should also be documented and archived for future reference and reflection" (Silberman, 2008, 8). Here can also be mentioned the manifest (Frischer et al., 2002) for a Cultural Virtual Reality Organization (CVRO), a proposed organisation to, among other issues, develop "aesthetic, scientific, and technical standards for cultural virtual reality models" and a common "philology", or conventions and semantics, for metadata on archaeological 3D visualisations. Photography and drawings lack similar charters, conceivably at least partly because of the longer history of these media types that precedes the era of cultural heritage charters.

Similarly to other charters in the cultural field (Luxen, 2004), all of the above mentioned charters are open to multiple interpretations. Moreover, they overlap with each other and provide only limited practical guidance. For example, none of the texts goes into specific detail in what metadata items should be included to achieve the desired level of documentation. Perhaps unsurprisingly, as Sköld et al. (work in progress) show, the references to the charters have a tendency to remain as fairly generic and the proposed means to implement them vary considerably. At the same time, the charters are empathetically political documents, or as Wells (2007) remarks, discursive acts, that construct very particular types of significances in that their focus is on describing a desirable future state of affairs rather than providing technical guidance.

Besides the collective efforts to write charters, several individual authors have produced lists of technical and policy recommendations based on their practical or scholarly work. There is a relatively comprehensive body of literature on archaeological illustration with such advice (incl. Dorrell, 1994; Adkins and Adkins, 1989; Baltsavias, 2006) – even if as Morgan and Wright (2018) justly remark that despite its central role in archaeological work, visual media is often marginalised in archaeological contexts. A part of these recommendations enumerate principles of how visualisations should be documented whereas others advocate for the adoption of specific standards (e.g. for photographs, Atarashi et al. 2000; Toffalori 2016, or spatial data, Shaw et al. 2009; McKeague et al. 2020, 2019). Champion (2018) suggests that an infrastructure for virtual heritage models should provide documentation of 1) data accuracy, 2) format limitations (i.e. known limitations of used digital formats), 3) provenance, 4) community protocols (who gets to access the material and who decides), 5) authenticity, 6) cultural presence (cultural significance and value of the original site or artefact), 7) evaluation data, and the 8) purpose of creating a model. In addition to dedicated texts, comparable recommendations can be found in the extensive archaeological handbook literature (e.g. Corsi et al., 2016; Barratt, 2016; Dorrell, 1994; Drewett, 1999).

Metadata schemes and standards

Despite the asserted importance of adequate well-structured metadata, only a few general, widely adopted standards specific to archaeological visualisations exist. This is especially obvious when compared to the general profusion of metadata standards in the cultural field (cf. Skinner, 2014).

Many popular standards used to describe archaeological visualisations cover archaeology and heritage, and its digital and non-digital representations in broader terms, or focus on the documentation of heritage rather than its representations (e.g. Toffalori, 2016; Ryan, 2001; Signore, 2009; Aloia et al., 2017b). Many archaeological repositories use also generic standards, such as the Dublin Core metadata framework (e.g. Miller, 1999; Atarashi et al., 2000; Kulasekaran et al., 2014) for documenting digital objects, popular geoinformation standards (De Roo et al., 2013; Shaw et al., 2009) for spatial data, and various schemes for documenting cultural work, such as Getty vocabularies (Baca and Gill, 2015), the British museum documentation standard SPECTRUM (McKenna and Patsatzi, 2007), the Categories for the Description of the Works of Art (Harpring, 2019), and the Visual Resources Association (VRA) Core (Library of Congress, 2014) standard for the description of works of visual culture and images that document them. The Cataloging Cultural Objects: A Guide to Describing Cultural Works and Their Images (CCO) (Baca et al., 2006) specifies a guideline for compiling a cataloguing record that can be implemented in standardised metadata schemes such as Dublin Core or VRA CORE.

Many of the archaeology specific metadata specifications, for instance, the British MIDAS (English Heritage, 2012) and Italian PICO (Scuola Normale Superiore di Pisa, 2007, 2011), are national standards and related to country-specific sites and monuments records (Ronzino et al., 2013). Some others are best characterised as proposals, such as the Cultural Heritage Markup Language (CHML), a formal language developed for documenting 3D reconstructions and reconstruction processes (Hauck and Kuroczyński, 2015), CHARM, a conceptual model of visual representation (Gonzalez-Perez et al., 2012; Apollonio and Giovannini, 2015), and the Extended Matrix/Framework (EM and EMF) for formal documentation of scientific processes underpinning archaeological virtual reconstructions (Demetrescu and Fanini, 2017). The large majority of the schemes are, however, developed and adopted by individual projects and repositories (Richards, 2009; McKeague et al., 2019; Carlisle and Lee, 2016). Despite the on-going standardisation work, influences that traverse from project and country to another (e.g. as vividly described in the work of Pavel, 2010), and occasional links to recommendations, charters and earlier standards (e.g. Dieckmann et al., 2010; von Schwerin et al., 2016), archaeological documentation practices have been described for a good reason as parochial (Aitchison, 2017) rather than highly standardised.

Despite the prevalence of local variation, there are examples of successful archaeology-related metadata standardisation initiatives. One of them, explicitly described as successful (Champion, 2018), is the CARARE metadata scheme (Fernie et al., 2013). It is based (Fernie et al., 2013) on the British MIDAS heritage documentation standard (English Heritage, 2012), CIDOC-CRM (Doerr et al., 2007), Europeana Data Model (EDM) and CIDOC LIDO (Coburn et al., 2010) metadata harvesting scheme. Rather than being a foundational metadata scheme, it was developed for facilitating metadata aggregation to Europeana with a focus on collections rather than individual items (Papatheodorou et al., 2011). The ARIADNE catalogue model is another scheme describable as an interoperability standard with an explicit aim of bridging between local content standards. It was developed for the ARIADNE infrastructure to facilitate metadata aggregation relating to archaeological collections and focuses on resource-level metadata and authorship (publisher, creator, owner, responsible). While ARIADNE focuses on archaeological data, the broadly speaking comparable PARTHENOS Registry Data Model has a broader scope. It aims to bridge infrastructures and builds on existing standards in linguistics, humanities, heritage, history, archaeology and related fields including such generic registry standards as W3C DCAT and ISOCat, and schemes implemented by, for instance, CLARIN, META-SHARE, EHRI, LRE MAP, DARIAH, and CENDARI (Aloia et al., 2017b) projects. The resulting semantic framework, the PARTHENOS Entities, functions as a target data model for mapping metadata from multiple source infrastructures (Durco et al., 2018).

Many of the internationally influential standards are similar in that they focus on archaeological sites and monuments and their representations beyond visualisations. Many of them are interoperability schemes rather than content standards that echoes the shift of general focus in standardisation from aspirations to develop global documentation schemes to data interoperability and aggregation (e.g. Richards, 2009; Doerr et al., 2007; Aloia et al., 2017a) and mappings between different local standards and schemes (e.g. Meghini et al., 2017). As Richards (2009) points out, this does not, however, imply that a certain level of agreement on content level descriptions would not be necessary.

In addition to the published standards, the literature contains many proposals and enumerations of desirable metadata elements. A widely cited collection of guidelines is the Guides to Good Practice published by the UK-based Archaeology Data Service (ADS) in collaboration with the US-based Digital Archaeological Record (tDAR) (Archaeology Data Service and Digital Antiquity, 2009-). Others include, for instance, Addison's (2007) suggestion to include information on recording device parameters, data manipulation devices, environmental conditions, submitter, author and sponsor, date and location of data capture in virtual heritage metadata. Moreover, there is a sundry recommendations and proposals of metadata schemes developed and implemented for specific archives or repositories (e.g. Polig, 2017; Ryan, 2001; von Schwerin et al., 2016).

Unsurprisingly, considering the ambiguity of views regarding the standardisation of archaeological documentation, the existing schemes have not avoided critique. Much of the critique focuses, however, either on details, or is expressed as a generic criticism of the limits of standardisation. For instance, Champion (2018) argues that the CARARE standard lacks an element for describing the cultural significance of documented assets included in his own list of recommendations, and explicit consideration of indigenous perspectives. Another comparable point of critique is the preferred naming of metadata elements (Hu et al., 2019) and the (lack of) consistency of how they are used (e.g. Carlisle and Lee, 2016).

Conceptual models: CIDOC-CRM and extensions

The third category of standards for the documentation of archaeological visualisations is conceptual models. Due to the dominant position of the CIDOC Conceptual Reference Model (CIDOC-CRM) in archaeology and heritage, it is used in the following to exemplify this category. CIDOC-CRM is a formal ontology (in the sense of Guarino, 1999) developed under the auspices of International Committee for Documentation (CIDOC) of the International Council of Museums (ICOM) to facilitate data exchange in the cultural heritage domain. The model defines relationships rather than terms to support integrating existing and future metadata structures and data schemes (Doerr et al., 2007). The version 1.0 of the CRM (Crofts et al., 1998) based on CIDOC information categories (Grant et al., 1995) was published in 1998. A standardisation process was started in 2000 and the model was accepted in 2006 as an ISO standard ISO21127:2006 (Doerr et al., 2007).

As the aim of CIDOC-CRM is to function as a general ontology of the cultural heritage sector, it has been complemented during the years with extensions to cover more specific aspects of heritage, including archaeological excavations (CRMarchaeo, Doerr et al., 2018), provenance metadata (CRMdig Theodoridou et al., 2010; Doerr et al., 2016), cross-research-infrastructure metadata (CRMpe Bruseker et al., 2017b), metadata about scientific observation, measurements and processed data in descriptive and empirical sciences (CRMsci, Doerr et al., 2014), about argumentation and inference making in descriptive and empirical sciences (CRMinf, Stead and Doerr, 2015), and ancient textual editions (CRMtex, Doerr et al., 2020).

Close to how paradata is defined in the literature, Niccolucci and Felicetti (2018) propose a combination of CRMsci, CRMdig and CRMpe for documenting heritage science i.e. scientific activities in support of conservation, access and interpretation of cultural heritage. Guillem and colleagues (2015) put forward a comparable CIDOC-CRM based scheme for documenting reconstruction and reconstruction-related argumentation processes, and Amico et al. (2013), a combination of CIDOC-CRM and CRMdig to document the planning and creation of 3D models of cultural objects for quality management purposes.

Many ontologies and documentation schemes (e.g. Aloia et al., 2017a; Henninger, 2018; Felicetti et al., 2013; Marlet et al., 2019) from different heritage-related disciplines has been mapped into CIDOC-CRM (Moraitou et al., 2018). The model has also been used as a basis for developing new ones (e.g. Padfield et al., 2019; Giovannini, 2018; Moraitou et al., 2018; Felicetti et al., 2013). Moraitou and colleagues note that the current proliferation of extensions and alternative mappings means that it is possible to select the most useful semantic representations among several options. They argue that this can improve the quality of preserved information and facilitate its reuse. At the same time, the burgeoning of alternatives means that it is both more difficult and important to have an overview of available options (Moraitou et al., 2018).

Formal ontologies such as the CIDOC-CRM have multiple benefits when compared to protocol-based knowledge organisation systems such as metadata schemes (Bruseker et al., 2017a). Even if they do not *per se* solve the intricacies of describing and naming things, they can improve machine readability of descriptions and the transparency of ontological assumptions of how concepts are related to each other. The typical critique of CIDOC-CRM and formal ontologies tend to relate to their complexity and the inconsistencies in how they are interpreted and applied in practice (e.g. Bruseker et al., 2017a; Nussbaumer and Haslhofer, 1999, also e.g. Peponakis, 2012).

Processes in the standards

After a brief review of major categories of standards and recommendations relevant to archaeological visualisations, we proceed to inquire into how processes are represented in a selection of these guidelines (for the sake of simplicity, referred hereafter collectively as 'standards'). In comparison to dedicated standards for representing scientific processes like CERIF (Jörg et al., 2012) and OBOE (Madin et al., 2007) and comparable discipline-specific schemes (e.g. Niccolucci and Felicetti, 2018), the above reviewed archaeological standards engage with processes on multiple levels of specificity. The Table 1 synthesises observations on a set of standards and guidelines pertinent to archaeological visualisations, how they engage politically with processes and what means they provide for documenting processes in the form of paradata categories. As a limitation, it is necessary to emphasise that the selection does not cover all conceivable standards or guidelines that could be used for the purpose. The review is also limited to providing an overview of the general approach of the standard rather than a detailed list of all metadata elements or options. In spite of these provisions, we argue that the enumeration provides a useful glimpse of how contemporary standards and guidelines expound processes. The model for analysis also provides a basis for scrutinising additional schemes and their intrinsic and extrinsic politics.

Table 1: Standards relating to archaeological visualisations and how they engage with process metadata.

Standard or guideline	How processes are represented	What space the standard encompasses	Examples of references to other standards and guidelines
London Charter (The London Charter Organisation, 2009)	Documentation of decisions, development of documentation strategies, sources, paradata, relationships between research sources, implicit knowledge, explicit reasoning, and visualisation-based outcomes, description of methods	Computer-based visualisation methods in research, communication and preservation of cultural heritage	ADS and tDAR Guides to Good Practice, CVRO
Seville Principles (International Forum of Virtual Archaeology, 2011)	Transparent presentation of entire work process: objectives, methodology, techniques, reasoning, origin and characteristics of the sources of research, results and conclusions	Virtual archaeology (refers to The London Charter Organisation, 2009 as a broader charter)	The London Charter
ADS & tDAR Guides to Good Practice (Archaeology Data Service and Digital Antiquity, 2009-)	Project and resource-level documentation and administrative metadata, file-level metadata according to the specific type of visualisation e.g. workflow documentation, creator, instruments, purpose, software and devices, results	Archaeology, especially parties intending to deposit data in ADS or tDAR	Multiple incl. CARARE, CIDOC-CRM (incl. extensions), Dublin Core

Standard or guideline	How processes are represented	What space the standard encompasses	Examples of references to other standards and guidelines
CDWA (Harpring, 2019)	Creator, creation date, place, cultural context of creation, conservation/treatment and condition/examination history, (historical) events associated with the object, critical responses, ownership/collecting, exhibition/loan and cataloguing history	Works of art	E.g. VRA Core, CCO
VRA Core	Incl. agent, cultural context, source, date (of creation, design, production, presentation, performance, construction, or alteration), description, location, relations, techniques	Works of visual culture as well as the images	CDWA, CCO, Dublin Core
EM/EMF (Demetrescu, 2015; Demetrescu and Fanini, 2017)	Schemaless semantic graph (of a reconstruction process)	Virtual reconstructions	E.g. CIDOC-CRM, CHARM (as related work)
CHARM (Gonzalez-Perez et al., 2012; Gonzalez-Perez, 2018)	Performative entities, manifestations, occurrences (activities - processes, actions, projects, tasks)	Cultural heritage	E.g. CIDOC-CRM
CHML (Hauck and Kuroczyński, 2015)	Historic events, research activities	3D reconstructions	Multiple XML-based (incl. RadianceML)

Standard or guideline	How processes are represented	What space the standard encompasses	Examples of references to other standards and guidelines
CARARE (Fernie et al., 2013)	Activities, collections, heritage assets and their constituents and relations to each other	Heritage assets, in version 2.0 compatibility with Europeana Data Model	E.g. MIDAS, CIDOC-CRM, CRMdig, LIDO
CIDOC-CRM (Doerr et al., 2007)	Events (incl. activities) and their constituents and related entities	Integration, mediation and interchange of heterogeneous cultural heritage information (in museum context)	No explicit references in the definition
CRMsci (Doerr et al., 2014)	Activities, alterations, beginnings of existence and their constituents/related entities	Integrating metadata about scientific observation, measurements and processed data in descriptive and empirical sciences	Multiple incl. CIDOC-CRM, OBOE,
CRMinf (Stead and Doerr, 2015)	Activities, alterations, beginnings of existence and their constituents/related entities	Integrating metadata about argumentation and inference making in descriptive and empirical sciences	Multiple incl. CIDOC-CRM, CRMsci

Due to their generic nature, it is not surprising that charters and recommendations often include generic formulations relating to the documentation of processes. The London Charter posits that "[d]ocumentation of the evaluative, analytical, deductive, interpretative and creative decisions made in the course of computer-based visualisation should be disseminated in such a way that the relationship between research sources, implicit knowledge, explicit reasoning, and visualisation-based outcomes can be understood." (The London Charter Organisation, 2009, 8). The document contains comparable provisions on the documentation of methods and development of documentation strategies (The London Charter Organisation, 2009) but even they remain – likely on purpose – on a fairly abstract level to make the document as a whole valid for diverse stakeholder groups (Denard, 2013). The Seville Principles are more specific in that "clear, concise and easily available" internationally standardised metadata and paradata are vital for ensuring scientific transparency. The text refers further to earlier principles on how heritage sites should be documented and to a need to establish an international "database" of exemplary projects (International Forum of Virtual Archaeology, 2011).

Even if metadata standards and schemes tend to focus on objects (Signore, 2009), they provide varying means to represent processes. The ADS and tDAR Guides to Good Practice is a comprehensive document with somewhat varying instructions for the documentation of multiple types of visualisations and visual data. For example, according to guides, the documentation of vector-based graphics should contain information on provenance (origins of the image), software, purpose of creation, conventions used in the document, creator and creation date, whereas the guidelines to document 3D visualisations refer to CARARE and CRMdig standards and description of workflows. In addition to document-specific metadata, the Guides to Good Practice advise to include project and resource, administrative and file-level process metadata (Archaeology Data Service and Digital Antiquity, 2009-). Unlike many others, the CARARE standard incorporates a specific field for provenance information, instructed to be provided as a narrative (Fernie et al., 2013). CCO asks who created the work or what is its culture of origin, where and when it was created and discovered, where it has been located, where it is now, and what tools and techniques and creative activities (e.g. creation, design, execution) were involved (Baca et al., 2006). However, in the majority of the standards and repositories surveyed by the PARTHENOS project, metadata covers authors, agents or owners of collections (Aloia et al., 2017b) following the rationale of describing basic provenance data (creator, date, method, see Bizer et al., 2011) rather than means or expectations to elaborate processes in detail.

A common feature of the standards, independent of their emphasis of actors and contexts (e.g. CCO) or events (as in CENDARI CENDARI WP6, 2013a,b, and VRA CORE, Library of Congress, 2014), is their interest in the historical (e.g. CENDARI, VRA CORE) and curatorial processes (e.g. PICO, CCO) relating to archaeological sites, monuments and objects rather than to their representations. This impression is strengthened by review of cataloguing examples provided as a part of the documentation of the standards.

Ontologies unfold as a third distinct type of standard. Instead of elucidating what counts as significant process-related information, they provide guidance to approaching the ontological question of what is a process and how to represent it. CIDOC-CRM approaches the question through an events-based approach with Temporal Entity and Event hierarchies of classes that are used to represent events and activities. Together with classes referring to persistent items, time-spans, places, dimensions, spacetime volumes and primitive values they can be used to describe processes and their constituents. The core standard with its documentation examples does, much like CENDARI and CVRA CORE, emphasise historical events whereas many of the extensions focus specifically on scholarly processes. The work of, for instance, Guillem et al. (2015) and Niccolucci and Felicetti (2018) show that the model and its extensions provide versatile tools for representing and describing archaeological scholarly processes – including those relating to the making and use of archaeological visualisations.

Discussion

This paper has inquired into a selection of recommendations, metadata schemes and ontologies pertinent to archaeological visualisations and unveiled a heterogeneous array of approaches and perspectives to document their provenance and processing history (i.e. paradata). They all enact a distinct take on the politics of what is important to describe and what can be left out. Both standards and charters have their own politics even if the latter are more explicitly political documents, commonly used as a basis for requirements engineering (Carrillo Gea et al., 2013) or developing standards (as the Seville principles explicitly suggest International Forum of Virtual Archaeology, 2011) – measures that are often experienced as neutral and factual (Bowker and Star, 2000; Star and Lampland, 2009).

To discuss the influence of politics and bias in the reviewed set of documentation standards, we use three criteria: 1) what is standardised i.e. the whatness of the objects they are helping to maintain, 2) what types of spaces the different standards create, and 3) what becomes standardised in the process. The first apparent observation is – considering the lively debate – the relative lack of dedicated standards for documenting archaeological visualisations and their related paradata. This can be perhaps explained partly in terms of the absence of a single domain pertaining to that field (Doerr, 2009; Hjørland and Hartel, 2003) and the consequential, relative lack of consensus on the 'whatness' (Denis, 2018) of archaeological visualisations and the significant aspects of their processing history. As a result, the schemes standardise or make recommendations on the standardisation of widely different aspects of visualisations and their processing history.

A lack of consensus on what archaeological visualisations are, is however, unlikely the only or decisive cause of the diversity. Another, perhaps a more pertinent explanation is the heterogeneity of who develops standards, for whom and for what purpose. Paradata, like metadata, are more likely to be of interest for specialists rather than for an average archaeologist who would probably be more inclined to stress the importance of tools instead (Benardou and Dunning, 2018). The needs and priorities of specific stakeholder groups are visible both in the more openly political recommendations and in the metadata standards that are often formulated in a more neutral, matter-of-factual tone. In infrastructural standards (e.g. CARARE, Guides to Good Practice) the focus is unsurprisingly on digital provenance (Ross, 2018) whereas curatorial standards (e.g. VRA Core, CDWA) put emphasis on the documentation of custodial processes. There is nothing inherently wrong with such emphases but they do make flagrantly visible the contextual and political nature of metadata schemes. In this respect, the calls for increased flexibility (e.g. Löwenborg, 2007) *and* standardisation (e.g. Quintero and Eppich, 2016) do not need to be as contradictory as they are portrayed by their proponents. The key question is how to navigate between standardisation and flexibility (Huvila, 2012) in relation to the purposes of the standards and their users – or what to standardise, and when (and how) to open up for diversity to facilitate specific types of future activities. As a whole, it is important to document the provenance and processing history in more detail and to think increasingly explicitly about who the likely users of information are (e.g. Edmond and Morselli, 2020). Similarly, an increased emphasis on managing the social aspects of archaeological information (Huvila, 2019) is undoubtedly useful – but perhaps even more important than to try to anticipate the future would be to be cognisant of the premises of existing descriptions and their guiding principles. Further, it would be of value to extend this critical awareness to rethinking and describing the theoretical foundations of current and emerging standards and data descriptions as enabling one type of description at one point in time.

A second remark that can be made on the basis of the review is that the standards create widely different spaces of operation. Some of the standards are or have been local to specific systems like particular national sites and monuments records, project databases, or digital libraries like Europeana. Choosing between standards and pairing up with a particular information infrastructure is a political choice (cf. Star, 1995; Hjørland, 2020) with consequences even if it would be backed by seemingly matter-of-factual arguments. Extending the emphasis of Moraitou et al. (2018) of the importance to be aware of CIDOC-CRM and in general of metadata schemes, it is equally important to be cognisant of what type of standards they are: recommendations, metadata or paradata schemes, or conceptual models, and to what type of space they are referring. A standard makes the documentation compliant to and at home in its space in a similar sense how Pétursdóttir (2020) comments the fate of archaeological objects in the teeth of heritage discourse.

A third question to ask a standard is what becomes transparent in the process of standardisation. If a standard is followed to the point – which is not always the case as they embed and are embedded in local practices (Maron and Feinberg, 2018) – it guides to provide a description of a specific perspective to a process rather than the process in its entirety. For example, the most of the reviewed standards represent processes as chains or networks of events and/or activities that essentially turn them to enumerations of distinct actions and incidents rather than, for instance, a continuum. Even when standards, like CRMarchaeo (Doerr et al., 2018), explain that they are neutral to accommodating different traditions and schools of thought, they are still imposing a lot – quoting Hanseth and Monteiro, "in complex and non-transparent ways" (Hanseth and Monteiro, 1997, p. 183). It is not a secret that standards impose perspectives – they are supposed to do so – but it is still worth being aware of how standards and their accompanying regimes not only enable specific trajectories but also constrain them (Fuenfschilling and Binz, 2018). Moreover, as the present review of standards shows, the transparency varies depending on the type of the standard, its intended purpose, and the infrastructural and organisational context where it was developed.

As a whole, the analysis underlines the critical importance to understand standards, what they standardise, for whom, what is their context or space of standardisation and what becomes standardised and what is 'maintained' (Denis, 2018) when they are applied. Understanding metadata as a meshwork rather than a thing becomes increasingly significant in the on-going shift to entity rather than object-based linked metadata (Smith-Yoshimura, 2020) and links to the calls for a critical stance towards "naive" perceptions of paradata (Havemann, 2012) and metadata as complete and permanent representations of data and its processing history. Various strategies have been proposed to remedy the biases and shortcomings of existing catalogues and data descriptions. These include user-generated metadata (Conradi, 2010), automatic annotation (Foley et al., 2017) and, for instance, deliberate correcting of descriptions through 'queering of the catalogue' (Drabinski, 2013). Even if many of the proposed efforts are promising, remedies come easily with their own biases. However, if different types of descriptive data are treated from their distinctive premises (Jansson, 2018) and combined with an adequate understanding of the space where applied data standards are operating and what becomes transparent when they are used, combinations of diverse types of data descriptions can be expected to have real potential to add perspectives (Freund and Butterworth, 2008; Stvilia et al., 2012) to descriptions, and consequently, to contribute to the findability of described assets and the efficiency of information retrieval.

Finally, beyond elucidating what standards are aiming at documenting and where, there is one more question to explore that can provide insights into what is attainable with contemporary documentation standards: who decides what the standards' aims and the spaces of operation are. A partial answer is that it is the standard developing organisations and communities. Currently, a large part of the standardisation effort is in the hands of multinational European projects. Even if the projects tend to be large, with up to hundreds of participating organisations and individuals, and comprehensive outreach programmes, the development is still driven and coordinated by a fairly small number of key actors with many possible voices that might be and are probably missing. In broader terms, metadata (Gartner, 2016) and paradata themselves are ideologies and political promoters of interoperability (DeNardis, 2011) – the desirability that resources are described and identifiable, information is retrievable, manageable and managed, and (re)used for multiple purposes. In a narrower sense, it is worth being observant to disciplinary variants of this broader political idea. In addition to assessing standards imported from neighbouring disciplines in the context where they are applied rather than from the perspective of the discipline of their origin (Huggett, 2013), it is useful to remember that the same should apply to standards developed within a neighbouring archaeological frame of reference. Otherwise a specific activity within archaeology (e.g. landscape archaeology or pottery studies) – and in a broader sense, any borrowing field – risks to become 'colonised' and subject to the politics of another activity (e.g. data curation or spatial analysis) rather than capable of developing their own metadata and paradata policies.

Conclusions

Before concluding remarks, it is appropriate to stress that the purpose of the present analysis was not to evaluate the schemes for eventual shortcomings but to investigate into the politics of paradata and the representation of specific facets of data. It is apparent that the primary concern of most of the reviewed standards is not to document information and data making processes. This explains why processes are often either completely absent or only partially addressed in the schemes and their accompanying documentation. At the same time, however, many of the standards like the CIDOC-CRM and its extensions incorporate structures to represent processual information to an extent that they can effectively substitute dedicated standards (e.g. Niccolucci and Felicetti, 2018). Moreover, as many of the reviewed schemes show, they can be combined with each other to achieve a broader coverage of details.

The analysis also suggests that the inescapably political nature of knowledge organisation deserves to be taken seriously when working with paradata. Instead of agonising that all paradata (and metadata) is biassed, bad and needs to be fixed, it is more important to try to understand the contexts, choices and assumptions that underpin the development of specific descriptive schemes and their practical consequences. Accordingly, as the use of existing metadata (Feinberg, 2017) and paradata, also the use of metadata and paradata schemes should be sensitive to what they are and how they have been developed. If a standard is doing what it was expected to do (assuming that its users are following it to a reasonable degree) – for instance, facilitating information retrieval in a museum context or harmonising data for inclusion in a specific database – it is perhaps good enough and can be used productively – and ethically as Olson (2000) underlines – and does not need to be changed. As Hjørland (2020) reminds, to assume that standards can be corrected is to deny their political nature and to believe that there is an unbiased apolitical master standard to be found.

When considering the practice of documenting the processing history of archaeological visualisations and other data, the present review of standards shows also that there are limits to how far a single standard stretches. The explicit and implicit assumptions on what types of things or processes a standard should standardise, and for what purpose, set limits to its general applicability. A standard for documenting 'activities related to digital reconstructions of cultural heritage artefacts' turns a process into a series of 'activities related to digital reconstructions of cultural heritage artefacts'. Besides the whatness of a standard, a comparable aspect is the space within which the standard is meant to operate and it aims to cover and control, and when put in practice, where it is used. If a standard is developed to cover 'museum knowledge', its politics is geared to the very specific space of museum knowledge even when its outspoken aim would be to aim at a broader scope of relevance. Therefore a final question to ask before embracing a particular standard should be if it can be employed to document what needs to be documented (e.g. paradata), and if it provides the expected type of transparency.

Acknowledgements

We would like to thank two anonymous reviewers and the editors of this special issue for their invaluable comments on earlier versions of this text. This work has received funding from the European Research Council (ERC) under the European Union's Horizon 2020 research and innovation programme grant agreement No 818210 as a part of the project CApturing Paradata for documenTing data creation and Use for the REsearch of the future (CAPTURE).

References

Addison, A. 2007. The vanishing virtual. In *New Heritage*, eds. Y. Kalay, T. Kvan, and J. Afflek, pp. 43–55. London: Routledge.

Adkins, L. and R. Adkins. 1989. *Archaeological illustration*. Cambridge: Cambridge UP.

Adler, M. 2009. Transcending Library Catalogs. *Journal of Web Librarianship* 3 (4):309–331.

Agrifoglio, R. 2015. *Knowledge Preservation Through Community of Practice*. Cham: Springer.

Aitchison, K. 2017. On the outside looking in: What will Brexit mean for European archaeology? *The Historic Environment* 8 (3):194–198.

Aloia, N., , C. Binding, S. Cuy, M. Doerr, B. Fanini, A. Felicetti, J. Fihn, D. Gavrilis, G. Geser, H. Hollander, C. Meghini, F. Niccolucci, F. Nurra, C. Papatheodorou, J. Richards, P. Ronzino, R. Scopigno, M. Theodoridou, D. Tudhope, A. Vlachidis, and H. Wright. 2017 a. Enabling european archaeological research: The ARIADNE e-infrastructure. *Internet Archaeology* (43).

Aloia, N., L. Candela, F. Debole, L. Frosini, M. Lorenzini, and P. Pagano. 2017 b. *PARTHENOS D5.2 Design of the Joint Resource Registry*. Geneve: Zenodo. URL http://dx.doi.org/10.5281/ZENODO.2575450.

Amico, N., P. Ronzino, A. Felicetti, and F. Niccolucci. 2013. Quality management of 3d cultural heritage replicas with CIDOC-CRM. In *Proceedings of the Workshop Practical Experiences with CIDOC CRM and its Extensions, Valetta, Malta, September 26, 2013.*, eds. V. Alexiev, V. Ivanov, and M. Grinberg. URL http://ceur-ws.org/Vol-1117/.

Apollonio, F. and E. Giovannini. 2015. A paradata documentation methodology for the uncertainty visualization in digital reconstruction of CH artifacts. *SCIRES-IT* 5 (1):1–24.

Archaeology Data Service and Digital Antiquity, eds. 2009-. *Guides to Good Practice*. York and Tempe, AZ. URL https://guides.archaeologydataservice.ac.uk/g2gp/Main.

Atarashi, R., M. Imai, H. Sunahara, K. Chihara, and T. Katata. 2000. Building archaeological photograph library. In *Research and Advanced Technology for Digital Libraries*, pp. 456–460. Berlin: Springer.

Baca, M. and M. Gill. 2015. Encoding Multilingual Knowledge Systems in the Digital Age: the Getty Vocabularies. *Knowledge Organization* 42 (4):232–243.

Baca, M., P. Harpring, E. Lanzi, L. McRae, and A. Whiteside. 2006. *Cataloging Cultural Objects: A Guide to Describing Cultural Works and Their Images*. Chicago: ALA.

Baltsavias, E. 2006. *Recording, modeling and visualization of cultural heritage*. London: Routledge.

Barratt, R. 2016. Part3 - sources and paradata. *Photogrammetry in Archaeology* URL https://archphotogrammetry.com/2016/06/25/part-3-sources-and-paradata/.

Bates, J. 2018. The politics of data friction. *Journal of Documentation* 74 (2):412–429.

Benardou, A. and A. Dunning. 2018. From Europeana Cloud to Europeana Research Tools, users and methods. In *Cultural Heritage Infrastructures in Digital Humanities*, eds. A. Benardou, E. Champion, C. Dallas, and L. Hughes, pp. 136–152. London: Routledge.

Bendicho, V. 2013. International guidelines for virtual archaeology: The Seville principles. In *Good Practice in Archaeological Diagnostics*, pp. 269–283. Cham: Springer.

Bentkowska-Kafel, A. and H. Denard. 2012. Introduction. In *Paradata and transparency in virtual heritage*, eds. A. Bentkowska-Kafel, H. Denard, and D. Baker, pp. 1–4. Farnham: Ashgate.

Bizer, C., T. Heath, and T. Berners-Lee. 2011. Linked data. In *Semantic Services, Interoperability and Web Applications*, pp. 205–227. Hershey, PA: IGI Global.

Borrero, M. and L. Stroth. 2020. A proposal for the standardized reporting of error and paradata regarding structure from motion (SfM) 3D models used in recording and consolidating archaeological architecture. *Advances in Archaeological Practice*.

Bowker, G. and S. Star. 2000. Invisible mediators of action. *Mind, Culture, and Activity* 7 (1-2):147–163.

Bruseker, G., N. Carboni, and A. Guillem. 2017 a. Cultural heritage data management: The role of formal ontology and CIDOC CRM. In *Heritage and archaeology in the DigitalAge*, eds. M. Vincent, V. López-Menchero Bendicho, M. Ioannides, and T. Levy, pp. 93–131. Cham: Springer.

Bruseker, G., M. Doerr, and M. Theodoridou. 2017 b. *D5.1. Report on the Common Semantic Framework*. PARTHENOS.

Carlisle, P. and E. Lee. 2016. Recording the past. *Journal of Cultural Heritage Management and Sustainable Development* 6 (2):128–137.

Carrillo Gea, J., A. Toval, J. Alemán, J. Nicolás, and M. Flores. 2013. The London charter and the Seville principles as sources of requirements for e-archaeology systems development purposes. *Virtual Archaeology Review* 4 (9):205–211.

CENDARI WP6. 2013 a. *D6.1. Common Metadata Schema*. London: CENDARI. URL http://www.cendari.eu/sites/default/files/CENDARI_D6.1-Common-Metadata-Schema-final.pdf.

CENDARI WP6. 2013b. *D6.2 Guidelines for Applying the Schema*. London: CENDARI. URL http://www.cendari.eu/sites/default/files/CENDARI_D6.2%20Guidelines%20for%20applying%20the%20schema.pdf.

Champion, E. 2018. The role of 3d models in virtual heritage infrastructures. In *Cultural Heritage Infrastructures in Digital Humanities*, eds. A. Benardou, E. Champion, C. Dallas, and L. Hughes. London: Routledge.

Coburn, E., R. Light, G. McKenna, R. Stein, and A. Vitzthum. 2010. *LIDO - Lightweight Information Describing Objects Version 1.0*. Paris: CIDOC.

Conradi, E. 2010. to_be_classified: A Facet Analysis of a Folksonomy. *Journal of Information Architecture* 2 (2):5–23. URL http://journalofia.org/volume2/issue2/02-conradi/jofia-0202-02-conradi.pdf.

Corsi, C., B. Slapsak, and F. Vermeulen, eds. 2016. *Good Practice in Archaeological Diagnostics*. Cham: Springer.

Crofts, N., I. Dionissiadou, M. Doerr, and P. Reed, eds. 1998. *CIDOC Conceptual Reference Model - Information groups*. Paris: ICOM/CIDOC.

de Kleijn, M., R. de Hond, and O. Martinez-Rubi. 2016. A 3d spatial data infrastructure for mapping the Via Appia. *Digital Applications in Archaeology and Cultural Heritage* 3 (2):23–32.

De Roo, B., J. Bourgeois, and P. De Maeyer. 2013. A survey on the use of GIS and data standards in archaeology. *International Journal of Heritage in the Digital Era* 2 (4):491–507.

Demetrescu, E. 2015. Archaeological stratigraphy as a formal language for virtual reconstruction. theory and practice. *Journal of Archaeological Science* 57:42–55.

Demetrescu, E. and B. Fanini. 2017. A white-box framework to oversee archaeological virtual reconstructions in space and time. *Journal of Archaeological Science: Reports* 14 (SuplC):500–514.

Denard, H. 2013. Implementing best practice in cultural heritage visualisation: The London Charter. In *Good Practice in Archaeological Diagnostics*, pp. 255–268. Cham: Springer.

DeNardis, L. 2011. *Opening standards*. Cambridge, MA.: MIT Press.

Denis, J. 2018. The maintenance of what? the contrasted ontologies of objects that last. In *Artisanal Electronics, Jul 2018, Genève, Switzerland*. URL https://hal-mines-paristech.archives-ouvertes.fr/hal-01841468.

Dieckmann, L., A. Kliemann, and M. Warnke. 2010. Meta-image - a collaborative environment for image discourse. In *Proceedings of EVA 2010*. URL http://dx.doi.org/10.14236/ewic/EVA2010.29.

Doerr, M. 2009. Ontologies for cultural heritage. In *Handbook on Ontologies*, eds. S. S. and S. R., pp. 463–486. Berlin: Springer.

Doerr, M., A. Felicetti, S. Hermon, G. Hiebel, A. Kritsotaki, A. Masur, K. May, P. Ronzino, W. Schmidle, M. Theodoridou, D. Tsiafaki, E. Christaki, et al. 2018. *Definition of the CRMarchaeo*. Prato: PIN.

Doerr, M., A. Kritsotaki, Y. Rousakis, G. Hiebel, and M. Theodoridou. 2014. *CRMsci: the Scientific Observation Model An Extension of CIDOC-CRM to support scientific observation*. Heraklion: FORTH.

Doerr, M. and P. LeBoeuf. 2007. Modelling intellectual processes: The FRBR-CRM harmonization. In *Digital Libraries: Research and Development*, eds. C. Thanos, F. Borri, and L. Candela, pp. 114–123. Berlin: Springer.

Doerr, M., F. Murano, and A. Felicetti. 2020. *Definition of the CRMtex*. Paris: CIDOC.

Doerr, M., C.-E. Ore, and S. Stead. 2007. The CIDOC conceptual reference model - a new standard for knowledge sharing. In *ER 2007, Auckland, New Zealand.*, eds. J. Grundy, S. Hartmann, A. Laender, L. Maciaszek, and J. Roddick, pp. 51–56. Sydney: ACS.

Doerr, M., S. Stead, and M. Theodoridou. 2016. *Definition of the CRMdig*. Heraklion: FORTH., version 3.2.1 ed.

Dorrell, P. 1994. *Photography in Archaeology and Conservation*. Cambridge: Cambridge UP.

Drabinski, E. 2013. Queering the Catalog. *Library Quarterly* 83:94–111.

Drewett, P. 1999. *Field archaeology an introduction*. London: UCL Press.

DuBois, A. 2003. Close reading: an introduction. In *Close reading: a reader*, eds. F. Lentricchia and A. DuBois, pp. 1–40. Durham, NC: Duke UP.

Durco, M., M. Lorenzini, and G. Sugimoto. 2018. Something will be connected - semantic mapping from CMDI to Parthenos Entities. In *Selected papers from the CLARIN Annual Conference 2017*, pp. 25–35. Linköping: Linköping UEP.

Edmond, J. and F. Morselli. 2020. Sustainability of digital humanities projects as a publication and documentation challenge. *JDOC* 76 (5):1019–1031.

English Heritage. 2012. *MIDAS Heritage - The UK Historic Environment Data Standard, v1.1*. London.

Feinberg, M. 2011. Expressive Bibliography. *Knowledge Organization* 38 (2):123–134.

Feinberg, M. 2017. The value of discernment. *Information Research* 22 (1):paper 1649.

Felicetti, A., T. Scarselli, M. Mancinelli, and F. Niccolucci. 2013. Mapping ICCD archaeological data to CIDOC-CRM: the RA schema. In *CRMEX 201. Valetta, Malta, September 26, 2013*, eds. V. Alexiev, V. Ivanov, and M. Grinberg. Valletta.

Fernie, K., D. Gavrilis, and S. Angelis. 2013. *The CARARE metadata schema, v.2.0*. URL https://pro.carare.eu/lib/exe/fetch.php?media=support:the_carare_meta data_schema2.pdf.

Foley, J., P. Kwan, and M. Welch. 2017. A web-based infrastructure for the assisted annotation of heritage collections. *JCCH* 10 (3):14:1–14:25.

Foulonneau, M. and J. Riley. 2008. *Metadata for digital resources*. Oxford: Chandos.

Fox, M. 2016. Priorities of arrangement or a hierarchy of oppressions?:. *Knowledge Organization* 43 (5):373–383.

Freund, L. and R. Butterworth. 2008. Tagging for use. In *Proceedings of IIiX '08*, pp. 6–12. New York: ACM.

Frischer, B., F. Niccolucci, N. Ryan, and J. Barceló. 2002. From CVR to CVRO. The past, present, and future of cultural virtual reality. In *Proceedings of VAST 2000. BAR*, vol. 843, pp. 7–18. Archaeopress.

Fuenfschilling, L. and C. Binz. 2018. Global socio-technical regimes. *Research Policy* 47 (4):735–749.

Gardin, J.-C. 1980. *Archaeological constructs*. Cambridge: Cambridge UP.

Gartner, R. 2016. *Metadata: Shaping Knowledge from Antiquity to the Semantic Web*. Cham: Springer.

Gazzola, P., R. Lemaire, J. Bassegoda-Nonell, L. Benavente, D. Boskovic, H. Daifuku, P. de Vrieze, H. Langberg, M. Matteucci, J. Merlet, C. F. Marini, R. Pane, S. Pavel, P. Philippot, V. Pimentel, H. Plenderleith, D. de Campos, J. Sonnier, F. Sorlin, E. Stikas, G. Tripp, J. Zachwatowicz, and M. Zbiss. 1964. *International Charter for the Conservation and Restoration of Monuments and Sites (the Venice Charter 1964)*. Paris: ICOMOS.

Giovannini, E. 2018. *Virtual Reconstruction Information Management*. Phd Thesis, Università di Bologna, Bologna.

Gnoli, C. 2012. Metadata About What? *Knowledge Organization* 29 (4):268–275.

Gonzalez-Perez, C. 2018. *Information Modelling for Archaeology and Anthropology*. Cham: Springer.

Gonzalez-Perez, C., P. Martín-Rodilla, C. Parcero-Oubina, P. Fábrega-Álvarez, and A. Guimil-Farina. 2012. Extending an Abstract Reference Model for Transdisciplinary Work in Cultural Heritage. In *CICIS*, eds. J. Dodero, M. Palomo-Duarte, and P. Karampiperis, vol. 343, pp. 190–201. Berlin: Springer.

Grant, A., J. Nieuwenhuis, and T. Petersen, eds. 1995. *International Guidelines for Museum Object Information: The CIDOC Information Categories*. Paris: CIDOC.

Guarino, N. 1999. Formal ontology and information systems. In *Amended version of N. Guarino (ed.), Formal Ontology in Information Systems*. Amsterdam, IOS Press, pp. 3-15. URL http://www.cidoc-crm.org/sites/default/files/ontologies%20Guarino.pdf.

Guillem, A., R. Zarnic, and G. Bruseker. 2015. Building an argumentation platform for 3d reconstruction using CIDOC-CRM and Drupal. In *2015 Digital Heritage*, vol. 2, pp. 383–386.

Gunnarsson, F. 2020. Digitalisation and its impact on archaeological knowledge production. In *Doing Digital Humanities*, eds. J. Hansson and J. Svensson, pp. 27–44. Växjö: Linnaeus UP.

Hanseth, O. and E. Monteiro. 1997. Inscribing behaviour in information infrastructure standards. *Accounting, Management and Information Technologies* 7 (4):183–211.

Hansson, K., T. Pargman, and A. Dahlgren. 2020. Datafication and cultural heritage: provocations, threats, and design opportunities. In *ECSCW'20*. Siegen: EUSSET. URL http://dx.doi.org/10.18420/ecscw2020_ws05.

Harpring, P. 2019. *Categories for the Description of the Works of Art*. Los Angeles, CA: J. Paul Getty Trust.

Hauck, O. and P. Kuroczyński. 2015. Cultural heritage markup language-designing a domain ontology for digital reconstructions. In *Proceedings of the 2nd International Conference on Virtual Archaeology, Hermitage Museum, St. Petersburg/Russia*, pp. 250–255.

Havemann, S. 2012. Intricacies and potentials of gathering paradata in the 3D modelling workflow. In *Paradata and Transparency in Virtual Heritage*, eds. A. Bentkowska-Kafel, H. Denard, and D. Baker, pp. 145–160. Farnham: Ashgate.

Haynes, D. 2018. *Metadata for information management and retrieval*. London: Facet.

Henninger, M. 2018. From mud to the museum. *Journal of Information Science* 44 (5):658–670.

Hjørland, B. 2020. Political versus apolitical epistemologies in knowledge organization. *Knowledge Organization* 47 (6):461–485.

Hjørland, B. and J. Hartel. 2003. Ontological, Epistemological and Sociological Dimensions of Domains. *Knowledge Organization* 30 (3/4):239–245.

Hodder, I. 2000. *Towards reflexive method in archaeology*. Cambridge: McDonald Institute for Archaeological Research.

Hu, X., J. Ng, and S. Xia. 2019. User-centered evaluation of metadata schema for nonmovable cultural heritage. *JASIST* 69 (12):1476–1487.

Huggett, J. 2013. Disciplinary Issues: Challenging the Research and Practice of Computer Applications in Archaeology. In *Papers from CAA2012*, eds. G. Earl, T. Sly, A. Chrysanthi, P. Murrieta-Flores, C. Papadopoulos, I. Romanowska, and D. Wheatley, pp. 13–24. Amsterdam: Amsterdam UP.

Huvila, I. 2012. Being Formal and Flexible: Semantic Wiki as an Archaeological e-Science Infrastructure. In *Proceeding CAA 2011*, eds. M. Zhou, I. Romanowska, Z. Wu, P. Xu, and P. Verhagen, pp. 186–197. Amsterdam: Amsterdam UP.

Huvila, I. 2017. The subtle difference between knowledge and 3d knowledge. *Hamburger Journal für Kulturanthropologie* 7 (1):99–111.

Huvila, I. 2019. Management of archaeological information and knowledge in digital environment. In *Knowledge Management, Arts and Humanities*, ed. M. Handzic, pp. 147–169. Cham: Springer.

IFVA (International Forum of Virtual Archaeology). 2011. *The Seville Principles: International Principles of Virtual Archaeology*. URL http://smartheritage.com/seville-principles/seville-principles.

Jansson, I.-M. 2018. Negotiating participatory ko in crowdsourcing infrastructures. In *Proceedings of the ISKO2018*, eds. F. Ribeiro and M. Cerveira, pp. 863–870. Baden-Baden: Ergon-Verlag.

Jansson, I.-M. and I. Huvila. 2019. Social tagging and commenting: theoretical perspectives. In *Participatory Archives*, eds. E. Benoit and A. Eveleigh, pp. 33–44. London: Facet.

Jörg, B., K. Jeffery, J. Dvořák, N. Houssos, A. Asserson, G. van Grootel, et al. 2012. CERIF 1.3 full data model (FDM): introduction and specification. *euroCRIS* .

Kastanis, L. 2019. *Authenticity in Digital Archaeological Reconstructions*. Phd Thesis, Queensland University of Technology, Brisbane.

Kulasekaran, S., J. Trelogan, M. Esteva, and M. Johnson. 2014. Metadata integration for an archaeology collection architecture. *International Conference on Dublin Core and Metadata Applications* pp. 53–63. URL https://dcpapers.dublincore.org/pubs/article/view/3702.

LCO (The London Charter Organisation). 2009. *The London Charter for the computer-based visualisation of cultural heritage*. London.

Leazer, G. and R. Montoya. 2020. The politics of knowledge organization. *Knowledge Organization* 47 (5):367–371.

Library of Congress. 2014. *VRA CORE*. Washington, DC: LOC, 4th ed. URL https://www.loc.gov/standards/vracore/.

Lim, S. and C. Liew. 2011. Metadata quality and interoperability of GLAM digital images. *Aslib Proceedings* 63 (5):484–498.

Llebot, C. and S. Tuyl. 2019. Peer review of research data submissions to ScholarsArchive@OSU: How can we improve the curation of research datasets to enhance reusability? *Journal of eScience Librarianship* 8 (2):e1166.

López, F., P. Lerones, J. Llamas, J. Gómez-García-Bermejo, and E. Zalama. 2018. A review of heritage building information modeling (h-BIM). *Multimodal Technologies and Interaction* 2 (2):21.

Löwenborg, D. 2007. Flexibility instead of standards? how to make digital databases on cultural heritage useable to large audiences - a researchers perspective. In *Communicating Cultural Heritage in the 21st Century*, eds. S. Hermon and F. Niccolucci, pp. 12–17. Pisa: EPOCH.

Luxen, J.-L. 2004. Reflections on the use of heritage charters and conventions. *Conservation Perspectives, The GCI Newsletter* 19 (2).

Madin, J., S. Bowers, M. Schildhauer, S. Krivov, D. Pennington, and F. Villa. 2007. An ontology for describing and synthesizing ecological observation data. *Ecological Informatics* 2 (3):279–296.

Manovich, L. 2001. *The Language of New Media*. Cambridge, MA: MIT Press.

Marlet, O., E. Zadora-Rio, P.-Y. Buard, B. Markhoff, and X. Rodier. 2019. The archaeological excavation report of Rigny: An example of an interoperable logicist publication. *Heritage* 2 (1):761–773.

Maron, D. and M. Feinberg. 2018. What does it mean to adopt a metadata standard?. *JDOC* 74 (4):674–691.

Mayernik, M. 2015. Research data and metadata curation as institutional issues. *JASIST* 67 (4):973–993.

McKeague, P., A. Corns, Å. Larsson, A. Moreau, A. Posluschny, K. Daele, and T. Evans. 2020. One archaeology: A manifesto for the systematic and effective use of mapped data from archaeological fieldwork and research. *Information* 11 (4):222.

McKeague, P., R. van't Veer, I. Huvila, A. Moreau, P. Verhagen, L. Bernard, A. Cooper, C. Green, and N. van Manen. 2019. Mapping our heritage: Towards a sustainable future for digital spatial information and technologies in european archaeological heritage management. *JCAA* 2 (1):89–104.

McKenna, G. and E. Patsatzi, eds. 2007. *SPECTRUM: The UK Museum Documentation Standard*. Cambridge: MDA, 3rd ed.

Meghini, C., R. Scopigno, J. Richards, H. Wright, G. Geser, S. Cuy, J. Fihn, B. Fanini, H. Hollander, F. Niccolucci, A. Felicetti, P. Ronzino, F. Nurra, C. Papatheodorou, D. Gavrilis, M. Theodoridou, M. Doerr, D. Tudhope, C. Binding, and A. Vlachidis. 2017. Ariadne: A research infrastructure for archaeology. *J. Comput. Cult. Herit.* 10 (3):18:1–18:27.

Miller, P. 1999. The importance of metadata to archaeology: One view from within the Archaeology Data Service. In *Proceedings of the CAA 1997*, eds. L. Dingwall, S. Exon, V. Gaffney, S. Laflin, and M. van Leusen, pp. 133–136. Oxford: Archaeopress.

Millerand, F. and G. Bowker. 2008. Metadata, trajectoires et énaction. In *La cognition au prisme des sciences sociales*, eds. B. Lahire and C. Rosental, pp. 277–303. Paris: ÉAC.

Molenda, A. 2020. *The Use of Preservation Tools Among Dutch Heritage Organizations*. The Hague: DDHN.

Moncrieffe, J. and R. Eyben. 2007. *The power of labelling*. London: Earthscan.

Moraitou, E., J. Aliprantis, and G. Caridakis. 2018. Semantic bridging of cultural heritage disciplines and tasks. In *CIDOC 2018 Heraklion, Crete, Greece*, pp. 1–9.

Morgan, C. and H. Wright. 2018. Pencils and pixels: Drawing and digital media in archaeological field recording. *Journal of Field Archaeology* 43 (2):136–151.

Morgan, C. 2009. (Re)Building Çatalhöyük: Changing Virtual Reality in Archaeology. *Archaeologies* 5 (3):468–487.

Moser, S. 2012. Archaeological visualisation. In *Archaeological Theory Today*, ed. I. Hodder, pp. 292–322. Cambridge: Polity.

Niccolucci, F. 2012. Setting standards for 3D visualization of cultural heritage in Europe and beyond. In *Paradata and transparency in virtual heritage*, eds. A. Bentkowska-Kafel, H. Denard, and D. Baker, pp. 23–36. Farnham: Ashgate.

Niccolucci, F. and A. Felicetti. 2018. A CIDOC CRM-based model for the documentation of heritage sciences. In *DigitalHERITAGE 2018*, pp. 1–6.

Nussbaumer, P. and B. Haslhofer. 1999. *Putting the CIDOC CRM into Practice, Experiences and Challenges*. Vienna: Universität Wien.

Ogleby, C. 2007. The "truthlikeness" of virtual reality reconstructions of architectural heritage: concepts and metadata. In *Proceedings of the 3DARCH, 2007*, p. 3D.

Oikarinen, T. and T. Kortelainen. 2013. Challenges of Diversity, Consistency, and Globality in Indexing of Local Archeological Artifacts. *Knowledge Organization* 40 (2):123–135.

Olson, H. 2000. Difference, culture and change: The untapped potential of LCSH. *The Cataloging & Classification Quarterly* 29 (1/2):53–71.

Olson, H. 1994. Universal models. *Advances in Knowledge Organization* 4:72–80.

Olson, H. 2002. *The power to name*. Dordrecht: Kluwer.

Padfield, J., K. Kontiza, A. Bikakis, and A. Vlachidis. 2019. Semantic representation and location provenance of cultural heritage information. *Heritage* 2 (1):648–665.

Papadopoulos, C. and S. Schreibman. 2019. Towards 3d scholarly editions. *Digital Humanities Quarterly* 13 (1).

Papatheodorou, C., C. Dallas, C. Ertmann-Christiansen, K. Fernie, D. Gavrilis, M. Masci, P. Constantopoulos, and S. Angelis. 2011. A new architecture and approach to asset representation for Europeana aggregation: The CARARE way. In *Metadata and Semantic Research*, eds. E. García-Barriocanal, Z. Cebeci, M. Okur, and A. Öztürk, pp. 412–423. Berlin: Springer.

Pasquetto, I., C. Borgman, and M. Wofford. 2019. Uses and reuses of scientific data. *Harvard Data Science Review* 1 (2).

Pavel, C. 2010. *Describing and interpreting the past*. Bucuresti: Editura Universitatii din Bucuresti.

Peponakis, M. 2012. Conceptualizations of the cataloging object: A critique on current perceptions of FRBR group 1 entities. *Cataloging & Classification Quarterly* 50 (5-7):587–602.

Pétursdóttir, Þ. 2020. Anticipated futures?. *International Journal of Heritage Studies* 26 (1):87–103.

Petzet, M. and J. Ziesemer, eds. 2004. *International Charters for Conservation and Restoration*. München: ICOMOS.

Piccoli, C. 2017. Visualizing antiquity before the digital age. *Analecta Praehistorica Leidensia* 47:225–257.

Polig, M. 2017. 3D GIS for building archaeology - combining old and new data in a three-dimensional information system in the case study of Lund Cathedral. *Studies in Digital Heritage* 1 (2):225–238.

Quintero, M. and R. Eppich. 2016. Introduction - current trends in cultural heritage and documentation. In *3D Recording, Documentation and Management of Cultural Heritage*, eds. E. Stylianidis and F. Remondino, pp. 1–14. Dunbeath: Whittles.

Radio, E. 2018. Abstraction, concrescence, and identity in descriptive metadata. *Journal of Library Metadata* 18 (1):31–44.

Rejdovianova, Z., A. Žitňan, M. Horňák, J. Hrubý, and D. Hlásek. 2018. Brief overview of examples of VR projects. In *Virtual reconstructions and computer visualisations in archaeological practice*, eds. P. Novaković, N. Tasić, and M. Horňák, pp. 31–39. Ljubljana: Ljubljana UP.

Richards, J. 2009. From anarchy to good practice: the evolution of standards in archaeological computing. *Archeologia e Calcolatori* 20 (1):27–35.

Richards-Rissetto, H. and J. von Schwerin. 2017. A catch 22 of 3d data sustainability: Lessons in 3d archaeological data management & accessibility. *Digital Applications in Archaeology and Cultural Heritage* 6:38–48.

Ronzino, P., N. Amico, A. Felicetti, and F. Niccolucci. 2013. European standards for the documentation of historic buildings and their relationship with CIDOC-CRM. In *CRMEX 2013, Valetta, Malta, September 26, 2013.*, eds. V. Alexiev, V. Ivanov, and M. Grinberg, pp. 70–79. Valletta: CEUR-WS.org.

Ross, S. 2018. Digital humanities research needs from cultural heritage looking forward to 2025? In *Cultural Heritage Infrastructures in Digital Humanities*, eds. A. Benardou, E. Champion, C. Dallas, and L. Hughes, pp. 153–166. London: Routledge.

Ryan, N. 2001. Documenting and Validating Virtual Archaeology. *Archeologia e Calcolatori* 12:245–273.

Scuola Normale Superiore di Pisa. 2007. *Profilo Applicativo Pico - versione 1.0 - 19/07/2007*. Pisa. URL http://www.culturaitalia.it/opencms/export/sites/culturaitalia/attachments/documenti/picoap/picoap1.0.xml.

Scuola Normale Superiore di Pisa. 2011. *Thesaurus Pico - versione 4.3 - 01/03/2011*. Pisa. URL http://www.culturaitalia.it/opencms/export/sites/culturaitalia/attachments/thesaurus/4.3/thesaurus_4.3.0.skos.xml.

Shaw, R., A. Corns, and J. McAuley. 2009. Archiving Archaeological Spatial Data: Standards and Metadata. In *CAA2009, Williamsburg, Virginia*.

Signore, O. 2009. Representing knowledge in archaeology: from cataloguing cards to Semantic Web. *Archeologia e Calcolatori* 20:111–128.

Silberman, N. 2008. *ICOMOS Charter for the Interpretation and Presentation of Cultural Heritage Sites*. Paris: ICOMOS.

Skinner, J. 2014. Metadata in archival and cultural heritage settings: A review of the literature. *Journal of Library Metadata* 14 (1):52–68.

Sköld, O., Börjesson, L., Huvila, I. work in progress. Interrogating paradata.

Smiraglia, R. P. 2014. *The Elements of Knowledge Organization*. Cham: Springer.

Smith-Yoshimura, K. 2020. *Transitioning to the Next Generation of Metadata*. Dublin, OH: OCLC.

Star, S. 1995. The politics of formal representations. In *Ecologies of Knowledge*, pp. 88–118. Albany: SUNY Press.

Star, S. and M. Lampland. 2009. Reckoning with standards. In *Standards and their stories*, eds. M. Lampland and S. L. Star, pp. 3–24. Ithaca: Cornell UP.

Stead, S. and M. Doerr. 2015. *CRMinf: the Argumentation Model - An Extension of CIDOC-CRM to support argumentation*. Purley: Paveprime.

Stvilia, B., C. Jørgensen, and S. Wu. 2012. Establishing the value of socially-created metadata to image indexing. *Library & Information Science Research* 34 (2):99 – 109.

Szostak, R., C. Gnoli, and M. López-Huertas. 2016. *Interdisciplinary Knowledge Organization*. Cham: Springer.

Theodoridou, M., Y. Tzitzikas, M. Doerr, Y. Marketakis, and V. Melessanakis. 2010. Modeling and querying provenance by extending CIDOC CRM. *Distributed and Parallel Databases* 27 (2):169–210.

Toffalori, E. 2016. Best practices and tools to create archival image metadata. *Center for Digital Archaeology (blog)* URL https://digitalarch.org/blog/2017/4/7/ykag-6k2fvln7g1jo2923n0c7zdrryg.

von Schwerin, J., M. Lyons, L. Loos, N. Billen, M. Auer, and A. Zipf. 2016. Show me the data!: Structuring archaeological data to deliver interactive, transparent 3d reconstructions in a 3d webgis. In *3D Research Challenges in Cultural Heritage II*, eds. S. Münster, M. Pfarr-Harfst, P. Kuroczyński, and M. Ioannides, pp. 198–230. Cham: Springer.

Watterson, A. 2015. Beyond digital dwelling: Re-thinking interpretive visualisation in archaeology. *Open Archaeology* (1).

Wells, J. 2007. The plurality of truth in culture, context, and heritage. *City&Time* 3 (2).

Minor Politics, Major Consequences
Epistemic Challenges of Metadata and the Contribution of Image Recognition

Beate Löffler, Tino Mager

Abstract

Metadata is part of our knowledge systems and, so, represents and perpetuates political hierarchies and perceptions of relevance. While some of these have come up for scrutiny in the discourses on digitization, some 'minor' issues have gone unnoticed and a few new mechanisms of imbalance have escaped attention as well. Yet, all of these, too, influence the usability of digital image collections.

This paper traces three fields of 'minor politics' and their epistemic consequences, both in general and in particular, with respect to the study of architecture and its visual representation: first, the intrinsic logic of the original collections and their digital representation; second, the role of support staff in the course of digitization and data transfer; and, third, keywording as a matter of disciplinary habitus. It underlines the 'political' role of metadata within the context of knowledge production, even on the local level of a single database, and connects to the implementation of contemporary technologies like computer vision and artificial intelligence for image content classification and the creation of metadata.

Given the abundance of digitally available (historical) images, image content recognition and the creation of metadata by artificial intelligence are sheer necessities in order to make millions of hitherto unexplored images available for research. At the same time, the challenge to overcome existing colonial and other biases in the training of AI remains. Hence, we are once again tasked to reflect on the delicate criterion of objectivity. The second part of this paper focuses on research done in the ArchiMediaL project (archimedial.eu); it demonstrates both the potentials and the risks of applying artificial intelligence for metadata creation by addressing the three fields mentioned above through the magnifying glass of programming.

Keywords: architectural history, interdisciplinary, machine learning, image recognition, visual data bases, epistemic challenges, metadata

Introduction

Metadata is part of our knowledge systems. It, therefore, represents and perpetuates political hierarchies and perceptions of relevance. Some of this comes up whenever curators discuss corpora for digitization, or the means and limits of access, for example. It becomes apparent when the humanities and computer science negotiate the hierarchies of cooperation or the technical parameters of interfaces, ontologies, database design, and data storage. Hence, some factors have already been scrutinized in the discourses on digitization; their consequences are part of the everyday intellectual processes of digital humanities. This decision-making process represents the 'major politics' of metadata. At the same time, many 'minor' issues go largely unnoticed, or are only discussed in small circles of specialists. Yet, they influence the usability of digital image collections and the reliability of their content as well, and thereby have a significant impact on the epistemic meaning of the resultant research.

This paper is inspired by more than two decades of work for—and with—digital image collections between cultural studies and architectural history. It initially traces three fields of 'minor politics' of discussing and attributing metadata and their epistemic consequences, both in general in cultural studies, and in particular with regard to the study of architecture and its visual representation. The discussion underlines the critical role of metadata within the context of knowledge production, showing localized and/or particular issues as part of the overall challenges of metadata. Based on this, it argues for an additional, conceptionally non-textual level of metadata creation, as represented by the implementation of contemporary technologies like computer vision and artificial intelligence for image content classification.

The paper reflects on the motivations and insights of our work within the ArchiMediaL project (archimedial.eu) to demonstrate both the potentials and the risks of applying artificial intelligence (AI) for metadata creation by addressing the epistemic and epistemological challenges from a programming perspective. Here, it becomes evident how the seemingly minor decisions of programming become crucial for the 'major politics' of metadata.

Epistemic challenges of metadata production

When digitization of visual media became a feasible and fundable issue during the 1990s, it aimed to enable access to important cultural objects and materials, and to customize teaching and exchange in research. The digital items were tools that were thought to facilitate processes, and by no means to replace the original collections and the work with those. With the further development in storage capabilities, digital photography, and the introduction of Web 2.0, the framework changed considerably. The available material grew exponentially, and, soon, the lines between digitized and originally digital material blurred. Over time, ideas arose not to keep the analogue sources but to save archival space by substituting them with their digital representations. With this notion out, and in discussion, the epistemic specifics of both analogue and digitized databases, the intrinsic mechanisms of digitization, and the allocation of meta-text acquired crucial relevance (cf. Matyssek 2009). This is even more so, given the increasingly different work experiences, research approaches, and the expectations of different generations of scholars in interacting with different types of visual databases.

We address three select phenomena from the digitization process to point towards the complexity of 'metadata politics' at a localized and field-specific, and, so, 'minor' level. We reflect on epistemically relevant decision-making from the angle of architectural history: the intrinsic logic of the original collections and their digital representation; the role of support staff in the course of digitization and data transfer; and keywording as a matter of disciplinary habitus.

The intrinsic logic of the original collections and their digital representation

Analogue collections of visual material arose from the most diverse contexts, and went on to carry in themselves the resultant specifics. There are, for example, materials compiled for teaching and collections of visual material generated in the course of research that are primarily of epistemic interest today since they make it possible to trace the theories of knowledge throughout history. There is original material resulting from the research processes themselves, such as sketches, photographs, or diagrams, which are both irreplaceable sources and parts of an order of thought; and there are repositories, including visual and textual materials of different types, and even artefacts, the heterogeneity of which challenges the classification systems of librarians and archivists. Transferring these collections into digital representations should actually mean understanding their intrinsic logic and finding ways to represent it in the ensuing meta-text. Otherwise, the historic and epistemic relevance of the collection will disappear: the images remain in their digital reincarnation but their meaning and context will be lost.

The points of decision-making depend on the specific lot. Teaching collections usually contain secondary materials; their digitization is often a matter of convenience first, and becomes a research topic only in retrospect. Yet, the structure of a slide magazine—the order of motifs—is relevant. Ethnologists talking about a human's transition through life or about a religious festival consisting of a series of rituals need to reproduce the correct sequence in their narration. The sequence of events carries meaning in the biography and the ritual as well as for the rehearsal of research methods and analysis. The meta-text needs to reproduce the timeline represented in the slide archive in an appropriate way, enabling later users to grasp the idea of the original collection. In contrast, the temporal dimension is secondary for teaching slides concerning artefacts, such as architecture or the inventories of museum collections. The genesis of forms over time or the mechanisms of construction or production play a role as well. Yet, the structures of knowledge evolve not from processes but rather around objects, places, or actors. The order of images aims to provide a general picture of the object in question and follows an established pattern of approach and appropriation from long distance to close-up view, from exterior to interior, from general to specific. Here, the single image gains meaning through its relationship with other images of the same object or the same artist, the linking done in the mind of the experienced scholar, or helped along by the catalogue of the slide collection. Digitization needs to represent not only direct connections but secondary and tertiary levels of order as well. Despite this, teaching collections adhere to very ordered systems of knowledge, mirroring basic training in the respective fields. Hence, the transfer of the underlying reference system is comparatively easy since the database structures of digitization follow similar ideas and encourage the most common kinds of interlinking. Here, the minor policies of handling a specific collection align with the overarching policies of metadata.

This becomes different as soon as original research collections are taken into account. Here, the logical order of the collection meets with the intrinsic developments of research to make one file packed to the bursting point with content or even overflowing to another, while the next remains entirely empty. Original material mixes with copies and reproductions or redrawings. The visual material is easy enough to extract and digitize, but the layers of collecting, sorting, and ordering are nearly impossible to reproduce. There is a haptic and epistemic difference between a dozen photographs illustrating a specific building, glued individually on numbered index cards on the one hand, and the same number of photographs stuffed together in a manila envelope with a shared number on the other. After digitization, all the images become equal 'individuals'; their former belonging—their 'invisible meta-text'—is usually reduced to the citation of reference numbers alone. The crucial information to understand the historical formation of scholar and material, the 'becoming' of the original collection with its shifts and changes, its notes and crossed-out sections, remains but readable in the analogue material.

Such challenges are even more extensive when the collections have an actual spatial character, such as the *Dokumenten-Kabinett europäischer Geschichte, Gegenwart und Zukunftsplanung* [Document cabinet of European history, present and future planning] of German legal expert Alexander Dolezalek (1914–1999), or the Friedrich Achleitner Archiv in Vienna, and have to be removed from their original locations, restored, or reassembled to provide appropriate preservation (Kellner 2008). It would be possible to create a digital copy of the collections to 'describe' their spatial dimensions, as we are able to build 3D reconstructions of archaeological sites or crime scenes by now. Today, however, the economic and personnel expenditure for such an endeavour is limited largely to collections of relevance compared to World Heritage sites or to diverse kinds of pilot projects, exploring the possibilities or recent technological developments.

These brief thoughts point towards digital databases as not being 'identical twins' of the analogue collections. The two kinds of collections are autonomous entities with their respective strengths and weaknesses, for which we can but partially compensate by meta-text. Even more so, when material or spatial qualities undergo translation into visual or textual information, first into images and second into descriptions or keywords. In consequence, the meta-information on the origin and intrinsic order of an original collection of visual material is largely a black box, depending on the awareness of the acting curators, the aim of the specific digitization, and the local policies (cf. Kohle/Locher 2019). The latter is of critical importance for many visual databases containing digitized material since they depend on how much funding, time, and staff are available for the digitization itself and the transfer of metadata from one medium to the other.

The role of support staff in the course of digitization and data transfer

Digitization means bulk production. The curators, computer scientists, and funders create the general framework of digitization; they do not themselves digitize. Except for material of the utmost importance, support staff usually do the entire process of scanning, storing, labelling, keywording, and meta-texting. The work is understood as being a menial one for its repetitive character and low level of complexity. The largely anonymous staff members with their sparse and/ or performance-related payment enable the amount of digitization we experienced during the past few decades. At the same time, they create another black box with their decisions during the work processes: experience shows a number of situations where digitization is not only a practice of copying from one medium to another for the benefit of accessibility and convenience, but as a practice of actual information production. Yet, changes in content might remain unnoticed; data might be created, lost, or changed, unintentionally modifying the content of the source material. This is part of the natural way of collecting and ordering knowledge for which scholarship developed the advanced checks of source criticism. These, however, do not necessarily translate themselves into the digital era.

A slide might get scanned mirrored; the image editing might alter the image significantly or even beyond recognition; identical or seemingly identical images might both be scanned, or not. In a series of images stored together, an image or two might miss the notes on the backs that all the others have. Does this mean that these images are irrelevant, or is it sensible to transfer the information from the others to these as well since they are stored together anyway? Here, a broad field of minor decisions has the potential to impact the metadata. Are spelling errors in the original metadata transferred or corrected? How do we handle place names or territorial allocations that have changed over time? How about terms that are perceived as racist, militarist, otherwise politically incorrect, or only so old-fashioned that they have become incomprehensible to most of the audience?

For some of these issues, approaches to solutions are provided for in guidelines for digitization, often based on the experiences of libraries and archives. Concerning the location, for example, the linking to GPS coordinates today provides a second level of entirely digital spatial allocation. Other issues depend on the day-to-day decisions taken by the support staff, which, in fact, carries responsibility for the consistence of the data material and the quality of the database. There might be images, for example, that are evidently mislabelled, or unlabelled images, the content of which can be clearly identified, since they depict sights such as castles or famous practices such as, for instance, the Munich Beer Festival. Here, the competences of the support staff can make an important contribution. Their knowledge of places and objects depicted in the images might add contemporary meta-text to historical meta-text, thereby extending the epistemological depth of the database—if the work regime provides economic and intellectual leeway to do so.

Yet, three issues remain unsolved, no matter how carefully the transfer of data—visual and textual—proceeds. First, it is impossible to apply source criticism—the bread and butter of the humanities—to a dataset the digital authorship of which is, in fact, unknown. Second, mistakes such as spelling errors occur, and might make datasets undiscoverable in some means of filtering. Third, information already missing in the original corpus cannot be created in the course of digitization. Images sourced during ethnological research or travel are often full of content but short on detailed information; they only note the place or the main motif. Even if the keywords encompass the entire image content, including costumes or means of transport and architecture, in the background, the metadata remains insufficient.

The first two issues underline the necessity of using the analogue corpus and its digital representation in parallel. The third might be helped along if we succeed in utilizing AI and image recognition to interlink such datasets and enhance them beyond their initial information content and handling, as we will discuss in the second part of this paper. Yet, even then, image description and keywording remain crucial elements of meta-texting, and, therefore, of the usability of visual databases.

Keywording as a matter of disciplinary habitus

Keywording is a crucial element of data storage for analogue corpora and for databases of digitized images, both thematically and in respect of image content. While the thematic order is often part of the basic structure of the collection, the keywording of image content is an additional layer that provides significant shortcuts in the use of digital collections. There is, however, another black box of metadata related to this coding, another point where decision-making on a small level has an important impact on the overall character of meta-data: The system chosen to describe the images depends on the curatorial context of the original collection and the digitizing institution. The keywording itself might be the task of the general support staff or a specific responsibility of the curators. In any case, the ensuing knowledge production links to the disciplinary qualification and *habitus* of the actors and, so, is neither neutral nor easily accessible for source criticism.

Fig. 1 Farm in Trebendorf, about 1890 to 1897, Sorbian Cultural Archive at the Sorbian Institute Bautzen, Karl Schmidt (052420)

To give an example, there are two historical images depicting rural scenes at the end of the nineteenth century, held by the Sorbian Institute in Bautzen (Germany) (Fig. 1 and 2). They show similar environments of residential and farm buildings with actors in local attire going about their daily business in a more or less staged manner. However, the descriptions as transferred into meta-text differ in accordance with the position of the images within the field-specific order of the original collection. While one is titled *construction—farm buildings and farmsteads*, the other reads *traditional costume and hairstyle—folk costume*. Interestingly, the keywording followed the logic of the original allocation of the image title as either building-related or clothing-related, and not necessarily of the overall image content. In the first case, it listed the general construction method (timber construction, block building) and roofing (reeds) along with architectural details (balcony, gallery) while the clothing was not mentioned. In the other case, the costume is listed but information on the building missing but for the term *farm building*, though the roofing and construction method is the same as before and easily recognizable. Sadly, as the keywords are a reflection of the language of the original titles rather than the actual content, neither the costumes in the first image nor the building construction in the second one are detectable in the visual database.

Fig. 2 Farmers at work (in Bórkowy/Burg-Spreewald), 1900, Sorbian Cultural Archive at the Sorbian Institute Bautzen, Steffen (Burg) (053710)

These observations should not be taken as a reproach to any of the actors involved in the digitization but to reflect on the conditions and consequences of meta-texting. They aim to gain a clearer view of the benefits of easy access to formerly hidden source materials in the course of digitization; there are challenges involved, despite—or even because of—digitized visual materials. Digitization makes visual source material accessible and invites one to delve into hitherto unknown or barricaded-off collections. It does neither solve the intrinsic shortcomings of existing analogue corpora, reduce errors, nor free us from the day-to-day business of source criticism. The process of meta-texting is riddled with possibilities of the mistransfer of words and ideas, the results both alluring and imperfect, as with the following example.

The image titled *View of Main Street, Tokio* (Fig. 3) is kept at the New York Public Library (cf. Löffler/Hein/Mager 2018). The metadata does not provide address, time of day, date, or photographer, as can be observed for many of similar souvenir pictures of the late nineteenth and early twentieth century. The descriptive keywords are consequently sparse: *trees, rickshaws, row houses,* and *streets.* Yet, the image might be of significant interest for the study of architecture and urban environment of Japan as soon as we succeed to assign the location and to narrow down the period. In this case, experts' cross-references with other digitized holdings makes it possible to recognize Ginza, a famous business district in downtown Tokyo, rebuilt after a fire in 1872 and planted with trees. Even further research unearths a largely identical newspaper photograph dated 1874 (Mainichi Shimbun 1960: 11).

Fig. 3 View of Main Street, Tokio, Still image (albumen print), [Date Unavailable], The New York Public Library, The Miriam and Ira D. Wallach Division of Art, Prints and Photographs: Photography Collection (MFY 96-4255)

This approach, however, asks for a much larger workforce and specialized expertise than most institutions can provide and afford. However, it also leads to the question of whether computer technology is also capable of providing solutions to these problems associated with digitization: Is it possible to use image content recognition as a support to circumvent these weaknesses of metadata, and to support or replace the many time-consuming minor politics in favour of an overarching technological solution?

Beyond digitizing: automatic image content recognition

It seems that computer technology has the potential to be helpful in solving, or even avoiding, various problems associated with the creation of metadata. The field of computer vision plays a particularly important role here. Computer vision is a branch of artificial intelligence and deals with the understanding of images by computers. In combination with crowdsourcing and linked open data, it will not only be possible to automatically create metadata, but also create references between the content of different images from different collections.

Today, computers can reliably recognize faces or visually understand their surroundings so that they can e.g. steer a car through them. They also outperform humans in detecting cancer cells (Savage 2020). Applied to big data, computer vision can help us study large collections of visual information that reach a global scale. It can contribute to identifying objects or elements, making digital images searchable through content indexing. Researchers from the University of Heidelberg demonstrated the power of computer vision to identify objects and gestures in medieval miniatures (Bell/Schlecht/Ommer 2013). In their argumentation, they point out that this enables a visual scaling of queries that can hardly be defined linguistically and, so, can lead to new research questions and findings (Bell/Ommer 2018: 68). In the meantime, the automated classification of architectural standard elements in images (e.g. windows, doors, or roofs) is well advanced, and aspects such as partial occlusion or perspective distortion are not an obstacle to the assessment of the image content (cf. Nishida/Bousseau/Aliaga 2018; Kapoor/Larco/Kiveris 2019).

However, the automatic generation of metadata remains a challenge (Ioannides/Davies 2017: 176). It is not only necessary here to recognize certain classes of image content (e.g. reeds, gallery, street), but also explicitly identify objects. This means not only recognizing a house or a street, but also providing information about which house and which street it is. In the case of buildings, determining their location can also help one identify them and thereby generate meaningful metadata. The PlaNet model, for example, based on a deep network trained with millions of geotagged images, is able to predict the location of photos comparable to the performance of humans and partially even beyond (cf. Weyand/Kostrikov/Philbin 2016). Where previous work has concentrated on limited subsets, such as certain types of buildings, the availability of street-view images or locations with dense image coverage, PlaNet can locate photographed locations without restriction. However, the result is not a specific geolocalization, but an estimate within a larger region. For a playful competition with AI, users can estimate the location of any image and compare their guess with the result of the algorithm in an online tool of the Leibniz Information Centre for Science and Technology (Technische Informationsbibliothek).

Artificial intelligence and historic images

Precise identification is being researched by the ArchiMediaL project (TU Delft/ VU Amsterdam/ TU Dortmund). It investigates the use of computer vision to automatically identify buildings in a large number of historical images (ArchiMediaL). This might be particularly useful for accessing great quantities of unannotated images and for identifying previously little-researched architectures. Millions of images featuring built structures are lost to research because the buildings in such a large number of images cannot yet be adequately identified. Unfortunately, most of these structures belong to under-represented architectures outside the canon, and their unavailability also contributes to biases in architectural historiography. In addition, the project examines the vision of the computer itself: What does a computer see in architecture if its perception and processing is not based on human senses and language? How can a computer successfully recognize buildings in images if it knows nothing about columns, windows, or roofs as concepts? ArchiMediaL tracks these questions by applying Grad-Cam technology to multiple convolutional neural networks (CNN), trained to distinguish imagery from different cities, and analyses the resultant heat maps that highlight the most important architectural areas for recognition and differentiation (Shi/Khademi/ van Gemert 2019).

The project's main focus, however, is on the automated identification of buildings in historical photographs. The identification of buildings can be solved by their location: a building has only one address/geolocation. A limiting factor here is that buildings change over time, or are demolished or replaced by other structures. The location can be determined if a computer recognizes that the image content (building) of a historical image is identical to the image content of a geo-referenced image (e.g. from Google Street view or Mapillary). This allows for the identification of the building in the historical image by its location. Here, there is a number of challenges: 1. A suitable algorithm can only be created if there is a sufficiently good data situation. This concerns a large number of historical photographs showing buildings that still exist in the cityscape. 2. The algorithm must be robust against image data from different domains. In contrast to image data for e.g. face recognition, historical photographs are very varied: coloured or black and white, blurred or sharp, taken from a variety of perspectives and with different focal lengths and light situations. 3. A sufficient number (~1,000) of buildings must be recognized by humans in both the historical and the geo-referenced images to generate valid image pairs that serve as a training and verification set for deep learning.

The first challenge limits the application of current AI solutions for image content recognition to collections that meet these criteria. ArchiMediaL has selected the Beeldbank collection of the Amsterdam City Archives (Stadsarchief Amsterdam). Here, on more than 400,000 photographs from the nineteenth and twentieth centuries, buildings of Amsterdam can be found, some of them with geographical information in varying degrees of detail. In most cases, they still exist, and are also visible in the georeferenced images provided on Mapillary. The collection contains image material from a broad variety of sources. Like online image material found through queries, there is hardly an intrinsic logic. The purposes for the creation of the images and their inclusion in subcollections are manifold. It was not a scope of the project to examine their nature but to make use of their diverse nature in respect of the investigation of the built environment of the past.

The second challenge concerns the design of machine learning. For this purpose, ArchiMediaL developed a novel age-invariant feature learning CNN (Wang/Li/Khademi/van Gemert 2019).

The third challenge reconnects AI performance to human knowledge and experience. This is also the entry point for biases and prejudices that are embedded in human thinking. These shortcomings can find their way into AI solutions, as research shows (Koene 2017, ALGB-WG 2017). Specifically, this means that when creating the training sets, not only will errors be incorporated into the training of the CNNs, but, furthermore, only the knowledge that has been acquired beforehand can be integrated. Here, dominant canons, professional habits, or prevailing cultural perceptions are of great weight, which makes it clear that the use of AI can hardly be considered a truly objective method. Hence, acknowledgement of the minor politics in the processes of digitization are vital. ArchiMediaL's strategy of harvesting the human knowledge required to build the training set was focused on crowdsourcing. This made it possible to get input from a variety of people with different cultural and educational backgrounds. This is because we were able to harvest image-specific knowledge provided by people with many different backgrounds—for example, architecture students, historians, computer specialists, as also local residents and interested lay people. They all have a different approach to urban scenes captured in the image. An online tool enabled invited users to view a historical picture and a Mapillary street view from a nearby area on a split screen (Fig. 4). The Mapillary screen allows for navigation along the streets and camera pan and tilt. The user's task is to navigate the camera to a position that roughly corresponds to the historical image on the other side of the screen. In this way, the location of the building can be captured using Mapillary's geodata, which enables identification, and the resultant image pair becomes usable for CNN training. Moreover, this changes the abovementioned role of the support staff, as now large and diverse crowds contribute to the extraction of knowledge from image material. They still operate within a frame of requested details but are able to contribute their own observations and interest via a response form.

In order to keep the resultant errors to a minimum, it was necessary to verify the results individually. An architectural historian reviewed the identified image pairs and also verified possible pre-set comments (e.g. building or parts of it covered/building removed/building added/building not accessible/no street view scene). It became clear that many situations are ambiguous: participants with little architectural knowledge have confused similar buildings with one another, experts have recognized completely changed structures on the basis of neighbouring buildings, residents have verified the correct location without the structure still being there, and so on. These and other cases led to matches that were useless for training the algorithm. But they have provided two crucial insights. On the one hand, they underscored the complexity of human image recognition and related knowledge management. On the other hand, they showed the need to describe the task precisely in order to give very different participants the opportunity to contribute meaningful results. Scholars of the humanities will need to invest a lot of time and supervision in preparing new technologies if they expect these to lead to useful methods. However, in this case, the investment in basic research will pay off when the automated recognition of content in millions of images becomes a reality, which is already a vision within reach.

Fig. 4 A screenshot from the online annotation tool showing a historical image from the Beeldbank collection (middle), the same building today in navigable Mapillary street-level imagery (left), and the locations of the building and camera on the map of Amsterdam. Ronald Siebes: ArchiMediaL annotation tool (http://archimedial.eu/beeldbank/marker-clustering-geojson2.php)

Towards alternative metadata for architecture

Without analysing the process and the results in detail, it becomes clear that research into computer methods for generating metadata for image material requires both profound knowledge of the humanities and visual sciences as well as intensive and smooth communications between the scientists involved in the various disciplines. Instead of just adding digital aspects to current research or using computer scientists as contributors to solve IT-related problems, it is crucial to further develop mixed method approaches. On the one hand, this does justice to the common roots of humanities and science (Mager/Hein 2019). On the other hand, it is the best way to secure a place for the interest of the humanities in the technology-driven development of the future: Computer science, with all its funding opportunities both from science organisations and industry, will continue to develop without great dependence on the interests of the humanities and state-funded organizations like universities (Shamir 2020). If the humanities want to participate in this development and are interested in the applicability of future IT methods for their own research, they must actively participate in this development. This can only happen if, for example, architectural historians and IT scientists develop common research interests or research questions and challenges, with benefits for both disciplines. Progressive mixed-method research can arouse further interest from computer science to contribute to historical and cultural research and supports the creation of a basis for a future-proof orientation of the humanities. In the case of ArchiMediaL, the training of CNN is currently underway, and initial results still show low accuracy. Yet, they demonstrate that the approach is working.

What would it mean if AI was able to recognize the same building in different images from different eras?

It would then be possible to reconstruct the visual representation of architecture over time and locate even less-researched, or not-yet-unidentified, sites worldwide. It could also become a tool for questioning structural parts of meta-texts—illuminating these minor politics—by pointing out epistemological connections that we are not yet aware of. Concerning the issues of keywording as disciplinary habitus, as outlined above, the identification of image content based on visual comparison raises questions about the interconnection of image and text, and leads to considerations about the character of metadata, which are 'strictly related to semantics' (Ioannides 2017: 178). When novel technologies allow more direct access to visual information, such as for comparing image content or visually defined queries (e.g. Bell/Ommer 2018, p. 68), this bypasses textual information/metatags to the extent that meanings of image content do not have to be explicitly formulated in order to establish references or relationships with other visual content(s). Here, linguistic inadequacies resulting from the translation of visual into textual information can be circumvented and new connections created. The designation of the information in the image is not restricted any longer to the interests of a specific discipline, as visually defined queries operate independently of semantic restrictions. On the other hand, this possibility also entails the risk of a loss of control if things no longer have to be named precisely, and are rather associatively linked, based on visual congruences. The automatically created associations and relations could also slip into the realm of decisions by artificial intelligence—because of the sheer number of objects, it might be difficult to keep control on this process, which could lead to another black box.

Conclusion

AI-based image content recognition has the potential to establish novel interlinkages between image material. It can provide text-based mechanisms and their partly known, partly unknown weaknesses with an alternative and seemingly neutral data access that bypasses the meta-text and ultimately enriches it at the same time. The neutrality of technology—which requires a lot of training data that is as unbiased as possible and must, therefore, be highly diverse—could, in contrast to the acceptance of subjectivity in the humanities, be something like a guide behind the narratives of metadata.

Which of the issues of minor politics outlined above will this alleviate, which will it worsen, and what are the new ones that could emerge?

Rather than keeping and reinstalling the intrinsic logic of the original collections and their digital representation, AI may find and propose novel logics that even interconnect multiple collections across disciplinary borders. The potential to recognize similarities and make classifications between millions of visual objects goes far beyond human capabilities. AI may not be very helpful in exploring small collections and the personal interests of their collectors. But it can help make these small and rather unknown collections accessible to a worldwide audience of researchers and give the material of these collections a meaningful and complementary place in the global visual sphere.

In the course of digitization and data transfer, support staff will continue to play a role. Even if computers seem able to compare and analyse without being biased and without having to fall back on hegemonic connections and categories, they are still made by humans. This means that biases embedded in our communications and perceptions of the world become part of the algorithms and artificial intelligences that we create (Hao 2019). The sheer size of the datasets used to train these intelligences can be useful in overcoming bias, as data from very different sources can be used. Nevertheless, there is a need for research in the humanities that critically reflects on and questions the way new knowledge is produced and that accompanies every step of the process—even beyond its own original interests.

The use of AI to investigate image content has very different disciplinary reasons—even within the humanities. Hence, the applied solutions and algorithms are not independent of the disciplinary habitus. Rather, they depend on the epistemological interest of the subject. A strong contribution to the humanities can be seen in the possibility of establishing cross-disciplinary connections between all kinds of visual objects, including objects that might be new as objects of interest for certain disciplines. Spatial and cultural boundaries do not initially play a role in this observation of objects or their integration: ultimately, the global stock of visual material can become the subject of investigation for research that is open to an expansion of its disciplinary horizon.

Bibliography

ALGB-WG—Algorithmic Bias Working Group (2017): "P7003—Algorithmic Bias Considerations", September 29, 2020 (URL: https://standards.ieee.org/project/7003.html).

ArchiMediaL: "Enriching and linking historical architectural and urban image collections", September 5, 2020 (http://archimedial.eu/).

Bell, Peter/ Björn Ommer (2018): "Computer Vision und Kunstgeschichte – Dialog zweier Bildwissenschaften", In: Kuroczyński, Piotr, Peter Bell, Lisa Dieckmann (eds.), Computing Art Reader – Einführung in die digitale Kunstgeschichte, Heidelberg: arthistoricum.net, pp. 61-75.

Bell, Peter/ Joseph Schlecht/ Björn Ommer (2013): "Nonverbal Communication in Medieval Illustrations Revisited by Computer Vision and Art History", In: Visual Resources: An International Journal of Documentation 29/1-2, pp. 26-37.

Hao, Karen (2019): "This is how AI bias really happens—and why it's so hard to fix", In: MIT Technology Review, 4 February 2019, URL: https://www.technologyreview.com/s/612876/this-is-how-ai-bias-really-happensand-why-its-so-hard-to-fix/ Access: 30 September 2020.

Inoue, Shuhei (2010): „Strategien gegen Kulturverlust durch Katastrophen in Deutschland und Japan: Das Historische Archiv der Stadt Köln und das Shiryo-Net", In: Japanisch-Deutsches Zentrum Berlin (ed.), 3. Deutsch-japanisch-koreanisches Stipendiatenseminar, 2.-3.10.2009, Berlin: JDZB, pp. 99-108.

Ioannides, Marinos/ Davies, Rob et al. (2017) "3D Digital Libraries and Their Contribution in the Documentation of the Past", In: Ioannides, Marinos/ Magnenat-Thalmann, Nadia / Papagiannakis, George, "Mixed Reality and Gamification for Cultural Heritage", Cham: Springer, pp. 161-199.

Kapoor, Amol/ Hunter Larco/ Raimondas Kiveris (2019): "Nostalgin: Extracting 3D City Models from Historical Image Data", In: arXiv:1905.01772v1 Access: 28 September 2020.

Kellner, Marcel (2018): Die Musealisierung einer Privatsammlung. Provenienzforschung zur Sammlung Alexander Dolezaleks am Deutschen Historischen

Museum (DHM), presentation at the conference *collecting loss*, Weimar, 16.11.2018.

Kohle, Hubertus/ Locher, Hubert: "The Digital Image", Priority Programm of the German Research Foundation, https://www.digitalesbild.gwi.uni-muenchen.de/, 2019, Access: 28 September 2020.

Koene, Angar (2017): "Algorithmic bias: Addressing growing concerns". In: IEEE Technology and Society Magazine 36(2), pp. 31–32.

Löffler, Beate/ Hein, Carola/ Mager, Tino (2018): "Searching for Meiji-Tokyo. Heterogeneous Visual Media and the Turn to Global Urban History, Digitalization, and Deep Learning", blog entry, 20. March 2018, https://globalurbanhistory.com/2018/03/20/searching-for-meiji-tokyo-heterogeneous-visual-media-and-the-turn-to-global-urban-history-digitalization-and-deep-learning/#more-4038 [18.09.2020]

Mager, Tino/ Hein, Carola (2019): "Mathematics and/as Humanities – Linking humanistic historical to quantitative approaches", In: D'Acci, Luca (ed.): "The Mathematics of Urban Morphology", Basel: Birkhäuser.

Mainichi Shimbun (ed.) (1960): Nihon no hyaku nen. Shashin de miru fuzoku bunkashi, Tokyo: Mainichi Shimbun.

Matyssek, Angela (2009): „Der Verlust der Spur. Über die Halbwertszeiten in Bildarchiven", presentation at the conference *Depot und Plattform. Bildarchive im post-fotografischen Zeitalter*, Köln, 05.06.2009

Münster, Sander/ Terras, Melissa: "The visual side of digital humanities: a survey on topics, researchers, and epistemic cultures", In: Digital Scholarship in the Humanities, fqz022, 5 May 2019, p. 2 f., URL: https://doi.org/10.1093/llc/fqz022 Access: 1 October 2020.

Nishida, Gen/ Adrien Bousseau/ Daniel G. Aliaga (2018): "Procedural Modeling of a Building from a Single Image", In: Computer Graphics Forum 37/2, pp. 415-429.

Prescott, Andrew (2015): "The Future and the Digital Humanities", In: Medium, 27 July 2005, URL: https://medium.com/digital-riffs/the-future-and-the-digital-humanities-6c6b3f8a3295 Access: 1 October 2020.

Ruhl, Carsten (2014): "Autobiographie und ästhetische Erfahrung. John Soanes Künstlerhaus in Lincoln's Inn Fields", In: Salvatore Pisani; Elisabeth Oy-Marra (ed.), Ein Haus wie Ich. Die gebaute Autobiographie in der Moderne, Bielefeld: transcript, pp. 129-156.

Savage, Neil (2020): "How AI is improving cancer diagnostics – Artificial intelligence can spot subtle patterns that can easily be missed by humans." In: Nature, 15 March 2020. URL: https://www.nature.com/articles/d41586-020-00847-2 Access: 27 September 2020.

Shamir, Lior (2020): "A Case Against the STEM Rush." In: Inside Higher Ed, 3 February 2020. URL: https://www.insidehighered.com/views/2020/02/03/computer-scientist-urges-more-support-humanities-opinion Access: 15 January 2021.

Shi, Xiangwei/ Khademi, Seyran/ van Gemert, Jan (2019): "Deep Visual City Recognition Visualization", In: arXiv:1905.01932, 6 May 2019, URL: http://archimedial.net/wp-content/uploads/2019/06/1905.01932v1.pdf Access: 28 September 2020.

Stadsarchief Amsterdam: "Beeldbank", September 28, 2020. (https://archief.amsterdam/beeldbank/?mode=gallery&view=horizontal&sort=random%7B1601407054472%7D%20asc).

Technische Informationsbibliothek: "Geolocation Estimation", September 7, 2020 (https://labs.tib.eu/geoestimation/).

Visual Narrative Initiative: "Urban Panorama", September 27, 2020 (https://www.visualnarrative.ncsu.edu/projects/urban-panorama/).

Wang, Ziqi/ Li, Jiahui/ Khademi, Seyran/ van Gemert, Jan (2019): "Attention-Aware Age-Agnostic Visual Place Recognition", in: arXiv:1909.05163v1, URL: https://arxiv.org/pdf/1909.05163.pdf Access: 28 September 2020.

Weyand, Tobias/ Kostrikov, Ilya/ Philbin, James (2016): "PlaNet - Photo Geolocation with Convolutional Neural Networks", In: arXiv:1602.05314, URL: https://arxiv.org/abs/1602.05314 Access: 25 August 2020.

The Diversity Paradox
Conflicting Demands on Metadata Production in Cultural Heritage Collections.

Anna Dahlgren, Karin Hansson

Abstract

At the core of museum practice is the notion of diversity. However, as this analysis of different types of metadata production shows, contradictory ideas and ideals pervade both metadata production among information specialists (i.e. archivists, metadata managers, curators working in the heritage institutions), and the systems for, and practices of, participatory metadata production. While the discourse on metadata standards is permeated by ideas of objectivity and interoperability the field is, in practice, far from coherent, being marked by a great variety as regards templates, formats and vocabularies. Conversely, the discourse on digital participation in the cultural heritage is permeated with notions of diversity, as means to increase democracy and support variety. In practice, however, the available crowdsourcing platforms are often formulaic offering few possibilities for the crowd to add individual interpretations and their own agenda. This analysis of the practice of producing descriptive metadata reveals the complex, multifaceted implications of notions of diversity for the cultural heritage. Diversity, meaning great variety, is then not solely a positive end in itself but can in fact hinder the distribution and linkability of information and thereby the creation and building of new knowledge. Likewise, participatory activities where heritage institutions reach out to the crowd do not automatically generate diversity as there is no direct correlation between the magnitude of the group and variability. To understand this complexity and acknowledge the, sometimes, contradictory demands and effects related to the notion and norms of diversity is at the core of the making and preservation of our cultural heritage.

Keywords: cultural heritage image collections, museums, metadata, metadata standards, participatory metadata production, crowdsourcing, diversity, open data

Introduction

One of the cornerstones of museum collections is the idea of diversity. Both UNESCO and the International Council of Museums (ICOM) highlight diversity in their recommendations and definition of what a museum or a collection is. UNESCO recognizes, for example:

the importance of culture in its *diverse* forms in time and space, the benefit that peoples and societies draw from this *diversity*, and the need to strategically incorporate culture, in its *diversity*, into national and international development policies, in the interest of communities, peoples and countries [our italics]. (UNESCO, 2015)

Likewise, ICOM suggests a definition of a museum as continually emphasizing diversity:

Museums are democratising, inclusive and *polyphonic* spaces for critical dialogue about the pasts and the futures. Acknowledging and addressing the conflicts and challenges of the present, they hold artefacts and specimens in trust for society, safeguard *diverse* memories for future generations and guarantee equal rights and equal access to heritage for all people. Museums are not for profit. They are participatory and transparent, and work in active partnership with and for *diverse* communities to collect, preserve, research, interpret, exhibit, and enhance understandings of the world, aiming to contribute to human dignity and social justice, global equality and planetary wellbeing [our italics]. (*ICOM Museum Definition*, 2020)

Diversity is thus at the heart of the mission and role of the museum collection, meaning a multitude and large variety of knowledge, experiences, opinions and beliefs. This norm of diversity, in turn, implies that enhanced audience participation provides the means to include wider perspectives and to develop a more collaborative and open-ended understanding of cultural heritage (Ciolfi, 2018). The question is then how the above, political, overall goals match the production of descriptive metadata, both within in-house systems comprising the databases for managing collections produced by information specialists and the different online interfaces where the general public, the crowd, is invited to produce descriptive metadata for the collections.

In this article we seek to discuss the contradictory practices in metadata production in relation to the notion of diversity, with a particular focus on metadata for images in museum collections, but also including cultural heritage institutions at large. The following synthesis is based on our previous research as well as others' studies of metadata practices and heritage platforms online, primarily in Europe and the US. We will argue that different ideas and ideals about coherence and diversity pervade both metadata production among information specialists (i.e. archivists, metadata managers, curators working in the heritage institutions), and the systems for, and practices of, producing metadata through digital participation in crowdsourcing platforms, wikis and social media applications. It is important to note that the term diversity in the context of this study relates to its commonly used definition – varieties among humans – and diverging policies and practices. In effect, these diversity paradoxes illuminate the complex, multifaceted and partly contradictory implications for, and understanding of, diversity in the cultural heritage. In order to study the balance between political and institutional policies and practice it is vital to deepen our understanding of how we should and could develop inclusive and sustainable spaces for understanding both our past and our present.

Visual heritage and the politics of representation

Image collections in museums, archives and libraries are currently manually furnished with metadata in two key ways, either by professional information specialists working within the heritage institutions or by representatives of the general public – the crowd – through a variety of initiatives and platforms. The latter, what we in this article call 'participatory metadata production', is defined as the engagement of the general public in the production of metadata. This is closely connected to the development of Web 2.0 which has enabled heritage institutions to harvest metadata through individual institutions' websites, heritage portals, wikis or social media platforms.

Turning to the crowd has not only provided a way for cultural heritage institutions to compensate for insufficient staff and funds to furnish their image collections with metadata, it is also thought to enable increased plurality through new readings and interpretations, and has the potential to engage and involve different audiences. In fact participatory metadata production may even provide better search functions as these metadata better reflect user terminology, and can also include emerging vocabularies (Cairns, 2013; Ellis, 2014; Alemu *et al.*, 2015; Manzo *et al.*, 2015; Ridge, 2017; Shaw *et al.*, 2017). In short, participatory metadata production might strengthen democratic processes and develop critical reflection, while at the same time offering a cost-effective data collection mechanism.

Cultural heritage institutions have conflicting roles: as maintainers of an open dissemination of knowledge, as producers of authoritative knowledge, as historical institutions founded on obsolete categorizations and understandings, and even as surveillance systems. For example, they may be suspected of monitoring, excluding and marginalizing certain groups. At the same time, they can be agents that work actively for a more just and pluralistic society (Ciolfi, 2018). In effect, for every cultural heritage institution governing the past there is a tension between fairly or accurately representing the existing historical collection and presenting a more diverse and pluralistic heritage. An institution's mission is to display their collection in an unbiased way and gaps such as the lack of artefacts produced by women or minorities must be compensated for. At the same time, decisions must be made about possibly outdated, and now no longer tolerable, parts of the collection that are problematic: whether they remain on display or are buried in the institutions' depositories. These conflicting roles also permeate the production of descriptive metadata for image collections. Similarly, historical metadata may be outdated or even offensive, yet institutions have to strike a balance between preserving historical metadata as part of the cultural heritage and making just metadata based on state of the art knowledge.

Image Metadata Creation

Seeman and Dean have highlighted fundamental differences between libraries and archives with regard to the purpose and content of metadata:

For libraries the purpose of metadata is to facilitate discovery and scholarship. Archival metadata, on the other hand, is doing more: it is responsible for enabling discovery of its content by patrons, but also has a duty to be faithful to the structure and context of the archives, and in turn, the presumption of authenticity of a particular fonds [...] While much of library metadata is explicitly derived from the object in hand – such as title and author – archival metadata is created by an archivist in response to what they can infer from an object (Seeman and Dean, 2019, pp. 8–9).

Museums in turn combine the openness and potentially large audiences of the libraries – through public exhibitions of the collection – with a strong focus on provenance, much like archives. In addition, many museum institutions include an archive, a library and museum collections of images and other artefacts. In short, museums are particularly complex types of collections not only because their holdings are very heterogenous but because they have diverging missions, being depositories for scholarly knowledge while also targeting the broader general public.

Metadata are always coloured by the institution or agent that governs the image collection – which is the focus here. The interest and agendas of these agents differ, depending on whether they are the original image producers, information specialist in the collecting institutions, scholars or the general public adding metadata (Schwartz, 1995; Schwartz and Cook, 2002; Baylis, 2014; Adler and Harper, 2018; Loukissas, 2019). This is true for all categories of metadata, indeed for all types of categorizations, but is especially so for descriptive metadata which is the main route for making image collections accessible. Descriptive metadata is "information about the content of a resource that aids in finding or understanding it" (Gilliland, 2016; Riley, 2017). Because this metadata also steer understanding and interpretation of a visual source it is central to the discussion on diversity and cultural heritage.

All types of material need descriptive metadata. They have particular significance for images as there is no one-to-one relationship between the transcribed and the transcription as there is often with text. Typically, the latter includes identifying letters or individual words in handwritten texts, or texts in images that are entered on a computer where all these letters and words are searchable. Images are too ambiguous, too nebulous and have the potential for a multitude of meanings which are too complex to harvest in a predefined template. This may be one reason why many participatory metadata production initiatives in the cultural heritage sector focus on text transcriptions rather than the handling of images. Likewise this may explain why participatory metadata production of images rarely feed back to the collection databases. Such metadata produced with the aid of the crowd are simply too diverse, too unstructured for machine reading and digitized searches, to be effective.

Diversity in standards and professional metadata practices

There is an increasing demand for the cultural heritage sector to pave way for a broad and heterogeneous representation of the past and the present. A number of studies have raised the problems of objectivity and the fact that classifying information often reproduces dominant norms that still bear the traces of their origin in the late nineteenth and early twentieth centuries, with obsolete and dusty notions about race, gender and sexuality, to cite the most apparent examples (Adler and Harper, 2018; Seeman and Dean, 2019, p. 6). For memory institutions like museums this entails sometimes irreconcilable demands. One the one hand the mission of the museum is to preserve old metadata as cultural expressions of historical periods. At the same time, they are obliged to promote and set an example as regards contemporary notions of gender, race and science, that is to provide progressive and informed interpretations of historical periods. As many collection databases do not include historical layers of metadata, the solution is typically to replace outdated metadata with new ones (Gilliland, 2016, p. 26).

While diversity forms the backbone of cultural heritage institutions, when it comes to collection accessions, display and public communication and audience target groups, issues of diversity are not always raised in the professional discourse on metadata standards. This is not unexpected as consistency is the main concern of metadata creation, to enhance searchability and usability. Consistency and interoperability are core values for metadata standards – not diversity (Gilliland, 2016). Indeed, the very language that describes metadata standards is filled with words relating to absolute values such as "objective", "clean" and "good" (Dahlgren, forthcoming). By using the same wording and format, that is, using metadata standards, it is possible to create coherence and thereby reliability across one collection or institution, or between different collections in different institutions. Glassman's handbook for librarianship even points out that "collections not using these standards create the need for considerable data clean-up and normalization if they are ever to be more than standalone projects" (Glassman and Dyki, 2017).

Despite the striving for homogeneity, in practice, the production of metadata among information specialists and the use of metadata standards is already marked by considerable diversity. This has come about for very pragmatic reasons. Different types of objects and collections require different types of metadata. The curatorial interest for particular information differs for example between images held in an art gallery and a library, as does the information specialists' domain expertise. Accordingly, diversity in metadata practice seems to be greatest in museums as they are the institutions that govern the most diverse collections. While the library sector has 'systematically and cooperatively created and shared' metadata standards since the 1960s, the museum sector, mostly handling images and objects, has been slower to establish such collaboration and consensus. Until relatively recently the museum sector did not share metadata formats, standards and catalogues to the same extent as the library sector (Gilliland, 2016). One reason for this may be that "many libraries holds what amounts to the same thing" (Seeman and Dean, 2019, p. 5), while museum holdings are much more diverse. In many cases museum objects are even unique, single examples of a category of objects. However, this does not hold for images, especially photographs or prints whose very essence are their multiplicity. Neither does it hold for all illustrations in books, magazines or other printed matter in library collections. This is particularly evident when images originating from the collections of different institutions appear on aggregated online platforms. Then the different metadata practices of different institutions and individuals are clearly exposed (Dahlgren, 2009).

Thus, there is a tension between coherence and diversity as regards metadata production among information specialists, which are both desirable qualities for cultural heritage institutions. While the aim of a standard is to impose uniform language practices in order to diminish the diversity of metadata, there are at present innumerable different metadata standards in use. Riley's detailed overview from 2009 outlines the most commonly used standards and their centrality in different types of cultural heritage institutions (museums, archives, libraries), for different types of material (visual resources, texts, cultural objects, moving images), and their primary function and importance (the extent of their use) (Riley, 2009). This overview maps no fewer than 105 different metadata standards. By cross-referencing the different categories in Riley's mapping of metadata standards it is possible to make a shortlist of the principal descriptive metadata standards for visual material. Still, one would end up with no fewer than thirteen different standards, including seven structure standards, one content standard and five controlled vocabularies (Table 1).

Table 1. Most commonly used standards for descriptive metadata for visual resources (based on Riley, 2009)

Metadata structure standards	CDWA (Categories for the Description of Works of Art)
	CDWA Lite (Categories for the Description of Works of Art)
	DC (Dublin Core)
	DIG35 (metadata for digital images)
	Ontology for media resource
	PBCore (Public Broadcasting Dublin Core)
	QDC (Qualified Dublin Core)
Metadata content standards	CCO (Cataloging Cultural Objects)
Controlled vocabularies	AAT (The Art & Architecture Thesaurus)
	TGM 1, TGM II (Thesaurus for Graphic Materials)
	TGN (Getty Thesaurus of Geographic Names)
	ULAN (Union List of Artist Names).

In sum, the sheer variety of metadata standards indicates that there is no consensus, no common template that would actually make collections fully homogeneous and thereby linkable or fully interoperational. In addition, a considerable number of museums, archives and libraries do not follow a specific standard. According to Beaudoin this is partly because 'many of the schemas are in a constant state of flux and new ones continue to be developed' (Beaudoin, 2007). For museums in particular, this is also an effect of the great variety in their collections and of their audiences or users. This is apparent from a recent survey of 157 metadata specialists in the US conducted by the Visual Resources Association (VRA). In fact, the majority of the responding cataloguers, metadata specialists, librarians and curators did not use established standards but used their own in-house templates. According to the survey a large percentage of the respondents reported that they were using in-house data content standards (most common, 56%), and in-house metadata structure standards (second most common, 38%). The only types of metadata practices in which there appeared to be a greater consensus were in the use of controlled vocabularies, especially the vocabularies produced by Library of Congress (LSCH, LCNAF, TGM, LVGFT) and Getty Research Institute (AAT, ULAN, TGN, CONA), which were dominant (Waldron *et al.*, 2018). Thus there seems to be most diversity with regard to ontology development, established agreed-upon syntax for how to do descriptions – metadata structure standards – while coherence in vocabulary and content standards, that is established agreed-upon nouns to use within that syntax, show both large coherence and large diversity.

Table 2. Most commonly used standards for descriptive metadata for visual resources based on VRA survey 2017 (Waldron et al., 2018) per cent of the 157 responding information specialists.

Metadata structure standards		
	DC (Dublin Core)	42%
	In-house	38%
	Marc 21	37%
	VRA Core 4	29%
	EAD (Encoded Archival Description)	21%
Metadata content standards	In-house	56%
	CCO (Cataloging Cultural Objects)	42%
Controlled vocabularies	AAT (The Art & Architecture Thesaurus)	73%
	LCSH (Library of Congress Subject Headings)	72%
	LCNAF (Library of Congress Names)	62%
	ULAN (Union List of Artist Names).	53%
	TGN (Getty Thesaurus of Geographic Names)	48%
	TGM 1, TGM II (Thesaurus for Graphic Materials)	28%

So, while there are strong arguments and rationales for using metadata standards, there seems to be a constant tension between the coherence that the standards advocate and the variation between those many different standards, and the fact that individual institutions use different standards or even have their own unique systems.

Besides this unintentional diversity in the standards used there is also the unintentional diversity arising from the fact that different collections or institutions have different origins, types of collections, aims and audiences. As noted, archivists have historically worked under the flag of objectivity yet there is today a keen awareness of the biases in any archival practice in the archival discourse (Seeman and Dean, 2019, pp. 3–4). In this context digitization and online access is making these differences more apparent and have indirectly raised the requirements on interoperability not only within one and the same institution or collection but across individual institutions, cohorts of different types of museums, and between nations and continents.[1]

As pointed out in previous studies, descriptive metadata produced by the general public "lack synonym control, can be polysemic, abbreviated, plural or

---

1 See for example the contribution to this special issue by Carlotta Cappurro and Gertjan Plets, "Europeana, EDM, and the Europeanisation of Cultural Heritage Institutions", p. 165 – 191.

singular, mis-spelled, or even simply wrong" (Cairns, 2013, p. 111). However, our detailed study of the Swedish museum online portal DigitaltMuseum.se discloses the exact same palette of inaccuracies even though they are produced by museum professionals or information specialists (Petersson and Dahlgren, forthcoming). Here it is important to distinguish between schemas and content, or metadata structure standards and metadata content standards as these disparities primarily pertain to content not structure standards. Put differently, the schemas, what information categories to use, are agreed upon by different heritage institutions in DigitaltMuseum. However, the contents of these boxes often appear to be highly dependant on the work of the individual institutions or even the individual information specialist. Thus despite the use of agreed-upon schemas or metadata structure standards (i.e. what fields, what type of information should be included and in what order), it appears that individual institutions or information specialist interpret categories like "creator", "subject", "title" and "type" very differently – to take the widely used categories from the Dublin Core as examples (*Dublin Core*, 2020). It is understood that information specialist are experts in the craft of cataloguing and classification, but not necessarily domain experts equipped to semantically describe the content of the material (Alemu *et al.*, 2012). The vital difference, then, is not that information specialists are objective or unbiased but that they are "trained to be oriented first and foremost to the creator and the archives" (Seeman and Dean, 2019, p. 4) and not to their own persons, personal thoughts, opinions or experiences and so on. However, one could argue that no individual can completely act outside his or her personal experiences and therefore that any metadata is at least partially socially constructed, both those produced by "professionals" and those produced by "amateurs".

Coherence in participatory metadata production

Given that there is not a common, defined understanding of the term crowdsourcing we have chosen to use the term 'participatory metadata production'. Consequently, the term as used in this article includes a miscellany of partly overlapping methods to produce metadata with the aid of the crowd such as crowdsourcing platforms, wikis and social media applications where resulting metadata can either be folksonomies – that is user-generated, bottom–up created vocabularies – or taxonomies created by information specialists. This could include anything from large-scale anonymous crowds to small and personal projects, initiated by large public heritage institutions or entirely originating from voluntary private initiatives. Moreover, it includes a variety of tasks from simple micro-tasks, like formatted correction and classifications, to co-curation and complementing of collections (Estellés-Arolas and González-Ladrón-de-Guevara, 2012; Hansson, Ludwig and Aitamurto, 2019).

Historically, crowdsourcing platforms have been particularly strong in science, more so than in information collections for the humanities and social sciences. Platforms like Zooniverse, for example, have a strong dominance in biology and astronomy where the crowd is mainly tasked with visually singling out occurences of different types of natural phenomena. In other words, this can be described, that it is primarily the visual perceptual discrimination of the crowd who are sought for not their personal, individual history, experiences or opinions. As most of these digital crowdsourcing platforms have been developed to serve the needs of science rather than the humanities they are based on science's needs to identify numbers of a certain species or formations. Such limited crowdsourcing tasks force ontological restriction, only offering a small set of possible fields to complete. However, it is important to note that although they concern micro-tasks they might still vary as regards vocabulary diversity. Either they welcome it – enter any term you can think of – or they impose strong lexical restrictions with multiple-choice interfaces. In both cases, however, the potential for diverse interpretations and perspectives are not fully realized.

A case in point is the Smithsonian Museum's Transcription Center whose 23 000+ active volunteers and a well-developed interface and effective system are among the major agents in the field. In this interface participants are invited to transcribe texts in handwritten documents, printed material and images. Thus, contributions are limited and offer little scope for individual experience, knowledge or interest. However, it is important to note that such tightly curated top–down designs may include other important democratic aspects for participation such as clear decision-making and credibility, although they do not support diversity to any great extent (Hansson and Dahlgren, forthcoming a).

The limitations in what is asked from the crowd also holds for the relatively free crowdsourcing platform Kbhbilleder.dk at the Copenhagen City Archive. Yet, despite Kbhbilleder.dk having a more open interface where the crowd can potentially add any terms or words, they, like many other participatory metadata production projects, prefer to ask for data that can be easily divided into smaller parts and collected, like single words, preferably nouns, describing depicted objects or geodata (Hansson and Dahlgren, forthcoming b). There is generally no room for lengthier information in the interface design, not only because it is space-consuming but because it would supposedly create metadata with low interoperability, which, in turn, means limited utility for a broader user group and for aggregated statistics. Naturally, this type of participatory metadata production for historical images has its limits which might explain why more open-ended collaborations and grassroots initiatives develop in the context of cultural heritage material. As argued by Cairns, folksonomies, whether this implies single words or lengthier stories, bring bottom–up collaborative classification methods that are the "antithetical to the formal and hegemonic taxonomies that museums have relied on to give objects context" and "[w]hile taxonomies are hierarchical and linear, folksonomies are uncentered and rhizomatic" (Cairns, 2013, p. 109). However, as we argue below, although the platforms do not prescribe the exact input from the crowd the outcome may likewise remain not very diverse.

While the structures for metadata, that is what type of information, what categories of information, image collection should be organized around are defined by information specialists, and in many cases agreed upon across different institutions, the crowd is used to help fill these categories with content. Most participatory metadata production can therefore be said to focus on item level in collections and not in their relation to other items. Issues of context, meaning historical, societal, cultural situation, is defined by information specialists not the crowd. The idea that what the crowd could add is either item-level description or context, meaning their personal, individual reflections, has two implications. First, it may gear the existent context information to institution-related issues rather than a broader historical, societal, cultural context. Second, it does not take advantage of the aggregated knowledge of the crowd, meaning giving cultural, historical context. In short, the crowd, if given free rein, will bring personal reactions and opinions.

Participatory metadata production has been valued for its potential to reduce the workload of the heritage institutions and make possible speedier digitization. However, in practice, little of the resulting metadata has been reinserted into the institutions databases and used in-house by information specialists. There are several projects which include co-curation and a discursive development of the collections, for example through Flickr Commons or Wikimedia Commons, but the information from such attempts are seldom reintegrated in the museum's collection databases (Hansson and Dahlgren, forthcoming a). Projects that are more integrated in the museum's practices regarding metadata are most often about micro-tasks, where the crowd contributes answers to clearly defined questions provided by the institution, and where the institutions keep tight control of the content that is being added.

Arguments for initiating interfaces for participatory metadata production have also been rooted in participatory discourses (Gil-Fuentetaja and Economou, 2019). It can make use of the crowd's extensive knowledge, enabling the enhancement and expansion of the information on the collections and pave the way for deliberative processes which at best mix the 'institutional expertise with the discussions, experiences, and insights of broad audiences' (Oomen and Aroyo, 2011; Estermann, 2014). Some of the most successful initiatives also entail a free-standing position in relation to established heritage institutions. A number of these have actually created new readings and understandings of visual heritage. One is the Mukurtu platform which is a community-centred collection management system engaging in the work of describing collections. This is not an isolated crowdsourcing project but a long-term engagement with specified communities outside the museum to drive core collection description infrastructure. In this platform, communities may not only define their own vocabularies, but also define their own ontologies by establishing their own schemae of fields in a far more capacious manner (*Mukurtu*, no date). Another example is Homosaurus, a community-driven vocabulary for use across many institutions as a counterpoint to hegemonic authorities such as LCSH. It is a key example of a well-organized domain-specific vocabulary compiled to oppose the erasure of critical LGBTQ+ communities and concepts in standard vocabularies (*Homosaurus*, no date).

In relation to participatory metadata production there are thus two related paradoxes. First, as mentioned, is the often tightly curated top–down design of crowdsourcing platforms where participation is wide in terms of numbers of participants but small in terms of what those participants are allowed to do. The second involves the preconception that the crowd per se, because of its sheer size, in some ways represents a diversity of perspectives and experiences, an idea which is often put forward as one of the benefits of participatory metadata production. Online participation, just like any other kind of participation, is subject to inequalities and discrimination which may disable representative participation, even though a large number of people are involved. However, the notion of diversity here suggests that overt differences between individuals, such as nationality, gender or race, automatically imply different perspectives. Several studies of crowdsourcing platforms and wikis indicate a lack of diversity in terms of age, gender, education, nationality, language, professional and religious background (Fort, Adda and Cohen, 2011; Zook, Graham and Boulton, 2015; Roued-Cunliffe, 2017). While the discourses around digital participation tend to treat the 'crowd' as a heterogeneous group of amateurs participating in their free time, research indicates that these crowds are not representative of the general public and that, rather than amateurs, consist of self-selected professionals and experts that typically comprise college educated, middle-class, white, English-speaking individuals (Brabham, 2012). Added to this is the fact that much of the output in crowdsourcing interfaces is most likely produced by a small core group of dedicated users, so-called super-users or super-taggers, who carry the major part of the workload. For example, among over 2 500 active crowdsourcers at Copenhagen City Archive which we have studied, the seven most active users account for 94 per cent of all edits – in other words, a very small group (Hansson and Dahlgren, forthcoming b).

Thus although the crowd is free to add whatever metadata they like through a more participatory regime, inequalities and particular viewpoints may be reinforced and diversity will not increase. Consequently, the sheer size of crowd does not mean that it is necessarily representative of a diverse range of people and perspective, rather that its core group of active users may consist of a handful of people who share similar perspectives and experiences.

The dilemmas of diversity and production of metadata

In this article we have outlined the contradictions that rest on the production of descriptive metadata, both for trained and specialized information professionals working within cultural heritage institutions and for the general public taking part in the cultural heritage sector's participatory metadata production initiatives. In essence, we argue that this can be described as a tension between ideals on the one hand, and practice on the other.

It is true that the metadata produced by the public differ from those created by information specialist. For example in a study by the Steve Project between 2006 and 2008 no less than 86 per cent of the terms provided by the crowd were not found in museum documentation (Trant, 2008). This does not indicate that the larger the crowd the larger are the diversity of tags. In theory, enrolling the crowd in metadata production through online interfaces entails "breadth of information and diversity of perspectives" (Gruber, 2008). However, in practice the crowd may in fact be composed of a very limited number of individuals and it is not certain that the sheer number of people involved – when the crowd is a really large group – automatically brings more diverse knowledge production. It could just as well result in more of the same. On another note, folksomonies exist among information specialists and museum professionals too. Just as folksonomies are characterized as "interpretations of, and reactions to" museum artefacts, the tags produced by information specialists are also influenced by their individual expertise and interest. In fact, this way of describing the crowd and the professionals emphasizes that the former have individual agency while the latter rather have a group agency. The crowd typically gives personal responses – if not highly circumscribed by templates online – while the information specialist does not.

Paradoxically, the professional, in-house institutional discourse on metadata is permeated by ideas of objectivity and interoperability while, in practice, the field is far from coherent, being marked by a great diversity as regards templates, formats and vocabularies. The degree of individuality and diversity is substantial. Conversely, and as paradoxically, the discourse on participatory metadata production in the cultural heritage sector is often presented as a way to harvest new readings and greater variety. However, many interfaces are often quite formulaic, based on micro-tasks which offer few possibilities for the crowd to add individual interpretations and their own agenda. Although museums have rapidly opened up during the past decade and are increasingly sharing their collections online, the participatory museum meaning where 'the voice of the user informs and influences processes of the museum itself' exists but is still quite rare (Gil-Fuentetaja and Economou, 2019). This means that audiences have typically been given greater and free access to the cultural heritage institutions but are not yet free to create it. The crowd is invited to participate but most commonly on the terms of the inviting heritage institution. This results in a very limited level of participation steered by established norms and the will of the governors of those institutions, which is far from the vision of a truly pluralistic cultural heritage. In fact, this reveals the significant difference between free-standing grassroots organizations and heritage institutions, even though one might expect that participation would be at core of the established heritage institutions too (Roued-Cunliffe and Copeland, 2017).

Adding to this, one might ponder on the possible implications of these inherent contradictions. We argue that these conflicts between ideal and practice may in fact explain a number of issues related to the production of metadata through participatory actions in cultural heritage institutions' collections. It may, for example, explain why many initiatives are run as temporary projects and assigned to the institutions' educational and communication departments rather than being connected to the core collection management of the institutions.

Some institutions, like the Smithsonian and Library of Congress, for example, harvest metadata information produced through crowdsourcing, but others keep these data strictly separate from their main catalogue records by using the Wikipedia platform for harvesting metadata or by running crowdsourcing platforms in-house, but separate from the primary activities of the institution. The Metropolitan Museum and National Gallery of Art are examples of the former while The New York Public Library and the Tenement Museum are examples of the latter. Glassman's warning about the uselessness of collections which do not align to standards and are deemed be 'standalone projects' if they are not improved by considerable processing by professionals (Glassman and Dyki, 2017), can in fact be read as an indirect characterization of several crowdsourcing platforms. Probably for the same reason (i.e. the lack of interoperability or, in other words, 'professionalism'), many crowdsourcing platforms are designed and showcased as games and pastimes. The expected results, the metadata created by the crowd, are therefore relatively simple. They are primarily 'surface tags' that describe formal features and depicted object and are seldom 'deep semantic tags' like abstract concepts requiring interpretation or expertise (Wieser et al., 2013). As such they are most probably useful for machine-learning applications, but less useful to current and future scholars, specialists and laymen.

In sum, this analysis of the practice of producing descriptive metadata reveals the complex, multifaceted implications of notions of diversity for the cultural heritage. Diversity, meaning great variety, is then not solely a positive end in itself but can in fact hinder the distribution and linkability of information and thereby the creation and building of new knowledge. Likewise, participatory activities where heritage institutions reach out to the crowd do not automatically generate diversity as there is no direct correlation between the magnitude of the group and variability. To understand this complexity and acknowledge the, sometimes, contradictory demands and effects related to the notion and norms of diversity is at the core of the making and preservation of our cultural heritage.

There are some conclusions which visual cultural heritage collecting institutions may draw that truly would support diversity. First, it is central to critically reflect on what participation means in terms of power and diversity. It is not enough to use technologies like crowdsourcing platforms or wikis, or to interact with the audience on social media to achieve the goals of diversity. On the contrary, this type of method can even be counterproductive. Instead, a thorough developed strategy based on a well-thought-out view of democracy is needed, where one looks at all parts of the institution's systems and decision-making processes, in terms of influence, co-determination and co-creation. Second, if the museums are to be "democratizing, inclusive and polyphonic spaces", it is far more than about giving the audience "open data". Above all, it is about opening the institution to new impressions and other stories from diverse communities. This means not only opening data content but also opening the data infrastructure itself for negotiation and variability. At the core of this is the issue of power, and here lies the challenge. The price for increased diversity is the loss of control. Thus in order to include wider perspectives and to develop a more collaborative and open-ended understanding of cultural heritage, what we need is trust.

Acknowledgments

The research for this article was conducted within the project The Politics of Metadata at the department of Culture and Aesthetics at Stockholm University, funded by the Swedish Research Council (No 2018-01068).

Bibliography

Adler, M. and Harper, L. M. (2018) 'Race and Ethnicity in Classification Systems: Teaching Knowledge Organization from a Social Justice Perspective', *Library Trends*, 67(1), pp. 52–73. doi: 10.1353/lib.2018.0025.

Alemu, G. *et al.* (2012) 'The Social Space of Metadata: Perspectives of LIS Academics and Postgraduates on Standards-Based and Socially Constructed Metadata Approaches', *Journal of Library Metadata*, 12(4), pp. 311–344.

Alemu, G. *et al.* (2015) 'The Use of a Constructivist Grounded Theory Method to Explore the Role of Socially-Constructed Metadata (Web 2.0) Approaches', *Qualitative and Quantiative Methods in Libraries*, 4(3), pp. 517–540.

Baylis, G. (2014) 'A Few Too Many Photographs? Indexing Digital Histories', *History of Photography*, 38(1), pp. 3–20. doi: 10.1080/03087298.2013.828481.

Beaudoin, J. E. (2007) 'Visual Materials and Online Access: Issues Concerning Content Representation', *Art Documentation: Journal of the Art Libraries Society of North America*, 26(2), pp. 24–28. doi: 10.1086/adx.26.2.27949466.

Brabham, D. C. (2012) 'The Myth of Amateur Crowds: A Critical Discourse Analysis of Crowdsourcing Coverage', *Information, Communication & Society*, 15(3), pp. 394–410. doi: 10.1080/1369118X.2011.641991.

Cairns, S. (2013) 'Mutualizing Museum Knowledge: Folksonomies and the Changing Shape of Expertise', *Curator: The Museum Journal*, 56(1), pp. 107–119. doi: 10.1111/cura.12011.

Ciolfi, L. (2018) 'Can Digital Interactions Support new Dialogue Around Heritage?', *Interactions*, 25(2), pp. 24–25. doi: 10.1145/3181368.

Dahlgren, A. (2009) 'Tankar om tillgänglighet och fotografier i arkiv', in Dahlgren, A. and Snickars, P. (eds) *I bildarkivet: om fotografi och digitaliseringens effekter*. Stockholm: Mediehistoriskt arkiv, 13, pp. 59–89.

Dahlgren, A. (forthcoming) 'Metadata as interpretation. Rethinking diversity in information systems for image collections'.

Dublin Core (2020). Available at: https://www.ietf.org/rfc/rfc2413.txt.

Ellis, S. (2014) 'A History of Collaboration, a Future in Crowdsourcing: Positive Impacts of Cooperation on British Librarianship', *Libri*, 64(1), pp. 1–10. doi: 10.1515/libri-20140–001.

Estellés-Arolas, E. and González-Ladrón-de-Guevara, F. (2012) 'Towards an Integrated Crowdsourcing Definition', *Journal of Information Science*, 38(2), pp. 189–200. doi: 10.1177/0165551512437638.

Estermann, B. (2014) 'Diffusion of Open Data and Crowdsourcing among Heritage Institutions: Results of a Pilot Survey in Switzerland', *Journal of Theoretical and Applied Electronic Commerce Research*, 9(3), pp. 15–31. doi: 10.4067/S0718187620140003000003.

Fort, K., Adda, G. and Cohen, K. B. (2011) 'Amazon Mechanical Turk: Gold Mine or Coal Mine?', *Computational Linguistics*, 37(2), pp. 413–420. doi: 10.1162/COLI_a_00057.

Gil-Fuentetaja, I. and Economou, M. (2019) 'Communicating Museum Collections Information Online: Analysis of the Philosophy of Communication Extending the Constructivist Approach', *Journal on Computing and Cultural Heritage*, 12(1), pp. 1–16. doi: 10.1145/3283253.

Gilliland, A. J. (2016) 'Setting the Stage', in Murtha Baca (ed.) *Introduction to Metadata*. 3rd edn. Los Angeles: Getty Publications, pp. 1–20.

Glassman, P. and Dyki, J. (eds) (2017) *The Handbook of Art and Design Librarianship*. 2nd edn. Chicago: Neal-Schuman, an imprint of the American Library Association.

Gruber, T. (2008) 'Collective Knowledge Systems: Where the Social Web Meets the Semantic Web', *SSRN Electronic Journal*. doi: 10.2139/ssrn.3199378.

Hansson, K. and Dahlgren, A. (forthcoming a) 'Choice, Negotiation and Conflict: An analytical Model for Participatory Technologies in the Cultural Heritage'.

Hansson, K. and Dahlgren, A. (forthcoming b) 'Crowdsourcing historical Photographs: Motivation and Infrastructure at the Copenhagen City Archives', *Computer Supported Cooperative Work (CSCW)*.

Hansson, K., Ludwig, T. and Aitamurto, T. (2019) 'Capitalizing Relationships: Modes of Participation in Crowdsourcing', *Computer Supported Cooperative Work (CSCW)*, 28(5), pp. 977–1000. doi: 10.1007/s10606-018-9341-1.

Homosaurus (no date). Available at: https://homosaurus.org. (Accessed: 3 February 2020).

ICOM Museum Definition (2020). Available at: https://icom.museum/en/resources/standards-guidelines/museum-definition/ (Accessed: 23 April 2020).

Loukissas, Y. A. (2019) *All Data are Local: Thinking Critically in a Data-driven Society*. Cambridge, Massachusetts: The MIT Press.

Manzo, C. et al. (2015) '"By the People, For the People": Assessing the Value of Crowdsourced, User-Generated Metadata,' *Digital Humanities Quarterly*, 9(1).

Mukurtu (no date). Available at: https://mukurtu.org/ (Accessed: 3 February 2020).

Oomen, J. and Aroyo, L. (2011) 'Crowdsourcing in the Cultural Heritage Domain: Opportunities and Challenges', in *Proceedings of the 5th International Conference on Communities and Technologies – C&T '11. the 5th International Conference*, Brisbane, Australia: ACM Press, pp. 138–149. doi: 10.1145/2103354.2103373.

Petersson, S. and Dahlgren, A. (forthcoming) 'Seeing Images: Metadata and Mediation in the Digital Archive.'

Ridge, M. (ed.) (2017) *Crowdsourcing our Cultural Heritage*. First issued in paperback. London, New York: Routledge (Digital research in the arts and humanities).

Riley, J. (2009) *Seeng Standards: A Visualization of the Metadata Universe*. Available at: http://jennriley.com/metadatamap/.

Riley, J. (2017) *Understanding Metadata. What is Metadata and What is it for?* Baltimore: National Information Standards Organization (NISO). Available at: https://www.niso.org/publications/understanding-metadata-2017.

Roued-Cunliffe, H. (2017) 'Forgotten History on Wikipedia', in Roued-Cunliffe, H. and Copeland, A. (eds) *Participatory Heritage*. London: Facet Publishing, pp. 67–76.

Roued-Cunliffe, H. and Copeland, A. (eds) (2017) 'Introduction. What is Participatory Heritage?', in *Participatory Heritage*. London: Facet Publishing, pp. xv–xxi.

Schwartz, J. M. (1995) '"We Make our Tools and our Tools make us". Lessons from Photographs for the Practice, Politics and Poetics of Diplomatics', *Archivaria*, 40, pp. 42–46.

Schwartz, J. M. and Cook, T. (2002) 'Archives, Records, and Power: The Making of Modern Memory', *Archival Science*, 2(1–2), pp. 1–19. doi: 10.1007/BF02435628.

Seeman, D. and Dean, H. (2019) 'Open Social Knowledge Creation and Library and Archival Metadata', *KULA: Knowledge Creation, Dissemination, and Preservation Studies*, 3, 13. doi: 10.5334/kula.51.

Shaw, B. J. et al. (2017) 'Contributions of Citizen Science to Landscape Democracy: Potentials and Challenges of Current Approaches', *Landscape Research*, 42(8), pp. 831–844. doi: 10.1080/01426397.2017.1385750.

Trant, J. (2008) 'Curating Collections Knowledge: Museums on the Cyberinfrastructure', in Marty P. F. and Jones K. B. (eds) *Museum informatics: people, information, and technology in museums.* New York: Routledge (Routledge studies in library and information science, 2), pp. 275–291.

UNESCO (2015) 'Recommendation Concerning the Protection and Promotion of Museums and Collections, their Diversity and their Role in Society. Adopted by the General Conference at its 38th Session'. UNESCO.

Waldron, Z. *et al.* (2018) 'Cataloging and Metadata Practices Survey Report', *Visual Resources Association Bulletin*, 45(1) article 3.

Wieser, C. *et al.* (2013) 'ARTigo: Building an Artwork Search Engine With Games and Higher-Order Latent Semantic Analysis', in *AAAI 2013*.

Zook, M., Graham, M. and Boulton, A. (2015) 'Crowd-Sourced Augmented Realities: Social Media and the Power of Digital Representation', in Mains, S. P., Cupples, J. and Lukinbeal, C. (eds) *Mediated Geographies and Geographies of Media*. Dordrecht, Heidelberg, New York: Springer, pp. 223–240.

Field Research
and Case Studies

Enabling Multiple Voices in the Museum: Challenges and Approaches

Paul Mulholland, Enrico Daga, Marilena Daquino, Lily Díaz-Kommonen, Aldo Gangemi, Tsvi Kulfik, Alan J. Wecker, Mark Maguire, Silvio Peroni and Sofia Pescarin

Within the recently launched SPICE project, citizen curation methods and tools are being co-designed through five museum case studies in Finland, Ireland, Spain, Italy and Israel. In each case study a museum is working with partner groups and organisations to introduce tools and methods that support citizen curation for visitor groups that tend to be underrepresented in cultural engagement, including people living with disability, older people, asylum seekers and minority religious communities.

Museums, rather than providing an authoritative account, increasingly attempt to present multiple voices related to their collection and exhibitions. Our question is "how can museum visitors be helped to engage with multiple voices?" Citizen curation is proposed as a way of achieving this aim by supporting citizens to share their own interpretations of museum objects and reflect on the variety of interpretations contributed by others.

We define citizen curation as *users applying curatorial methods to archival materials available in heritage and memory institutions as well as to items depicted in exhibitions in order to develop their own interpretations, share their own perspective and appreciate the perspectives of others*. Related uses of the term can be found in the work of Mauer (2017) and Hill et al (2018). Mauer (2017) defines citizen curating as enlisting citizens to curate exhibitions using archival materials available in museums and other institutions.

Within the SPICE project we aim to operationalize citizen curation more broadly, to encompass participatory museum activities in which citizens can productively contribute and share their personal perspectives, potentially on a larger scale and without prior training in curatorial methods. The following sections outline three challenges to be addressed in order that citizen curation can be used to create an active space for interweaving voices and perspectives.

Representing multiple subjective perspectives with metadata standards

Museum cataloguing and metadata standards (Harpring et al. 2006; Baca and Harpring 2009; Coburn et al. 2010; Cowles 2014) are primarily designed to focus on the description of denotative aspects while connotative aspects is less extensively carried out, and mainly focuses on a (more or less) shareable classification of iconographic terms in thesauri, taxonomies, or folksonomies (van de Waal 1973; Warnke 2000; Harpring 2010). Indeed, connotation as a subject of cataloguing is often meant to support discovery across collections by association, rather than to foster understanding and development of personal and subjective viewpoints.

Collecting such information during visitors' encounters with artifacts (whether these happen in presence or online) as structured data would allow more relevant or familiar concepts to be leveraged in museum decision and policy-making, providing a solid ground when developing innovative engagement strategies.

Currently, Linked Data technologies (Bizer, Heath and Berners-Lee 2011; Hyvönen 2012) allow us to formally represent complex situations as structured metadata that can be leveraged in reasoning and knowledge discovery applications. Lately, research on vocabularies and ontologies for describing aspects related to the Cultural Heritage domain has been focusing on denotative attributes (Doerr 2003; Doerr et al. 2010; Daquino et al. 2017; Carriero et al. 2019), connotative (iconographical) attributes (Carboni and de Luca 2019), provenance of information (Moreau et al. 2015), and competing (contradictory) interpretations about cultural heritage objects (Daquino and Tomasi 2015).

The challenge in the SPICE project is to design a flexible architecture of ontology design patterns (Gangemi and Presutti 2009) addressing all the aspects underlying personal encounters with artifacts in a way that new (latent) information on users' reflection can be inferred. In particular, the aim of the SPICE ontology framework is twofold: to represent interpretations having different settings and intentions, i.e. interpretations that are voluntarily shared (e.g. a user interacting with a museum curator in a forum) or indirectly shared (e.g. a user's posting on a social media platform about a museum visit) to understand differences in users' behaviours; to represent relations between connotations originally shared by artists and curators and connotations that are developed by users (as influenced by artists and museums or independently developed by users), so as to highlight the dialectic between institutions and citizens and how power dynamics may affect reflection.

In SPICE we propose a holistic, bottom-up approach based on data collection during engagement events with museum visitors and social media data analysis for framing all the aspects that are relevant to our problem. Based on the analysis of collected data, we plan to define methods and models for representing citizen curation activities, and to link this information back to museum catalogues. To validate our approach, five project case studies with museum partners have been set up, wherein data mined and analysed in the knowledge acquisition phase are leveraged in online and in physically present engagement activities for encouraging visitors to share, compare, and develop their own perspectives. However, we need to consider these issues within the context of a technical infrastructure for sharing, publishing, accessing, and connecting cultural heritage collections. This is discussed in the next section.

Enabling museum and citizen control of data and identities

Social media platforms are ill-suited for reflective experiences that draw on individual or collective social media histories. This has led Facebook to devise methods for bringing social media history into people's timelines. However, inadequate access to social media history, the diversity of platforms (e.g. Twitter, Facebook, Instagram) and their various APIs and terms and conditions, produce fragmentation which is a barrier to the creation of social spaces bringing together museum artefacts and resources with the responses of visitors. There is also a fundamental imbalance in the power relation between content producers and social media service providers, where the latter makes all efforts to enable free user expression but reject liability for the messages. Additionally, museum Collection Management Systems (e.g. TMS Collections, MuseumIndex+) have limited visitor-facing functionality, separating the collection from the responses of the visitors.

Within the framework of the SPICE project, we seek to develop a distributed Linked Data layer to support the management of content (museum objects, related museum resources, citizens' contributions, and models of citizens and groups). This will build on the principles of Social Linked Data (SOLID) (Mansour 2016). In SOLID, agents (both users and organisations) are identified by a decentralized protocol for identity management, such as WebID, and agents can expose their content on the Web using self-managed repositories, known as Solid PODs, and declare access control policies. The basic building blocks of SOLID allow the development of applications that are fully decentralised, where the data can remain stored on the user's device, for example, the mobile phone, without needing to be transferred to a central hosting organisation. However, the requirements of citizen curation go beyond the use case of decentralised identity and data access control management. For example, heritage institutions will need to access and process user contributions at scale, connecting simultaneously to a potentially very large number of devices - a known problem of distributed database systems (Özsu 1999). The role of systems acting as mediators will be of crucial importance in supporting this data ecosystem.

Clearly, users and organisations need to share also *non-open data* and choose who can access or reuse them, by making rights statements and enabling and revoking usage rights to some or all of the assets and associated metadata. However, this issue goes beyond access control and touches the problem of expressing and negotiating terms and conditions tailored to each unique situation. This is common practice in museum organisations, when assets are asked to be used for certain activities, for example, to build derived assets for the advertisement industry or, closer to our domain of interest, to allow a school teacher to make photographs of an artwork in the context of a workshop, for educational purposes. Many of these constraints can be limited in time. One may have the right to display a certain image on a screen during a special event but not one month after the event has finished. The management of copyright is a significant part of the administration of cultural heritage that falls under the scope of copyright law, such as contemporary art and design. Being able to express constraints such as time and place when some usage right is granted is of fundamental importance. For these reasons it is necessary that the digital ecosystem is capable of supporting the expression, exchange, and negotiation of usage policies, so that organisations can request access to digital assets and express why they want to do that, how they are going to use the asset, how long, for what purpose, and so on. Similarly, museum organisations may want to express the general requirements to be satisfied, by detailing how the integrity of the digital assets need to be preserved, or how to report on attribution.

Recommending diverse voices to the museum visitor

As citizen curation enables citizens to express their perspectives about cultural objects, current Information and Communication Technology (ICT) may be applied to engage the visitor in further discussion with the content provided by other visitors about the object of interest. With technology, visitors may be able to interact with museums, exhibitions and exhibits (Ciolfi et al., 2008). Visitors may share their impressions and perspectives about exhibits on social media. If the museum (or the exhibition) has a website, then visitors may respond and comment on the exhibits – if this is possible. By analysing the textual content provided by a visitor as a post about a cultural object, one may learn about the perspectives expressed in the text and its sentiment, whether it is positive or negative – whether the visitor liked or disliked the object and / or the explanation. The ability to comment about exhibits may enable discussion between visitors and, moreover, enable the museum to guide the interaction (Black, 2010). Once the text (or audio) of the visitor's comment is analysed, the museum system, by applying classical content-based recommendation techniques (Pazzani & Billsus, 2007) (which means using similarity of textual content for recommending additional content to users), may consider suggesting additional information (if the visitor expressed an interest to learn more), or present comments of other visitors expressing similar/different perspectives (if there is an interest to present visitors with diversity of perspectives). In this way, the museum may achieve the goal of engaging visitors and fostering interaction of visitors with the museum and between them about objects of interests, expressing and sharing perspectives, reflecting on their experience and in general, enabling discussion and expression of diverse perspectives. By reasoning on the visitors' contributions and especially if they are returning visitors that are known to the museum, a system may be able to understand who they are and what they are interested in and act accordingly to engage them in further discussion about cultural heritage, their experience as well as others' experience.

It is worth noting the different approach taken by the SPICE project, compared with classical applications of recommender systems (even though the techniques are similar). In classical applications of recommender systems, the goal of the system is to provide the "best" or the "highest rated" suggestion (or the "top k") to its user (Ricci et al., 2015). The "highest" may be according to the end user or according to the site owner. Usually, the actual reasoning process is not known to the end user, even though sometimes explanations are provided. This includes product recommendations in e-commerce applications, points of interest in tourism applications, content in news applications and people to follow on social media. Specifically, these techniques were also applied in cultural heritage for enhancing the museum visit experience (Kuflik et al., 2010; Ardissono et al., 2012; Kuflik et al., 2015). In recent years, "beyond accuracy" criteria have been applied to recommendation systems such as diversity, serendipity, novelty and coverage (Kaminskas et al 2016, Kolkov et al, 2020). SPICE builds on these trends by aiming to increase awareness of the variety of perspectives about a specific topic – not just "more of the same", highly rated items, but by suggesting to the user to explore a diversity of perspectives - to understand, respect, and acknowledge other points of view. In order to do that, in SPICE we will present the user a selection of alternatives, following interaction scripts and taking into account the user's characteristics – the "user model" (Wahlster and Kobsa, 1989, Nguyen et al 2018), with the aim to persuade the user to explore the diversity of existing perspectives rather than the highest-rated or most similar to their own. The criteria for success are not just user satisfaction but also the increase in awareness and understanding of other perspectives.

Acknowledgements

This project has received funding from the European Research Council (ERC) under the European Union's Horizon 2020 research and innovation programme (grant agreement n° 870811).

References

Ardissono, L., Kuflik, T., & Petrelli, D. (2012). Personalization in cultural heritage: the road travelled and the one ahead. User modeling and user-adapted interaction, 22(1-2), 73-99.

Baca, M., & Harpring, P. (2009). Categories for the Description of Works of Art (CDWA).

Bizer, C., Heath, T., & Berners-Lee, T. (2011). Linked data: The story so far. In Semantic services, interoperability and web applications: emerging concepts (pp. 205-227). IGI global.

Black, G. (2010). Embedding civil engagement in museums. Museum management and curatorship, 25(2), 129-146.

Carboni, N., & de Luca, L. (2019). An Ontological Approach to the Description of Visual and Iconographical Representations. Heritage, 2(2), 1191-1210.

Carriero, V. A., Gangemi, A., Mancinelli, M. L., Marinucci, L., Nuzzolese, A. G., Presutti, V., & Veninata, C. (2019, October). ArCo: The Italian cultural heritage knowledge graph. In International Semantic Web Conference (pp. 36-52). Springer, Cham.

Ciolfi, L., Bannon, L. J., & Fernström, M. (2008). Including visitor contributions in cultural heritage installations: designing for participation. Museum Management and Curatorship, 23(4), 353-365.

Coburn, E., Light, R., McKenna, G., Stein, R., & Vitzthum, A. (2010). LIDO-lightweight information describing objects version 1.0. ICOM International Committee of Museums.

Cowles, E. (2014). *VRA Core Schemas and Documentation.*

Daquino, M., & Tomasi, F. (2015, September). Historical Context Ontology (HiCO): a conceptual model for describing context information of cultural heritage objects. In Research Conference on Metadata and Semantics Research (pp. 424-436). Springer, Cham.

Daquino, M., Mambelli, F., Peroni, S., Tomasi, F., & Vitali, F. (2017). Enhancing semantic expressivity in the cultural heritage domain: exposing the Zeri Photo Archive as Linked Open Data. Journal on Computing and Cultural Heritage (JOCCH), 10(4), 1-21.

Doerr, M. (2003). The CIDOC conceptual reference module: an ontological approach to semantic interoperability of metadata. AI magazine, 24(3), 75-75.

Doerr, M., Gradmann, S., Hennicke, S., Isaac, A., Meghini, C., & Van de Sompel, H. (2010, August). The europeana data model (edm). In World Library and Information Congress: 76th IFLA general conference and assembly (Vol. 10, p. 15).

Fuchs, C. (2012). The political economy of privacy on Facebook. Television & New Media, 13(2), 139-159.

Gangemi, A., & Presutti, V. (2009). Ontology design patterns. In Handbook on ontologies (pp. 221-243). Springer, Berlin, Heidelberg

Harpring, P. (2010). Development of the Getty vocabularies: AAT, TGN, ULAN, and CONA. Art Documentation: Journal of the Art Libraries Society of North America, 29(1), 67-72.

Harpring, P., Lanzi, E., & McRae, L. (2006). Cataloging cultural objects: A guide to describing cultural works and their images. American Library Association.

Hill, A., Kretzschmar, M., Morton, D., & Raffel, S. (2018). "Eenie Meenie Miney Mose": Using Experimental Citizen Curating to Engage Visitors with Racial Ephemera. *Florida Studies Review*, 62.

Hyvönen, E. (2012). Publishing and using cultural heritage linked data on the semantic web. Synthesis Lectures on the Semantic Web: Theory and Technology, 2(1), 1-159.

Kaminskas, M., & Bridge, D. (2016). Diversity, serendipity, novelty, and coverage: a survey and empirical analysis of beyond-accuracy objectives in recommender systems. ACM Transactions on Interactive Intelligent Systems (TiiS), 7(1), 1-42.

Kuflik, T., Kay, J., & Kummerfeld, B. (2010). Lifelong personalized museum experiences. *Proc. Pervasive User Modeling and Personalization (PUMP'10)*, 9-16.

Kuflik, T., Wecker, A. J., Lanir, J., & Stock, O. (2015). An integrative framework for extending the boundaries of the museum visit experience: linking the pre, during and post visit phases. *Information Technology & Tourism*, 15(1), 17-47.

Mansour, E., Sambra, A. V., Hawke, S., Zereba, M., Capadisli, S., Ghanem, A., ... & Berners-Lee, T. (2016, April). A demonstration of the solid platform for social web applications. In Proceedings of the 25th International Conference Companion on World Wide Web (pp. 223-226).

Mauer, B. J. (2017). The Citizen Curating Project Confronts the Pulse Nightclub Shooting. Special Issue on The Humanities as Activism, M. Carosone guest editor, *The St. John's University Humanities Review*, 14 (1), Spring 2017.

Moreau, L., Groth, P., Cheney, J., Lebo, T., & Miles, S. (2015). The rationale of PROV. *Journal of Web Semantics, 35*, 235-257.

Nguyen, T. T., Harper, F. M., Terveen, L., & Konstan, J. A. (2018). User personality and user satisfaction with recommender systems. *Information Systems Frontiers, 20*(6), 1173-1189.

Özsu, M. T., & Valduriez, P. (1999). Principles of distributed database systems (Vol. 2). Englewood Cliffs: Prentice Hall.

Pazzani, M. J., & Billsus, D. (2007). Content-based recommendation systems. In *The adaptive web* (pp. 325-341). Springer, Berlin, Heidelberg.

Ricci, F., Rokach, L., & Shapira, B. (2015). Recommender systems: introduction and challenges. In *Recommender systems handbook* (pp. 1-34). Springer, Boston, MA.

Wahlster, W., & Kobsa, A. (1989). User models in dialog systems. In *User models in dialog systems* (pp. 4-34). Springer, Berlin, Heidelberg.

Warnke M. (ed.) (2000). *Der Bilderatlas Mnemosyne*. Akademie Verlag: Berlin.

Biographical Notes

Jane Birkin is a researcher at the Winchester School of Art and works on exhibitions in the Special Collections Division, University of Southampton. She is author of Archive, Photography and the Language of Administration [ital], Amsterdam University Press, 2021.

Lisa Börjesson works as a researcher at the Department of ALM at Uppsala University in Sweden. Her research focuses on research information including research information management systems, data descriptions, data publishing and use.

Carlotta Capurro is a PhD candidate at Utrecht University, in the Department of History and Art History.

Enrico Daga is Research Fellow in the Knowledge Media Institute, The Open University, UK. His research is exploring novel methods for metadata curation (integrating policies and process knowledge) and the application of computational, knowledge-based methods in the humanities.

Anna Dahlgren is professor of Art History at the Department of Culture and Aesthetics, Stockholm University. She has written extensively on different aspects of photography and visual culture, the digital turn, archives and museum practices. She is PI of the project The Politics of Metadata [metadataculture.se] focusing different aspects of metadata production in cultural heritage institutions image collections online. Recent publications include *Fashioned from the North. Agents, Images and Histories of Nordic Fashion Photography* (ed., Nordic Academic Press, 2020) and *Travelling Images. Looking Across the Borderlands of Art, Media and Visual Culture* (Manchester University Press, 2018).

Lily Diaz-Kommonen is professor of New Media at Aalto University in Finland. She is interested in the use of practice-led research methods in art, design and digital cultural heritage and in virtual reality as a new genre for artistic expression.

Kathrin Friedrich is professor of Digital Media Culture at the University of Bonn in Germany. Before she worked as a media studies postdoc and scientific coordinator in the research group SENSING: The Knowledge of Sensitive Media (funded by the Volkswagen Foundation) at the Brandenburg Centre for Media Studies. She is a member of the DFG-research project "Adaptive Images. Technology and

Aesthetics of Situative Digital Imaging" as well as co-founder of the Adaptive Imaging Group.

Aldo Gangemi is full professor at the University of Bologna, and director of the Institute for Cognitive Sciences and Technologies of Italian National Research Council (ISTC-CNR). His research focuses on semantic technologies as an integration of methods from knowledge engineering, the semantic web, cognitive science, and natural language processing.

Karin Hansson is associate professor in Computer and Systems Sciences at the Department of Culture and Aesthetics, Stockholm University. She has written extensively about technology-based participation from a design perspective. She is PI of the project The Politics of Metadata[metadataculture.se] focusing different aspects of metadata production in cultural heritage institutions image collections online. Recent publications include "Capitalizing Relationships: Modes of Participation in Crowdsourcing" (*JCSCW* 28 (5), 2019). She has recently edited the Special issue: Crowd Dynamics: Conflicts, Contradictions, and Cooperation, *The Journal of Collaborative Computing and Work Practices* (*JCSCW* 28, 2019).

Isto Huvila is professor in Information Studies at the Department of ALM at Uppsala University in Sweden. Huvila is chairing the COST Action ARKWORK and is directing the ERC funded research project CAPTURE. His primary areas of research include information and knowledge management, information work, knowledge organisation, documentation, and social and participatory information practices.

Rebecca Kahn is an associate researcher at the Alexander von Humboldt Institute for Internet and Society in Berlin. Her work focusses on the documentation, data models and internal ontologies of cultural heritage institutions and their digital assets. Since 2017 she has been Director of Collections for the Pelagios Network, a collaborative research project which uses linked open geodata to build connections between digital historical sources and cultural heritage collections.

Mette Kia Krabbe Meyer is senior research fellow, PhD in Special Collections at The Royal Danish Library. Her work is interdisciplinary, and she combines the theory of photography and media studies, cultural history and the history of science as well as digital cultural heritage. At the moment she is investigating the visual culture of the former Danish West Indies as part of the project The Art of Nordic Colonialism: Writing Transcultural Art Histories. She recently published "Contested paradise: exhibiting images from the former Danish West Indies" in *Curatorial Challenges: Interdisciplinary Perspectives on Contemporary Curating* (eds. Henningsen, Vest Hansen, Gregersen), Routledge, 2019.

Biographical Notes   269

Tsvi Kulfik is a professor of Information Systems at the University of Haifa, Israel. His research interests include the application of novel technology to Cultural Heritage, Digital Humanities, User Modelling and Intelligent User Interfaces.

Beate Löffler received an engineering degree in Architecture and majored in Medieval History and the History of Art afterwards; 2009 PhD in architectural history. She was a long-serving employee and project manager of an ethnological digitalization project, leader of a research group on urban East Asia (University of Duisburg-Essen) and realized research projects and fellowships in Bochum, Duisburg, and Dortmund; 2020 PD for history and theory of architecture and construction. Currently, she works as a postdoctoral researcher on *Transformations of Sacredness: Religious Architecture in Urban Space in 21st Century Germany* (DFG) at the TU Dortmund.

Tino Mager is Assistant Professor of the History and Theory of Architecture and Urbanism at the University of Groningen. He studied media technology in Leipzig and art history and communication science in Berlin, Barcelona and Tokyo; 2015 PhD in architectural history. After research stays in Japan and at the University of California, Los Angeles, he was a lecturer at the Technical University of Berlin and the ITU Istanbul, scientific assistant at the Chair of History and Theory of Architecture at the TU Dortmund, fellow of the Leibniz Association and the University of Queensland, and postdoc at the Faculty of Architecture and the Built Environment at TU Delft.

Mark Maguire holds a BA in Fine Art Painting from the National College of Art and Design, Ireland. He is currently Assistant Curator: Schools and Family in the Engagement and Learning department, Irish Museum of Modern Art (IMMA).

Paul Mulholland is a senior research fellow at the Knowledge Media Institute, The Open University, UK. His research interests include technology enhanced learning, digital humanities and human computer interaction.

Temi Odumosu is an art historian and senior lecturer in Cultural Studies at Malmö University. She is author of the book Africans in English Caricature 1769-1819: Black Jokes White Humour (2017). Her interdisciplinary research and curatorial practices are concerned with colonial archives/archiving, slavery and visuality, race and visual coding in popular culture, post-memorial art and performance, image ethics and politics of digitisation. Overall, she is focused on the way art can mediate social transformation and healing.

Silvio Peroni is assistant professor at the University of Bologna, Italy. His research interests include the development of ontologies for representing bibliographic information, scientometrics studies, and visualisation and browsing interfaces for semantic data.

Rachel Pierce is a researcher at the Swedish School of Library and Information Science at the University of Borås. She has a PhD in women's history from the University of Virginia and a MSc in Library and Information Science from the University of Borås. Her publications include articles on the politics of sexuality and feminism during the Cold War and articles on digitized photography and metadata, with a focus on feminist descriptive practices.

Gertjan Plets is assistant professor at Utrecht University, in the Department of History and Art History.

Olle Sköld is a senior lecturer at the Department of ALM and the director of Uppsala University's Master's Programme in Digital Humanities. His research is characterized by a broad interest in the ALM field, research data creation and use, and digital humanities. This paper was written with support from CAPTURE (ERC 818210) where Sköld works as researcher.

Ramón Reichert is a research assistant professor at the Department of Art and Education at the University of Art and Design in Linz. He currently works as a senior researcher and EU-project coordinator. He is the program director of the M.Sc. Data Studies at Danube University Krems, Austria. He works as a researcher with a particular focus on media change and social changes in the fields of theory and history of digital media, history of knowledge and media history of digital cultures, and media aesthetics. He is author of *New Media Reader* (2007, co-edited), *Amateurs in the Web* (2008), *Big Data* (2014, ed.), *Social Machine Facebook* (2019, co-edited) and *Selfie Culture* (2021).

Alina Volynskaya studied philosophy, literature and cultural studies in Moscow and Digital Humanities in Lausanne. She is currently a doctoral assistant at the Laboratory for the history of science and technology at the Ecole Polytechnique Fédérale de Lausanne (EPFL). Supported by the Swiss National Foundation, her PhD project questions digital archives of science as an agency of memory and knowledge production.

Amanda Wasielewski is a postdoctoral researcher in Art History at the Department of Culture and Aesthetics, Stockholm University. She is currently part of the Metadata Culture project Sharing the Visual Heritage, focusing on the impact of digital tools in art historical scholarship and collections. She is the author of *Made in Brooklyn: Artists, Hipsters, Makers, Gentrifiers* (2018) and *From City Space to Cyberspace: Squatting, Art, and Internet Culture in the Netherlands* (forthcoming).

Alan J. Wecker is a research fellow at University of Haifa (UH). Research interests include: User Modelling and Cultural Heritage, HCI, mobile museum guides, recommendations and trust, component modelling, online books, XML, Remote User Interfaces and software engineering.

Medienwissenschaft

Christoph Engemann, Andreas Sudmann (Hg.)
**Machine Learning –
Medien, Infrastrukturen und Technologien
der Künstlichen Intelligenz**
2018, 392 S., kart.
32,99 € (DE), 978-3-8376-3530-0
E-Book:
PDF: 32,99 € (DE), ISBN 978-3-8394-3530-4
EPUB: 32,99 € (DE), ISBN 978-3-7328-3530-0

Tanja Köhler (Hg.)
**Fake News, Framing, Fact-Checking:
Nachrichten im digitalen Zeitalter**
Ein Handbuch

Juni 2020, 568 S., kart., 41 SW-Abbildungen
39,00 € (DE), 978-3-8376-5025-9
E-Book:
PDF: 38,99 € (DE), ISBN 978-3-8394-5025-3

Geert Lovink
Digitaler Nihilismus
Thesen zur dunklen Seite der Plattformen

2019, 242 S., kart.
24,99 € (DE), 978-3-8376-4975-8
E-Book:
PDF: 21,99 € (DE), ISBN 978-3-8394-4975-2
EPUB: 21,99 € (DE), ISBN 978-3-7328-4975-8

**Leseproben, weitere Informationen und Bestellmöglichkeiten
finden Sie unter www.transcript-verlag.de**

Medienwissenschaft

Mozilla Foundation
Internet Health Report 2019

2019, 118 p., pb., ill.
19,99 € (DE), 978-3-8376-4946-8
E-Book: available as free open access publication
PDF: ISBN 978-3-8394-4946-2

Pablo Abend, Sonia Fizek, Mathias Fuchs, Karin Wenz (eds.)
Digital Culture & Society (DCS)
Vol. 5, Issue 2/2019 – Laborious Play and Playful Work I

September 2020, 172 p., pb., ill.
29,99 € (DE), 978-3-8376-4479-1
E-Book:
PDF: 29,99 € (DE), ISBN 978-3-8394-4479-5

Gesellschaft für Medienwissenschaft (Hg.)
Zeitschrift für Medienwissenschaft 23
Jg. 12, Heft 2/2020: Zirkulation.
Mediale Ordnungen von Kreisläufen

September 2020, 218 S., kart.
24,99 € (DE), 978-3-8376-4924-6
E-Book: kostenlos erhältlich als Open-Access-Publikation
PDF: ISBN 978-3-8394-4924-0
ISBN 978-3-7328-4924-6

**Leseproben, weitere Informationen und Bestellmöglichkeiten
finden Sie unter www.transcript-verlag.de**